RAF TRAINERS
Volume 2
1945-2012

Written and Illustrated by Peter Freeman
with Tim Walsh

Series Editor Neil Robinson

First published in the UK in 2013 by

AIRfile Publications Ltd
Hoyle Mill
Barnsley
South Yorkshire S71 1HN

Compiled by Neil Robinson
AIRgen Publications

Illustrations Copyright Peter Freeman 2013

ISBN 978-0-9569802-9-8

The rights of Peter Freeman and Tim Walsh to be identified as illustrator/author and co-author of this work have been asserted by them in accordance with the Copyright Designs and Patents Act 1988

All rights reserved. No part of this book may be reproduced or transmitted in any form or by any means, electronic or mechanical, including photocopying, recording or by any information storage and retrieval system without permission from the Publisher in writing.

Design: Mark Hutchinson

Printed in the UK by
PHP Litho Printers Ltd
Hoyle Mill
Barnsley
South Yorkshire S71 1HN

Acknowledgments

Tim and I would like to thank all the people who have given us help in the research of this second volume of 'RAF Trainers'. With such a range of aircraft involved, it was obvious to us that all help would be appreciated, but special thanks must go to my son, Jon Freeman, and valued friends Mike Starmer and Paul Lister, for their consistent support throughout both the second and the first volumes. Finally, regardless of all the help that people have generously given us, any errors of fact or interpretation of the references used, are entirely our own.

Peter Freeman
June 2013

AIRfile
to inform and inspire

A range of illustrated camouflage and markings guides, full of well-researched, clear and unambiguous full colour illustrations, with detailed informative captions, produced by a cooperative of well-known aviation enthusiasts, authors and illustrators, designed to provide comprehensive camouflage scheme and markings coverage, culled from a variety of areas including previously published material, official and private documents and photo collections, and primary sources.

Used either as a one-stop reference source, or as an integral part of your research in to the fascinating study of colour schemes and markings carried by combat aircraft from World War One to the present day, each AIRfile aims to show the chronology and development of the schemes and markings of the aircraft in question, including the many anomalies and inevitable misinterpretations and errors occasionally to be found on operational military aircraft.

RAF Trainers
Volume 2 - 1945-2012

With the end of the Second World War in Europe and the conflict in the Pacific Theatre ending just months later, 1945 saw the RAF once again looking at a massive reduction in numbers. Unlike the period after the Great War, the Royal Air Force was now recognised as a major fighting force, second only to the United States Army Air Force, so its existence was assured, but as a peace time force it was massively over-manned and the majority of the 55,000 plus aircraft were quickly deemed surplus to requirements. As a result, many of the aircraft supplied under the Lend Lease scheme were returned to the United States. One of the exceptions to this rule was the North American Harvard, an aircraft held in such esteem by the training establishment, that it continued to serve in large numbers for a full decade after the end of the war.

Many training units in the post-war period disappeared, or were amalgamated with other units, and some took on different identities. The frontline squadrons also saw a steady decline as Government funding for the RAF was cut year after year. Despite this, the RAF once again found itself fighting in small conflicts around the world, as colonies of the larger countries began to fight for their independence. It would seem that history was repeating itself. In the three years after the end of the Second World War, the RAF was down to approximately one tenth of the front line aircraft numbers, at just over 1,000 aircraft, and personnel numbers had dropped by two thirds to just over 300,000

As previously noted, the post-war RAF had to survive on ever decreasing funding, and as a result, the technological lead that Britain had gained was quickly overtaken by the Americans and the Russians, especially in the jet engine field. Britain had been the first of the Allies to operationally use a jet aircraft, the Gloster Meteor, and this was quickly followed by a second, the de Havilland Vampire. By the time the Korean War broke out in 1950, the RAF realised that their jet aircraft did not match up to the American F-86 Sabre or the Russian MiG-15, and the training of its personnel left something to be desired, having lost so many experienced men in the post-war demobilisation.

As the RAF moved towards using jets more and more, there was an urgent need for pilots to be trained on jets, and the Gloster Meteor T.7 finally made an appearance in 1948, being used by the Advanced Flying Schools that had been set up to fill this need in the immediate post-war period. Some of these later became the Flying Training Schools from the mid 1950s onwards. In 1952 the Meteor trainer was joined by the Vampire T.11.

The mid-1950s saw the RAF increasing its use of more modern trainers. The de Havilland Tiger Moth was eventually replaced by the de Havilland Chipmunk in 1955, one iconic aircraft being replaced by another that would soon earn for itself an enviable reputation. The lacklustre Percival Prentice was replaced by the much more capable Percival Provost piston-engined trainer. Another aircraft that would become renowned for its longevity was the Vickers Valetta/Varsity, a design that would spend the next thirty years training pilots, navigators, electronic officers and other aircrew. The introduction of the Hunting/Percival (BAC) Jet Provost in the mid-1950s allowed the RAF to become the first air force in the world to have an all-through jet training regime.

As front line jet aircraft became more and more prevalent, the use of jet training aircraft became ever more relevant. The Folland Gnat joined the ranks in 1962, a small, nimble, tandem seat aircraft that was soon chosen to be the Red Arrows' first mount. Specific development of trainer variants was now becoming the norm. High powered, and increasingly more technical, aircraft such as the Hawker Hunter and English Electric Lightning were soon followed into service by their two seat trainer equivalents.

The fast moving advances in technology, aerodynamics and engine ability meant that types that had entered the RAF as cutting edge aircraft, were soon cast aside as ever more reliable and advanced aircraft were developed. Another factor that was beginning to come to the fore was the cost. As the RAF moved into the 1970s and 1980s, the cost of training a single pilot became astronomical. The Hawker Siddeley/BAe Hawk T.1 of the mid 1970s therefore, was an attempt to reduce the ever spiralling costs, and in the 1980s, the Brazilian Embraer EMB-312 Tucano two-seat turboprop basic trainer built under license by Shorts of Belfast, was an even greater attempt to save money.

This cost cutting was not confined only to Great Britain. Collaborations with France, Germany and Italy allowed the development of the next generation of jet aircraft without any one nation having to pay what was becoming an unsustainable output, resulting in aircraft such as the SEPECAT Jaguar, Panavia Tornado and Eurofighter Typhoon.

The continuing reduction of the RAF into the 1990s and 2000s saw many aircraft that had soldiered on long past their retirement date finally disappearing. Outsourcing of facilities and requirements also began to be seen, with private companies tendering for, and receiving, contracts to take over parts of the RAF. The current and contentious major development in aviation is 'the warplane without a pilot'. The expensively trained pilot is replaced with technology that allows combat missions to be flown from a safe, distant location. There are no aircrew to put into jeopardy, and if the remotely piloted vehicle is shot down, economically, there is no loss of valuable aircrew.

The cost of maintaining an independent Air Force is now an overriding factor in these money dominated times, and as the RAF's one hundredth year approaches, some of the questions to be answered are – Will it survive independently or will it become part of some Pan-European force? Are manned aircraft soon to be an expense that can no longer be afforded? As the RAF uses less and less aircraft, more and more capable and potent though they may be, the needs for aircrew training will become less. It is unlikely that manned aircraft will be replaced in the near future, but it is just as unlikely that the RAF will ever be at the equipment and staffing levels it enjoyed even in the three decades immediately after the Second World War. It will continue, but as a shadow of its former glory.

Training Colour Schemes

Coming out of the Second World War, all of the training aircraft were in the requisite upper surface camouflage schemes over standard yellow under surfaces. In an immediate attempt to make these aircraft even more visible, broad yellow trainer bands were applied over the wings and on the aft fuselage, creating some quite colourful aircraft.

Harking back to the glory days of the 1930s, silver dope and paint came back into fashion quite quickly after the war, still sporting yellow bands for the trainers. Squadron regalia also started to be re-introduced, slowly at first with things like checks to the nose, tail or wingtips, eventually leading up to squadron bars either side of the fuselage roundel, a practice that became more common, culminating in the heyday of the 1960s when squadron colours almost seemed to make up more of the aircraft surface than the original camouflage or bare metal.

In the 1950s a gloss polyurethane Light Aircraft Grey began to be used, at the same time as Day-glo Orange and Red were finding favour. These latter colours could be applied as a paint, or more conveniently, they were available in self adhesive paper strips, and if a combination of both were used on an aircraft, could result in great variations between one aircraft and another of a similar type.

The next colour scheme adopted for trainers was Red and White and Light Aircraft Grey. The surviving Chipmunks, along with the new two-seat, side-by-side primary trainer, the Scottish Aviation Bulldog and the Jet Provosts, all carried this scheme, once again with almost as many variations as there were aircraft types. The Folland Gnats and the Hunters could also be seen in the new livery. Red, White and Light Aircraft Grey was applied to the new BAe Hawk T.1 as it entered service, and very soon Blue was added to the trainer scheme for a very smart patriotic effect. When the Hawk was chosen to perform as a second line fighter, more fitting air superiority greys covered the entire aircraft. Even then, the squadrons managed to hold on to their identities with (now smaller) bars either side of the fuselage roundel, and fins and/or badges that related in some way to the squadron.

Tactical camouflage was not unknown on trainer aircraft, with Hunter T.7s, Hawks and Jet Provosts of the Tactical Weapons Units all donning a more warlike garb, and the Jaguars T.2s and Hawker Siddeley/BAe Harriers wearing only Dark Green and Dark Sea Grey (although there were the usual exceptions). On the whole though, conspicuousness was the name of the game for training aircraft, and in the 1990s trials were held to find a colour that could be quickly identified as belonging to an aircraft that was employed in a training role. While it might seem fairly obvious now, the Longview Trials came to the conclusion that black, and in a high gloss finish at that, was the most easily seen, both in the air and against the ground, and this colour has become the latest scheme for RAF training aircraft.

Peter Freeman and Tim Walsh - 2013

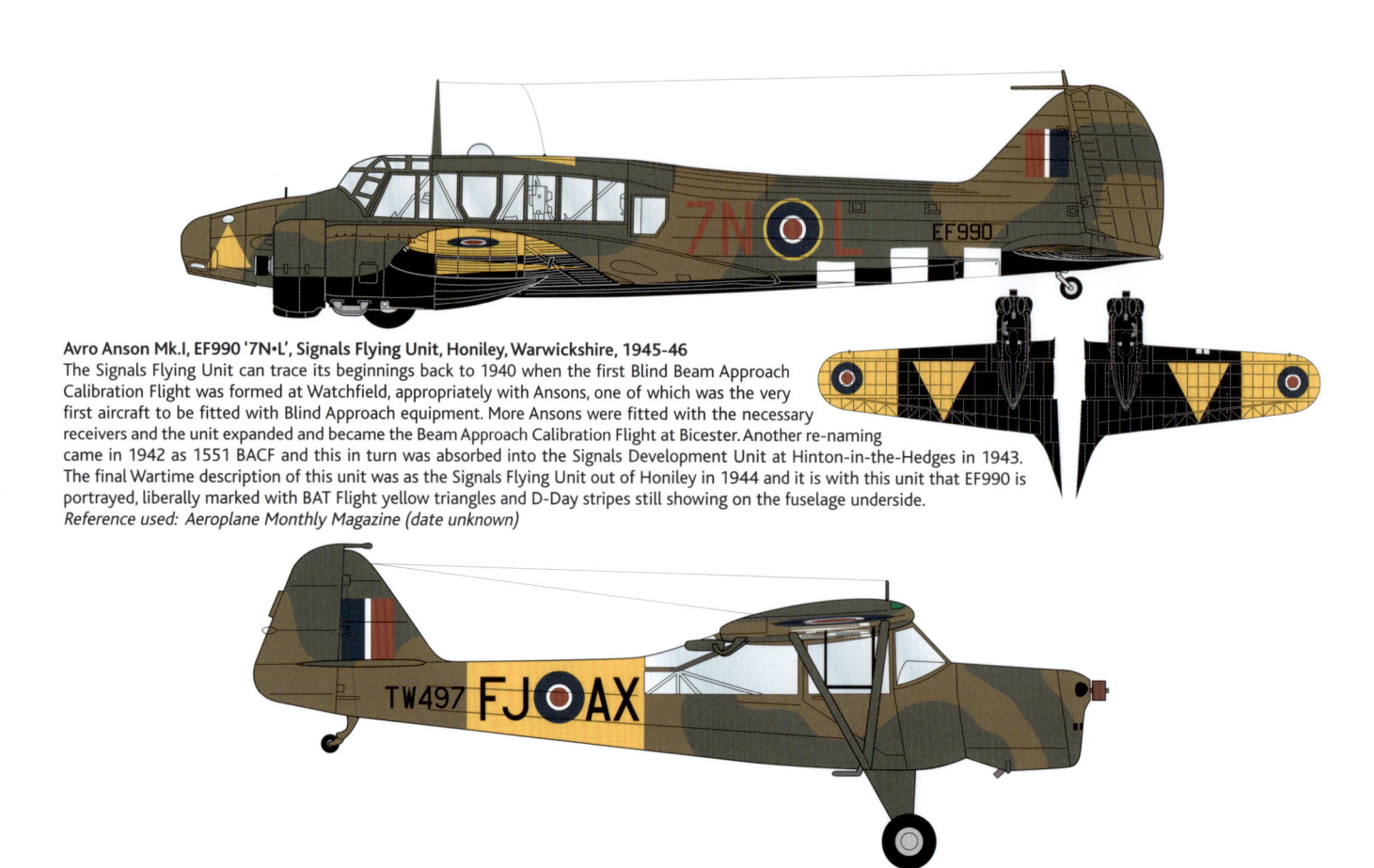

Avro Anson Mk.I, EF990 '7N•L', Signals Flying Unit, Honiley, Warwickshire, 1945-46
The Signals Flying Unit can trace its beginnings back to 1940 when the first Blind Beam Approach Calibration Flight was formed at Watchfield, appropriately with Ansons, one of which was the very first aircraft to be fitted with Blind Approach equipment. More Ansons were fitted with the necessary receivers and the unit expanded and became the Beam Approach Calibration Flight at Bicester. Another re-naming came in 1942 as 1551 BACF and this in turn was absorbed into the Signals Development Unit at Hinton-in-the-Hedges in 1943. The final Wartime description of this unit was as the Signals Flying Unit out of Honiley in 1944 and it is with this unit that EF990 is portrayed, liberally marked with BAT Flight yellow triangles and D-Day stripes still showing on the fuselage underside.
Reference used: Aeroplane Monthly Magazine (date unknown)

Auster AOP Mk.VI, TW497 FJA•X, No.22 Elementary Flying Training School, Cambridge, Cambridgeshire 1946
Right from the start of World War One, observing the enemy from the air was considered to be of great importance, so much so that missions to knock down the opposition's observation balloons were looked upon with dread, virtually suicide missions in the eyes of the pilots. With the advent of airborne radio (even in the crudest form a great advance over dropped messages), aircraft started to come into their own as observation platforms, spotting for the guns and reporting enemy movements. By the end of World War Two, the culmination of this particular facet of warfare resulted in aircraft such as the Piper L-4 and the Auster AOP Mk.VI. The Mk.VI was selected in the immediate post-war period to replace the previous Marks and incorporate all lessons learned from them. Whilst it was manufactured for the RAF and maintained by RAF personnel, the pilots themselves were recruited from the Royal Artillery.
Reference used: p25 'RAF Flying Training and Support Units since 1912' by Ray Sturtivant with John Hamlin, Air Britain (Historians) Ltd. 2007

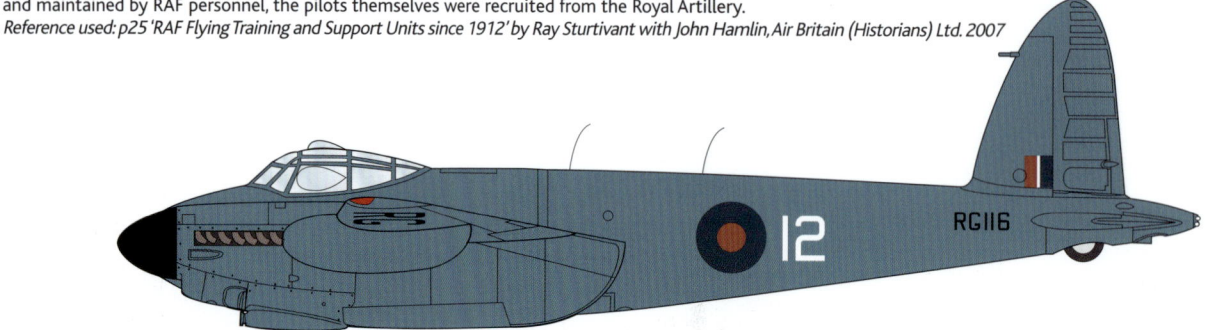

De Havilland Mosquito PR.34, RG116 '12', No 8 (Coastal) Operational Training Unit, Benson, Oxfordshire 1946
Originally formed at Fraserburgh from the OTU of No 1 PRU and the PRU Conversion Flight of No 3 School of General Reconnaissance, the unit's aim was to train pilots for photographic reconnaissance units on Spitfires. As the PR Mosquito gradually evolved as an equable photo reconnaissance machine, the unit's establishment of Mosquitoes increased. The PR.34 was the ultimate Mark in the series and it defined the peak of PR development at this time. The PR.34 was equipped with four F52 cameras, two forward and two aft of the belly tanks, together with either one F24 oblique camera or a vertical K17 camera for air survey work. The bomb-bay was filled with two huge tanks holding an additional 1192 gallons of fuel and, with the addition of two 200 gallon drop tanks on the wings, the range was extended to 3600 miles whilst flying at 300mph and 25,000ft.
Reference used: Collection of Mike Starmer

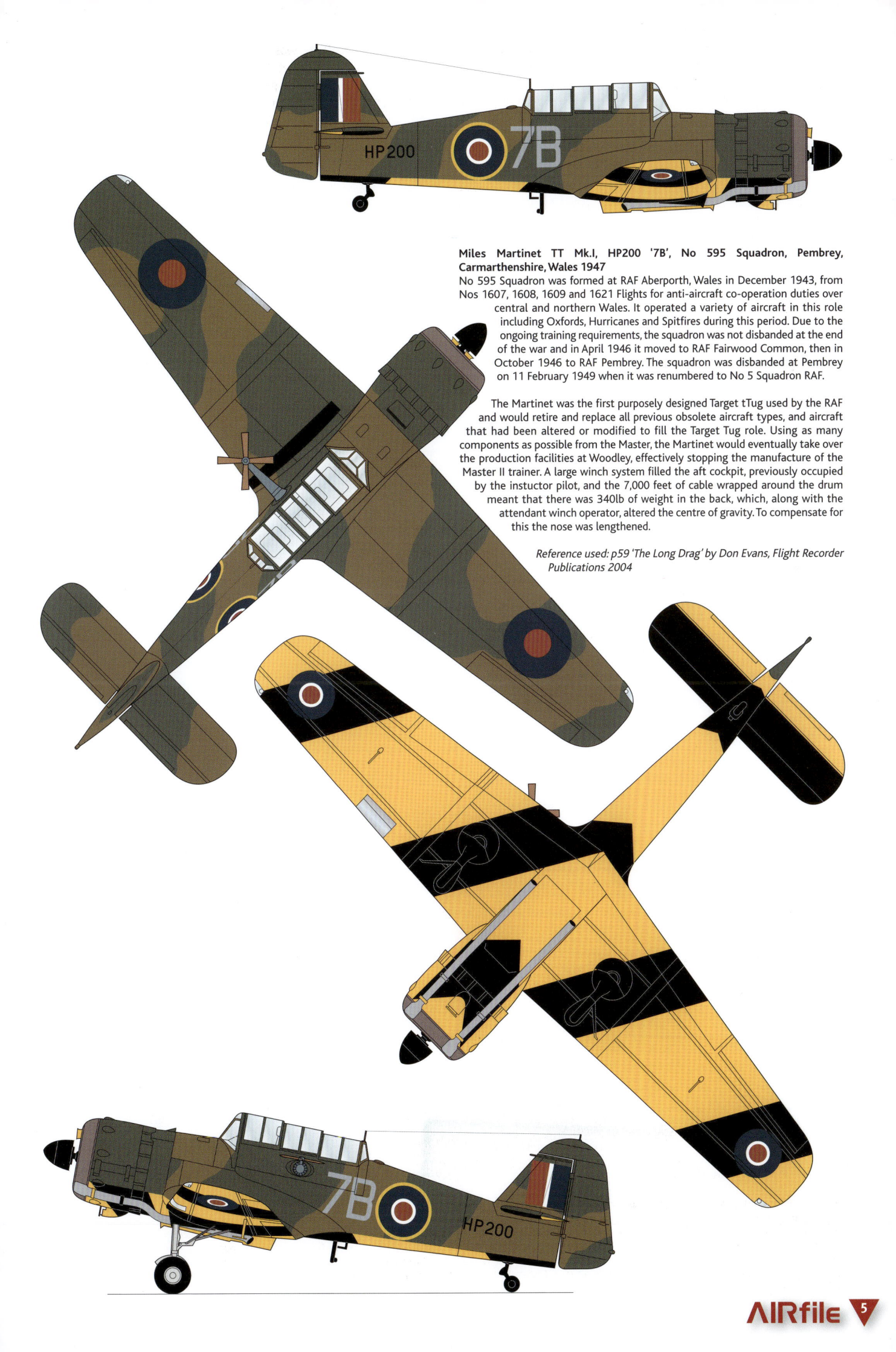

Miles Martinet TT Mk.I, HP200 '7B', No 595 Squadron, Pembrey, Carmarthenshire, Wales 1947

No 595 Squadron was formed at RAF Aberporth, Wales in December 1943, from Nos 1607, 1608, 1609 and 1621 Flights for anti-aircraft co-operation duties over central and northern Wales. It operated a variety of aircraft in this role including Oxfords, Hurricanes and Spitfires during this period. Due to the ongoing training requirements, the squadron was not disbanded at the end of the war and in April 1946 it moved to RAF Fairwood Common, then in October 1946 to RAF Pembrey. The squadron was disbanded at Pembrey on 11 February 1949 when it was renumbered to No 5 Squadron RAF.

The Martinet was the first purposely designed Target tTug used by the RAF and would retire and replace all previous obsolete aircraft types, and aircraft that had been altered or modified to fill the Target Tug role. Using as many components as possible from the Master, the Martinet would eventually take over the production facilities at Woodley, effectively stopping the manufacture of the Master II trainer. A large winch system filled the aft cockpit, previously occupied by the instuctor pilot, and the 7,000 feet of cable wrapped around the drum meant that there was 340lb of weight in the back, which, along with the attendant winch operator, altered the centre of gravity. To compensate for this the nose was lengthened.

Reference used: p59 'The Long Drag' by Don Evans, Flight Recorder Publications 2004

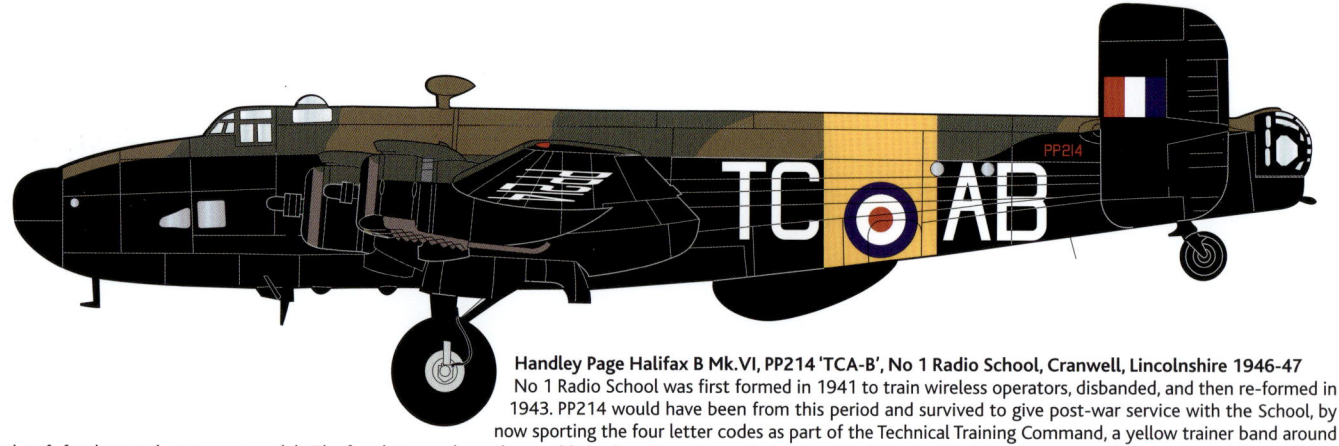

Handley Page Halifax B Mk.VI, PP214 'TCA-B', No 1 Radio School, Cranwell, Lincolnshire 1946-47
No 1 Radio School was first formed in 1941 to train wireless operators, disbanded, and then re-formed in 1943. PP214 would have been from this period and survived to give post-war service with the School, by now sporting the four letter codes as part of the Technical Training Command, a yellow trainer band around the aft fuselage and post-war roundels. The four letter code can be roughly broken down thus:- the 'T' stood for Technical Training Command, 'CA' represented Cranwell (CR was also used), and 'B' is the individual aircraft letter. Night flying instrumentation was fitted, resulting in a different profile to the nose.
Reference used: p102 'Halifax at War' by Brian J Rapier, Ian Allan Ltd, 1987

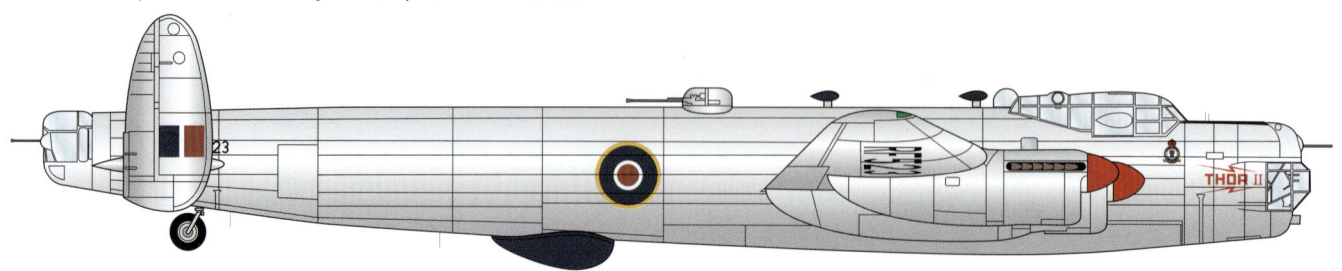

Avro Lincoln B Mk.II, RF523 'THOR II', Empire Air Armaments School, Manby, Lincolnshire 1947
The replacement for the Lancaster, the Lincoln, was designed to be bigger, faster, climb higher, carry more payload over a longer distance and be an instrumental part of the War against Japan. The dropping of the atomic bombs changed all that and suddenly the Lincoln went from what was to be a mass produced important strategic weapon, to an archaic anachronism, especially in light of the fact that the Americans had flown the futuristic looking B-47 Stratojet just two years after the service debut of the Lincoln. As a result, the RAF used the Lincoln for a mere twelve years, the final operational flight being undertaken in 1957. RF523 was used by the RAF to propound the doctrines, practices, theories and systems learned through five years of war, on long range missions to the USA, Canada, New Zealand, the Far East and South Africa.
Reference used: p35 'Avro Lincoln' by Tony Buttler, Warpaint Series No.34, Hall Park Books Ltd

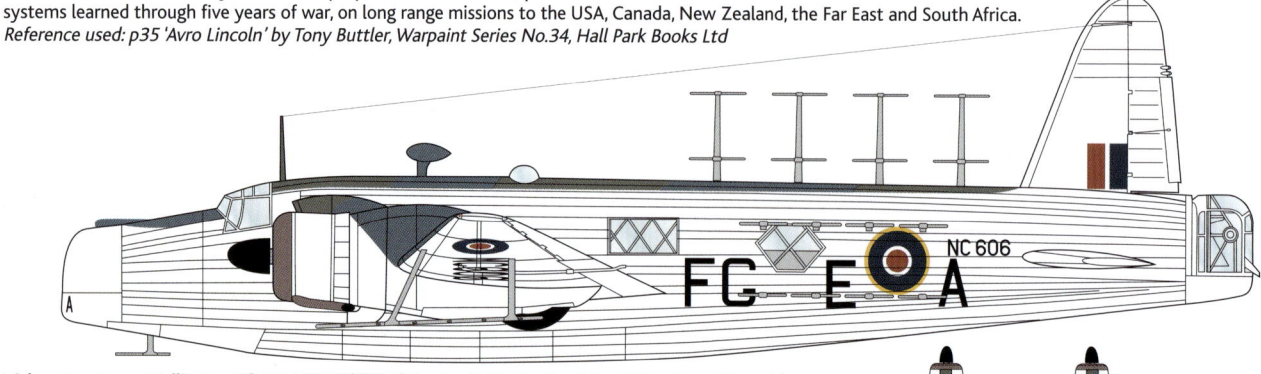

Vickers Armstrong Wellington Mk.XIII, NC606 'FGE•A', Empire Air Navigation School, Shawbury, Shropshire, 1947 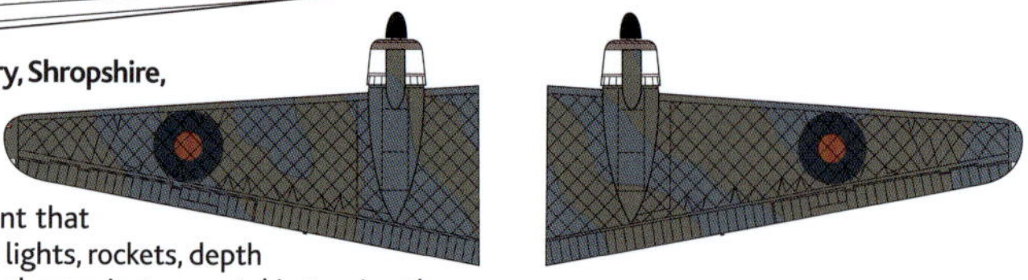
Over 11,400 Wellingtons were built and as such the type was a major contributor to the War effort, flying on all fronts. The adaptability of the design also meant that the aircraft was useful in roles other than just as a bomber. The submarine threat in the Atlantic meant that aircraft with a good range were utilised to combat the U-boats. Fitted with ASV radar, Leigh lights, rockets, depth charges and the like, Wellingtons, along with Catalinas, Sunderlands, Halifaxes, Whitleys et al, were instrumental in turning the tide against the submarines. NC606 was photographed after the war being used by the Empire Air Navigation School, with their four letter codes applied and all aerials still in place. One has to wonder wether the once top secret equipment was now being used as just another navigation training aid.
Reference used: p106 'RAF Flying Training and Support Units since 1912' by Ray Sturtivant, J Hamlin & J Halley Publications, 1st edition 1997

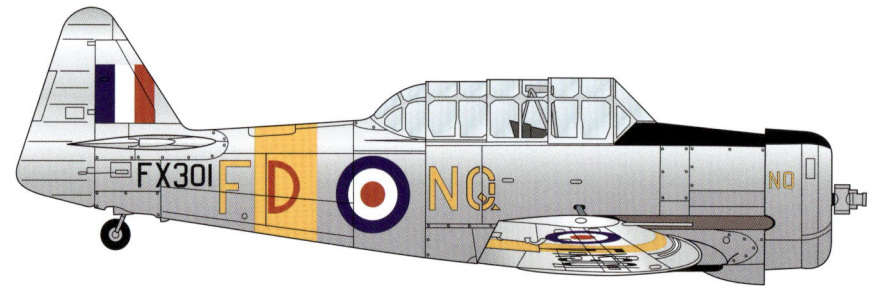

North American Harvard IIB, FX301, 'FDN•Q', Central Flying School, Little Rissington, Gloucestershire, circa 1947
One of the (few) early complaints about the Harvard was the poor cockpit heating. This was rectified by extending the exhaust pipe and running a second pipe from the inside of the exhaust and into the cockpit. FX301 also shows the other features that makes this the archetypal Harvard – the triangular fin and rudder, clipped wingtips and monocoque aluminium fuselage. The Harvard was the only American trainer to serve with the RAF on British soil, and would continue in the trainer role until replaced by Vampires in 1955. The Central Flying School had a long tenure at Little Rissington, from being established in 1946 until moving to Cranwell in 1976. Interesting features of this profile are the dissimilar size of the serial numbers, the red 'D' on the fuselage band and the stencil 'Q'.
Reference used: the Private Collection of Mike Starmer

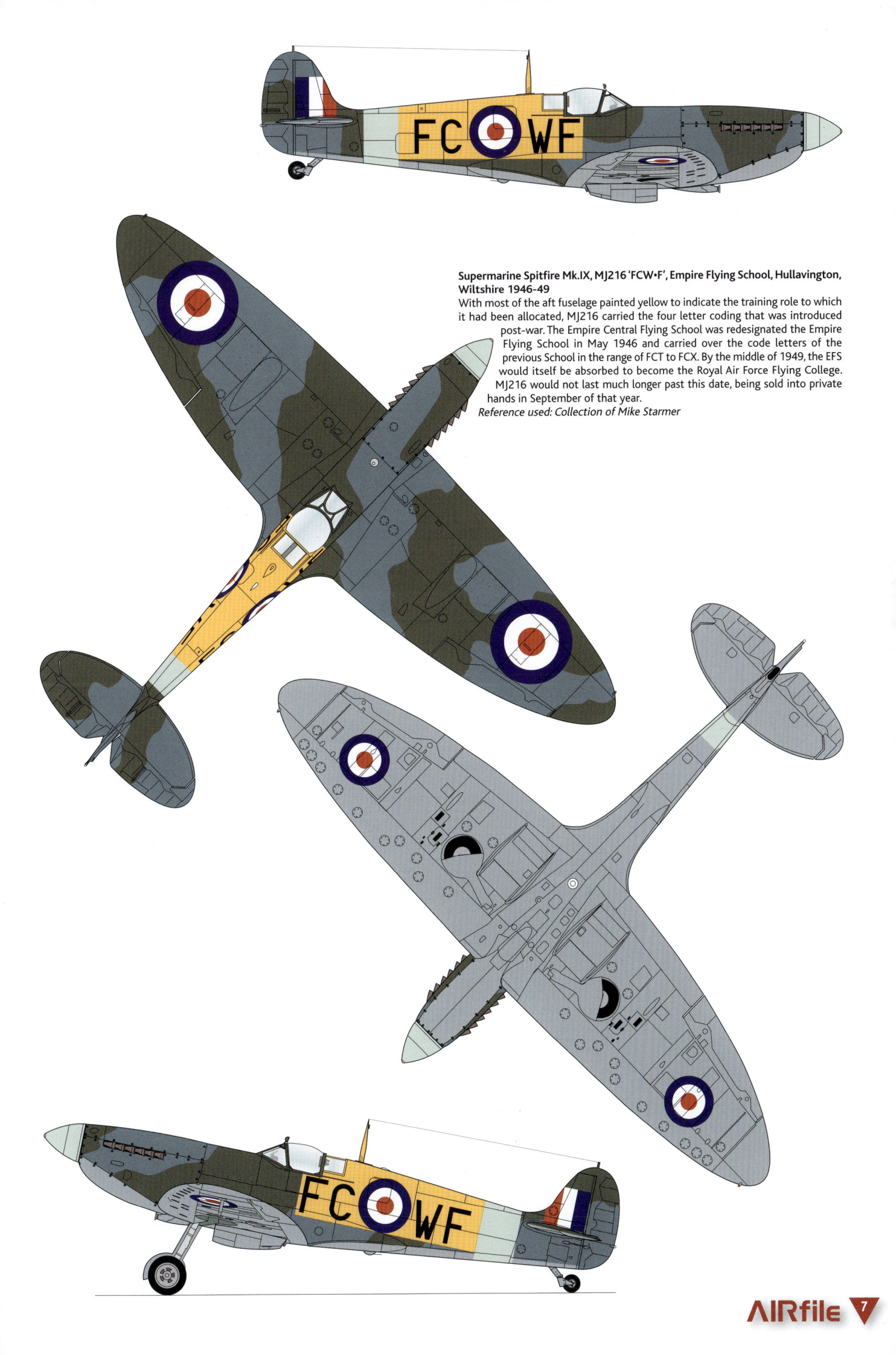

Supermarine Spitfire Mk.IX, MJ216 'FCW•F', Empire Flying School, Hullavington, Wiltshire 1946-49

With most of the aft fuselage painted yellow to indicate the training role to which it had been allocated, MJ216 carried the four letter coding that was introduced post-war. The Empire Central Flying School was redesignated the Empire Flying School in May 1946 and carried over the code letters of the previous School in the range of FCT to FCX. By the middle of 1949, the EFS would itself be absorbed to become the Royal Air Force Flying College. MJ216 would not last much longer past this date, being sold into private hands in September of that year.

Reference used: Collection of Mike Starmer

Handley Page Halifax B Mk.VI, (serial unknown), 'FEP•B', No 21 Heavy Glider Conversion Unit, North Luffenham, Rutland, 1947
The Halifax was the second four-engined bomber to go into service with the RAF, after the Stirling, and became the mainstay of Bomber Command alongside the soon to be introduced Lancaster. As increasing numbers of Lancasters became available, the Halifax became very much the lesser partner in the bombing campaign. It also did not help that AVM Arthur 'Bomber' Harris, C-in-C Bomber Command, was quite vociferously against the Halifax, considering it to be inferior to the Lancaster. Whilst this might have been true as regards performance and bomb load, the crews that flew it were more than happy with the aircraft, and the airframe had more potential for conversion to other roles than the Lancaster. This included a glider towing capability which was part of the Halifax design from the outset, a forward thinking approach that would allow the Halifax another secondary role. FEP•B was used in just such a role, as a glider tug Post War.
Reference used: p149 'Action Stations 2. Military airfields of Lincolnshire and the East Midlands' by Bruce Barrymore Halpenny, Patrick Stephens Limited 1981

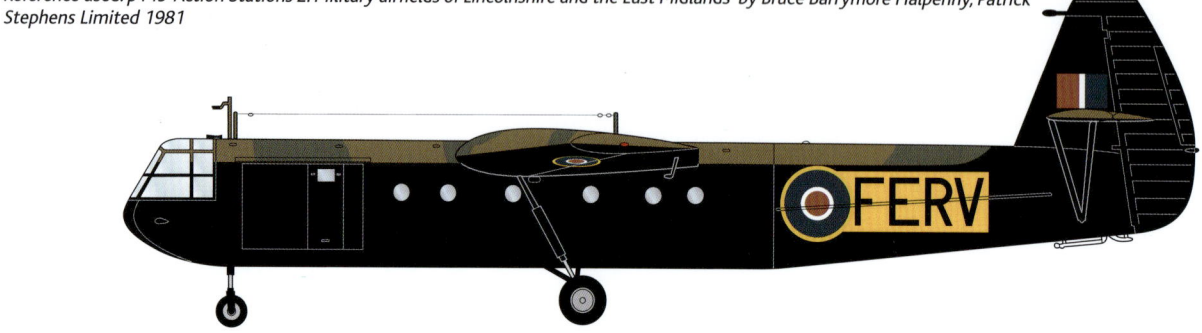

Airspeed Horsa I, (serial unknown), 'FER•V', No 21 Heavy Glider Conversion Unit, North Luffenham, Rutland May 1947
Training in heavy glider tactics continued post-war, but with the advent of helicopters of increasing power and capability, assault gliders would quickly fade from the scene, with only *ab initio* training gliders remaining with the RAF. This was the second sojourn at this base for No 21 HGCU, a period that would last just twelve months before disbandment in January 1948. Their first visit to North Luffenham in 1944 was much more important, training the glider pilots that would take part in the D-Day Landings.
Reference used: p149 'Action Stations 2. Military airfields of Lincolnshire and the East Midlands' by Bruce Barrymore Halpenny, Patrick Stephens Limited 1981

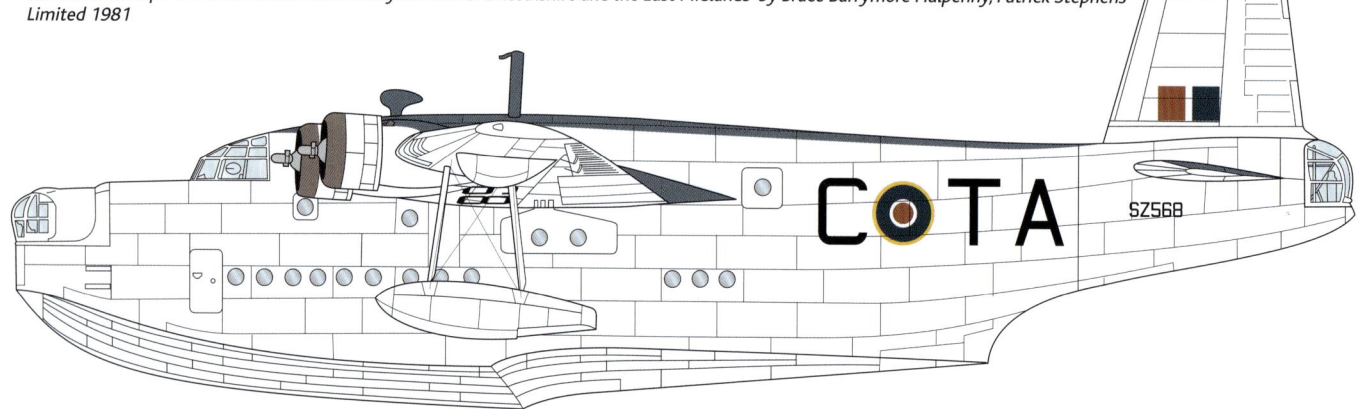

Short Sunderland GR.5, SZ568, 'TA•C', No 235 (Coastal) Operational Conversion Unit, Calshot, Hampshire, 1947
Calshot was the primary base for the training of flying boat crews, a role that the base maintained until the end of 1953. No 235 (C) OCU originally started as the Flying Boat Training Squadron in September of 1939. This became No 4 Operational Training Unit in March 1941 and remained so throughout the war and immediate post-war period, taking on OCU status in 1947. SZ568 was one of the last Sunderland aircraft built.
Reference used: p487 'Aircraft of the Royal Air Force since 1918' by Owen Thetford, Guild Publishing London, 1988.

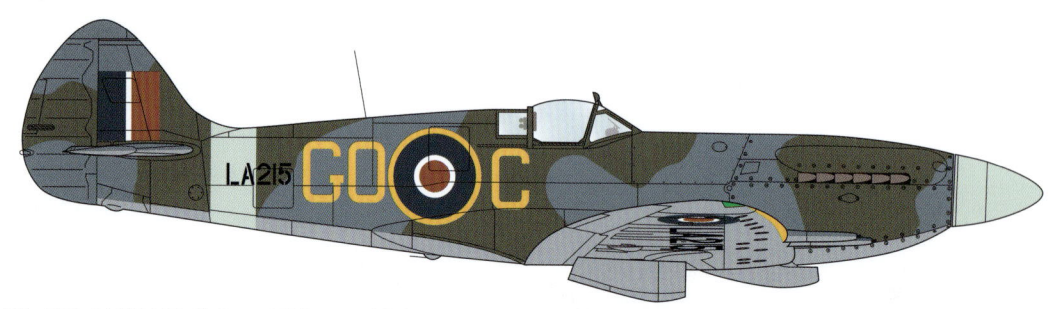

Supermarine Spitfire F.21, LA215, 'GO•C', Central Fighter Establishment, RAF Tangmere, Sussex, late 1940s
The CFE had been created in 1944 with the aim of bringing together all the Schools that had appeared during the war years, such as the Developmental Units, Training Squadrons and Units etc, whether they be Fighter affiliated, Bomber, Experimental or Instrument Units, Target Flights, even up to and including the Enemy Aircraft Flight. With such a diversity of units came an even wider diversity of aircraft, including Spitfires of all Marks, Typhoons and Tempests, Oxfords, Martinets and Mosquitoes, all the way up to the large bomber aircraft such as Liberators and Wellingtons. This late Mark Spitfire was probably attached to the Fighter Interception Development Squadron based at Ford.
Reference used: p525 'Aircraft of the Royal Air Force since 1918' by Owen Thetford, Guild Publishing London, 1988.

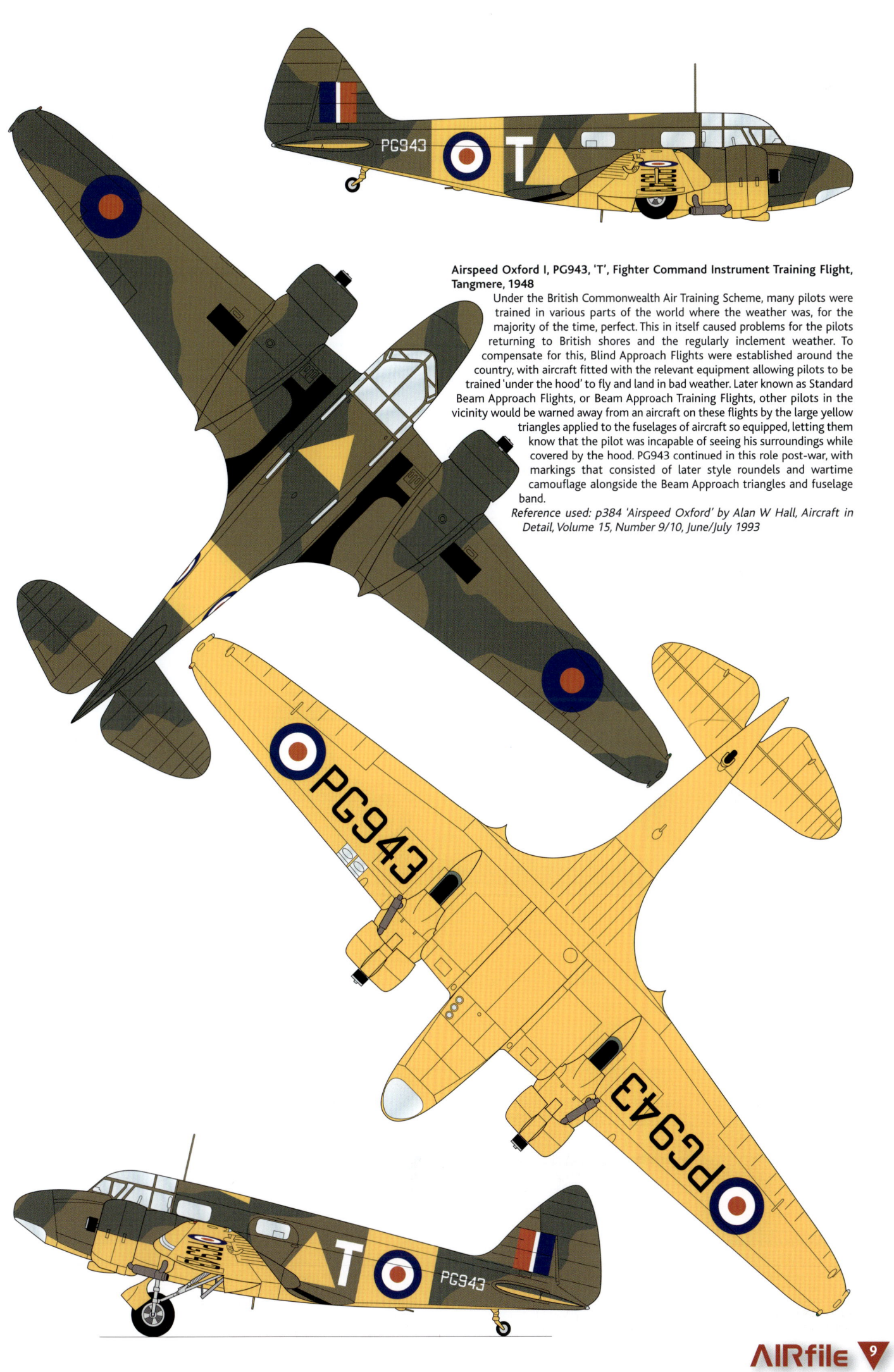

Airspeed Oxford I, PG943, 'T', Fighter Command Instrument Training Flight, Tangmere, 1948

Under the British Commonwealth Air Training Scheme, many pilots were trained in various parts of the world where the weather was, for the majority of the time, perfect. This in itself caused problems for the pilots returning to British shores and the regularly inclement weather. To compensate for this, Blind Approach Flights were established around the country, with aircraft fitted with the relevant equipment allowing pilots to be trained 'under the hood' to fly and land in bad weather. Later known as Standard Beam Approach Flights, or Beam Approach Training Flights, other pilots in the vicinity would be warned away from an aircraft on these flights by the large yellow triangles applied to the fuselages of aircraft so equipped, letting them know that the pilot was incapable of seeing his surroundings while covered by the hood. PG943 continued in this role post-war, with markings that consisted of later style roundels and wartime camouflage alongside the Beam Approach triangles and fuselage band.

Reference used: p384 'Airspeed Oxford' by Alan W Hall, Aircraft in Detail, Volume 15, Number 9/10, June/July 1993

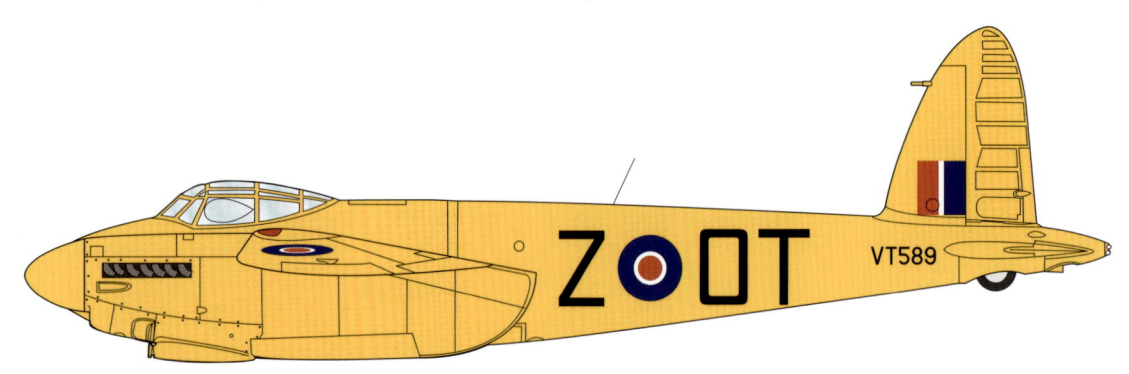

De Havilland Mosquito T.3, VT589, 'OT•Z', No 58 Squadron, Benson, Oxfordshire 1948
This T.3 Mosquito was on the strength of No 58 Squadron, probably to keep the pilots up to date with the PR.34 aircraft that was the standard equipment of the squadron. Formed late in 1946, No 58 Squadron was tasked with photographing post-war Britain in order to upgrade maps and do survey work. The squadron was appropriately based at Benson, which during the war years was the centre for RAF photo-reconnaissance. It was from Benson that photo-recon Spitfires recorded the damage after the Dam Busters raid and developed the photos of the *Tirpitz*. It continued in this task after hostilities, if anything being busier catering for civilian requests both at home and abroad for the recording of wartime damage. No 58 Squadron continued to use Mosquitoes until 1953, when they were replaced by Canberra PR.3s.
Reference used: p222 'Aircraft of the Royal Air Force since 1918' by Owen Thetford, published by Owen Thetford 1957

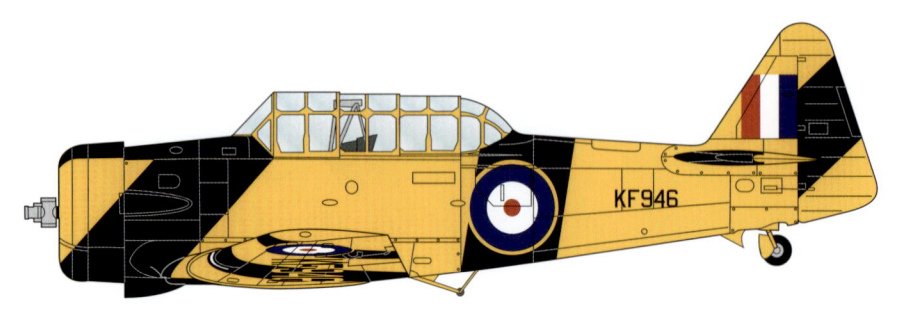

North American Harvard II, KF946, Station Flight, Nicosia, Cyprus 1948
The Target Tug version of the Harvard was developed by Noorduyn Aviation in 1944, and KF946 was one of an indeterminate number built and by 1948 was part of the Station Flight at Nicosia in Cyprus. This well worn airframe shows some anomalies to the standard Target Tug colour scheme, with the black stripes on the fuselage at varying angles to one another and was quite possibly a local 'paint job'. This particular aircraft was photographed on Malta, whilst transitioning through to Egypt where it served with the Ismailia Sation Flight in 1949. A year later it returned to Malta with No 73 Squadron, towing targets for that squadron's Vampire FB.3s to shoot at. It was eventually struck off charge in November 1950.
Reference used: p5 'Birds of Passage - Pictorial Memories of Visitors to Malta 1948/50' by Norman Lees, Air Enthusiast, March/April 1998, Number 74

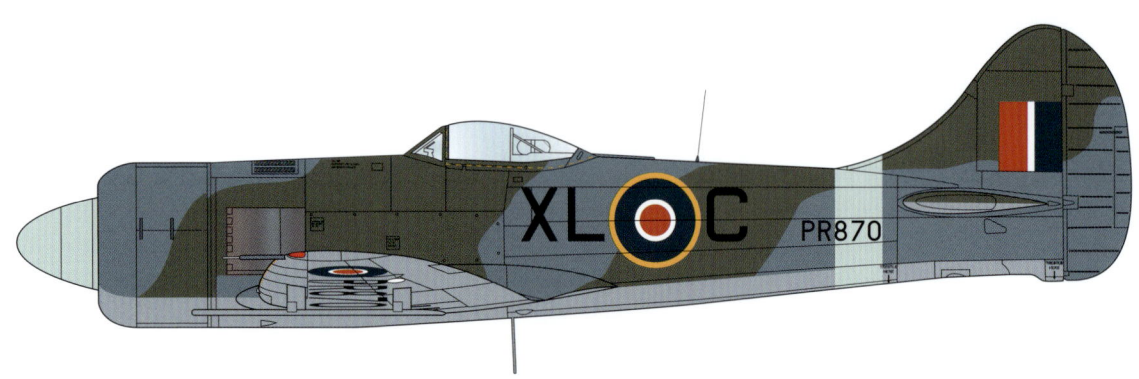

Hawker Tempest Mk.II, PR870, 'XL•C, No 226 Operational Conversion Unit, RAF Bentwaters, Suffolk, September 1948
As the final and ultimate variant of the Typhoon/Tempest V line, the Centaurus engine of the Tempest II made it the most powerful single-engined fighter at the end of World War Two. The long range capabilities of the Tempest II, (1,640 miles) meant that it was earmarked, along with the Hornet, to be used in the Pacific Theatre. The end of hostilities in the Far East, therefore meant that the majority of the order was cancelled. Even so, a total of 472 aircraft were built, most of these serving in the RAF overseas. PR870 was one that stayed on home soil, and was used for the operational training of fighter pilots. The dark coloured Squadron codes are unusual.
Reference used: p195 'RAF Flying Training and Support Units since 1912' by Ray Sturtivant with John Hamlin, Air-Britain (Historians) Ltd 2007

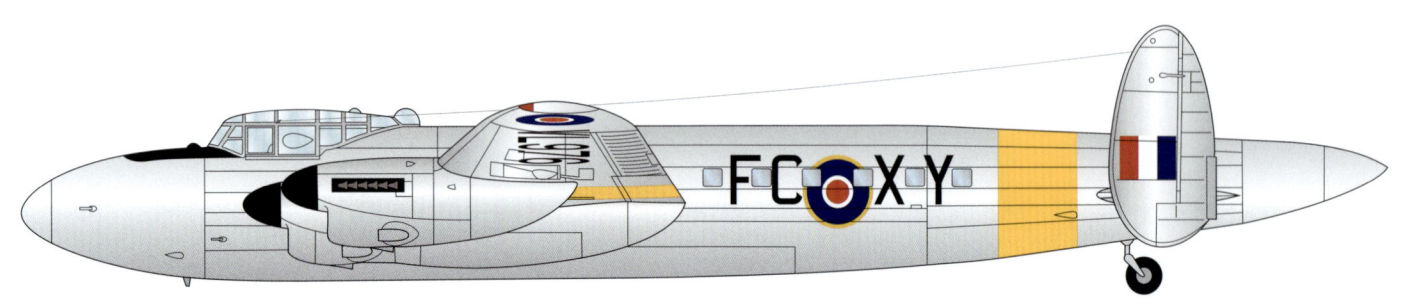

Avro Lancastrian C.2, VL976, 'FCX•Y', Empire Flying School, Hullavington, Wiltshire 1948
The original idea for converting the Lancaster airframe into a cargo aircraft came from Trans Canada Airlines, who saw potential in the long range and load carrying capabilities. The initial conversion proved to be a success, being used to transport mail and freight across the Atlantic in under 12½ hours. As a result of this success, more Lancaster airframes were allocated to be converted into what became known as the Lancastrian. RAF usage was limited to twenty-three C.1 aircraft (the majority of these went to BOAC after the war), thirty-three C.2 aircraft, and eight C.4 aircraft. Many long distance flights and records were established by the Lancastrian, especially those used by the Empire Air Navigation School – one notable flight being the circumnavigation of the globe in less than a week.
Reference used: p107 'RAF Flying Training and Support Units since 1912' by Ray Sturtivant with John Hamlin, Air-Britain (Historians) Ltd 2007

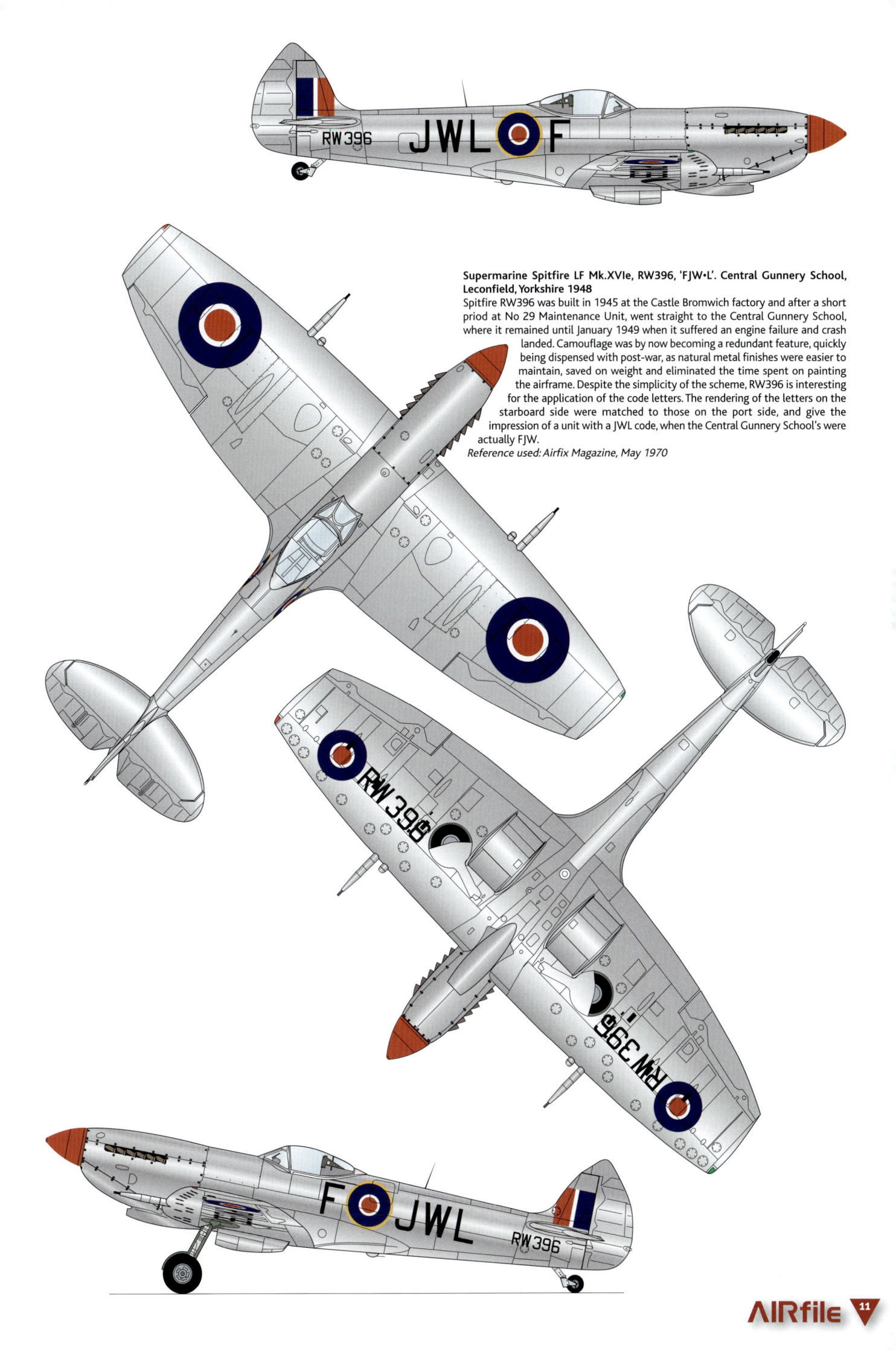

Supermarine Spitfire LF Mk.XVIe, RW396, 'FJW•L'. Central Gunnery School, Leconfield, Yorkshire 1948

Spitfire RW396 was built in 1945 at the Castle Bromwich factory and after a short priod at No 29 Maintenance Unit, went straight to the Central Gunnery School, where it remained until January 1949 when it suffered an engine failure and crash landed. Camouflage was by now becoming a redundant feature, quickly being dispensed with post-war, as natural metal finishes were easier to maintain, saved on weight and eliminated the time spent on painting the airframe. Despite the simplicity of the scheme, RW396 is interesting for the application of the code letters. The rendering of the letters on the starboard side were matched to those on the port side, and give the impression of a unit with a JWL code, when the Central Gunnery School's were actually FJW.

Reference used: Airfix Magazine, May 1970

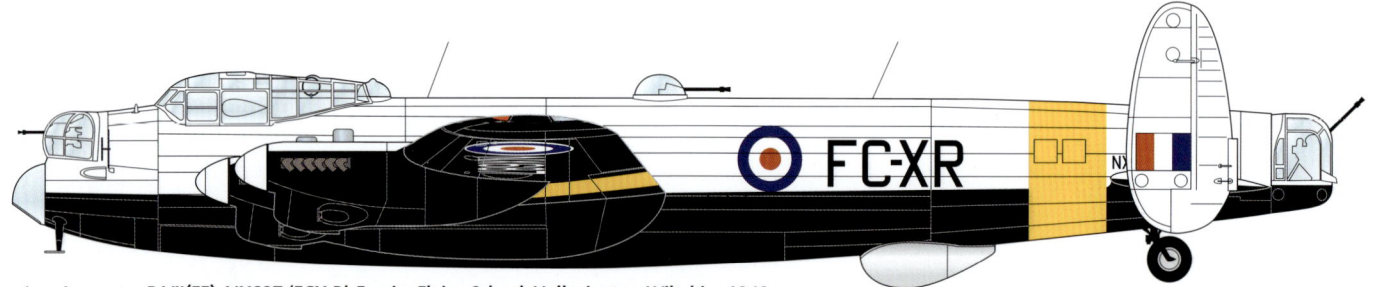

Avro Lancaster B.VII(FE), NX687, 'FCX·R', Empire Flying School, Hullavington, Wiltshire 1948
As can be ascertained from the Mark number f this aircraft, NX687 was one of the Lancaster force that was to go to the Far East to continue the war against the Japanese. The entire production run of 180 Mk VII aircraft were built by Austin Motors and all were eventually converted to FE requirements. NX687 was initially with No 15 Squadron RAF until they began to be re-equipped with Lincolns from 1947, at which point this aircraft went to No 5 Maintainance Unit and from there to the Empire Flying School. It then spent a period of time with the Empire Air Armament School until it crashed in France. Because of this, the aircraft ended its days as an instructional airframe.
Reference used: p26 'RAF Flying Training and Support Units since 1912' by Ray Sturtivant with John Hamlin, Air Britain (Historians) Ltd.,2007

Miles Master II, DK805, 'FJX·U'. Central Gunnery School, Leconfield, Yorkshire 1948-49
DK805 was built at Woodley, one of a batch of 500, and survived to see post-war service with the Central Gunnery School. The overall yellow colour scheme was adopted in 1946, as were the four letter squadron codes. The Central Gunnery School was a highly specialised and advanced unit, dealing with all aspects of air-to-air and air-to-ground gunnery techniques, from usage of gun sights, turrets, machine guns and cannon, to aircraft recognition, leadership training and radar. It was also the place during wartime that fighter pilots came to hone their skills, with Mustangs, Spitfires and Thunderbolts, making use of the facilities along with their pilots. Master DK805 would have been part of a huge and diverse collection of aircraft used both during and after the War.
Reference used: p374 'Miles Military Trainers' by Alan W Hall, Scale Military Modelling, Volume 19 Number 8 October 1997, Guideline Publications 1997

Percival Prentice, VS270, 'FA·FJ', RAF College, Cranwell, Lincolnshire 1949
The Prentice entered service with the RAF in 1947 as the replacement for the Tiger Moth. It allowed for basic training in the use of flaps, variable pitch propellers and radio, was obviously usable in adverse weather with the fully enclosed cockpit, and being a side-by-side trainer, the first with the RAF, allowed the instructor to better see the trainee's progress, all of these things impossible in the Tiger Moth. Of the numbers built for the RAF, (approximately 370), 125 were built under sub-contract by Blackburn Aircraft, and VS270 is from this company. With standard yellow trainer bands over silver, VS270 had an unusual rendering of the four letter code, splitting it into pairs, when the actual code for Cranwell should have been FAF-J.
Reference used: p131 'The History of Britain's Military Training Aircraft' by Ray Sturtivant, Haynes Publishing Group 1987

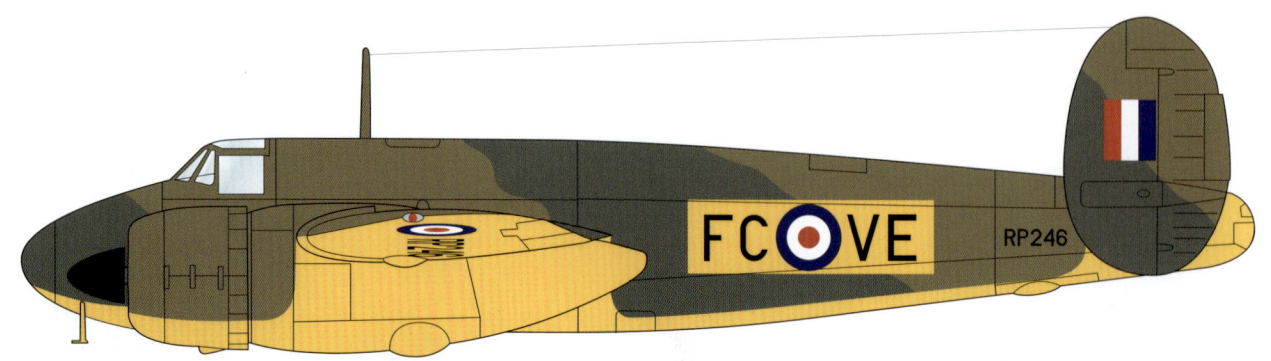

Bristol Buckmaster T.1, RP246, 'FC·VE', Empire Flying School, Hullavington, Wiltshire 1949
When the Buckmaster T.1 entered service at the end of World War Two, it was the fastest trainer that the RAF had up to that point. The existence of the Buckmaster came about by way of the Brigand, an aircraft intended to replace the Beaufighter. Whilst in development, the Air Ministry requested a dual control version of the Brigand. The Bristol Company were loathe to do this, for reasons of ease of development and production of the Brigand, and instead put forward the proposal of converting the Buckingham fast day bomber, an aircraft that had found its intended role taken by the Mosquito, with a subsequent reduction in production numbers. 110 Buckmasters were constructed from Buckingham components, a widening of the upper fuselage at the cockpit area allowing for side-by-side seating.
Reference used: p156 'Aircraft of the Royal Air Force since 1918' by Owen Thetford, published by Owen Thetford 1957

Vickers Armstrong Wellington Mk.X, RP550, 'FMB•Y', No 201 Advanced Flying School, Swinderby, Lincolnshire, January 1949

RP550 was one of 600 Wellingtons built at the shadow factory in Blackpool in 1943. After flying with No 20 Maintenance Unit, it moved to No 17 Operational Training Unit at Silverstone. It was whist at 17 OTU that RP550 was rudely 'mounted from behind' by another Wellington during night taxying, damaging the tail around the turret, tailfin and tailplanes.

No 17 OTU was re-designated No 201 Advanced Flying School in March 1947 and moved to Swinderby. RP550 had by now been repaired, marked with yellow trainer bands and the post-war four letter coding and a pointedly relevant warning under the tail code, 'Accident Prevention Concerns You'! In just two more years the Wellingtons would be gone, being replaced by the Vickers Varsity.

Reference used: p151 & 154 'Vickers-Armstrongs Wellington' by Ken Delve, Crowood Aviation Series, The Crowood Press Ltd, 1998

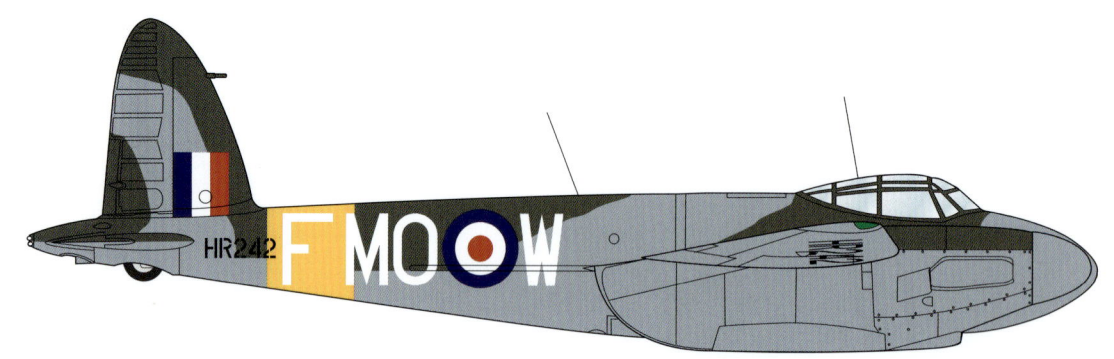

De Havilland Mosquito FB.VI, HR242, 'FMO•W', No 204 Advanced Flying School, Brize Norton, Oxfordshire 1949
No. 204 Advanced Flying School was formed from two Operational Training Units, Nos 13 and 16, specifically for the training of crews for this still potent aircraft, which was rightly regarded at the start of a long and varied career as one of the fastest operational aircraft in the world. The reference photo for HR242 shows it in a very sorry state, obviously having suffered a wheels-up landing, with spinners missing and propellers bent. The standard Night Fighter colour scheme is compromised by the post-war four letter coding and what could be a yellow band around the aft fuselage. The high speed whip aerials are of note.
Reference used: p35 'RAF Flying Training and Support Units since 1912' by Ray Sturtivant with John Hamlin, Air Britain Publications 2007

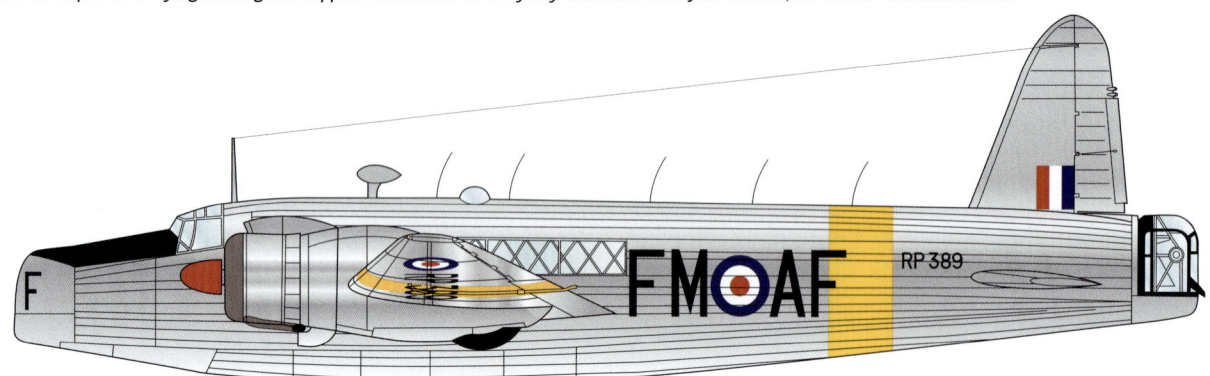

Vickers Armstrong Wellington T.10, RP389, 'FMA•F', No 201 Advanced Flying School, Swinderby, Lincolnshire 1950
By 1950 the Wellington was well past its prime, and would soon be replaced by the Valetta and Varsity. The last few examples would finally be given the standard colour scheme of yellow trainer bands over Aluminium (silver). RP389 was built at the shadow factory in Blackpool. These factories were Government sponsored and built, and were dispersed around the country and capable of continuing production if the parent company was put out of action, as did happen at the Weybridge factory when it was targeted by the *Luftwaffe*. The red spinners indicate that this aircraft flew with 'A' Squadron.
Reference used: p153 'Vickers-Armstrongs Wellington' by Ken Delve, Crowood Aviation Series, The Crowood Press Ltd, 1998

De Havilland Hornet F.3, PX362, 'MS•H', Hornet Conversion Flight, RAF Linton-on-Ouse, Yorkshire 1949/50
The Hornet can be considered to be the epitome of the twin piston-engined fighter. It was the fastest piston-engined fighter to serve with the RAF, and also the last. Incorporating all the knowledge and technology garnered from the Mosquito, and special, handed Merlin engines, that eliminated drag by reducing the frontal area, the Hornet had a range of over 2,500 miles and a top speed in excess of 470mph. These requirements were paramount to the intended role of the aircraft, to fight Japanese aircraft in the Pacific. The end of the war precluded any deployment, however the Hornet found a niche replacing Brigands in Malaya, and were successfully employed in rocket attacks. The Hornet Conversion Flight lasted for just a single year, and the Hornet itself was replaced by Vampires in 1955.
Reference used: p166 'RAF Flying Training and Support Units since 1912' by Ray Sturtivant with John Hamlin, Air-Britain (Historians) Ltd 2007

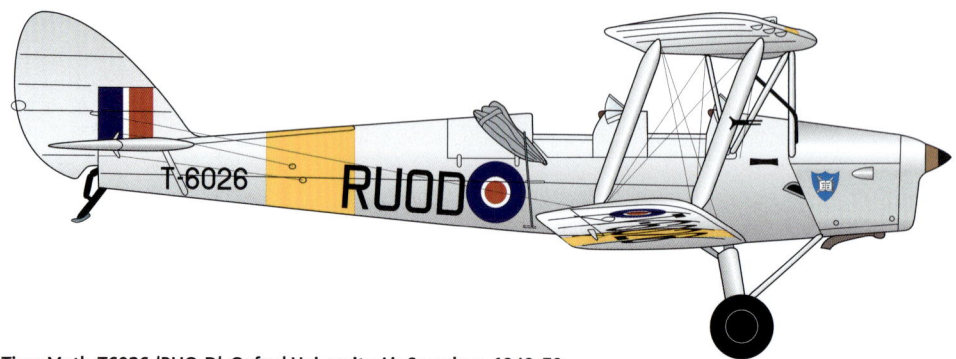

De Havilland DH 82A Tiger Moth, T6026, 'RUO•D', Oxford University Air Squadron, 1949-50
Tiger Moth T6026 displays the post-war colour scheme of silver overall with yellow bands to fuselage and wings that would be the standard trainer colouring for many years to come. The four letter code system was introduced post-war but would last only into the early 1950s. In this case the 'R' stood for Reserve Command, the 'U' was for the University Squadrons, while the 'O' represented the particular University, Oxford, and the 'D' was the individual aircraft letter. The 'T' prefix to the serial number shows that this aircraft was built by Morris Motors at Cowley.
Reference used: p34 'De Havilland Tiger Moth 1931-1945 (all marks) Owners' Workshop Manual' by Stephen Slater with assistance of the de Havilland Moth Club, Haynes Publishing 2009

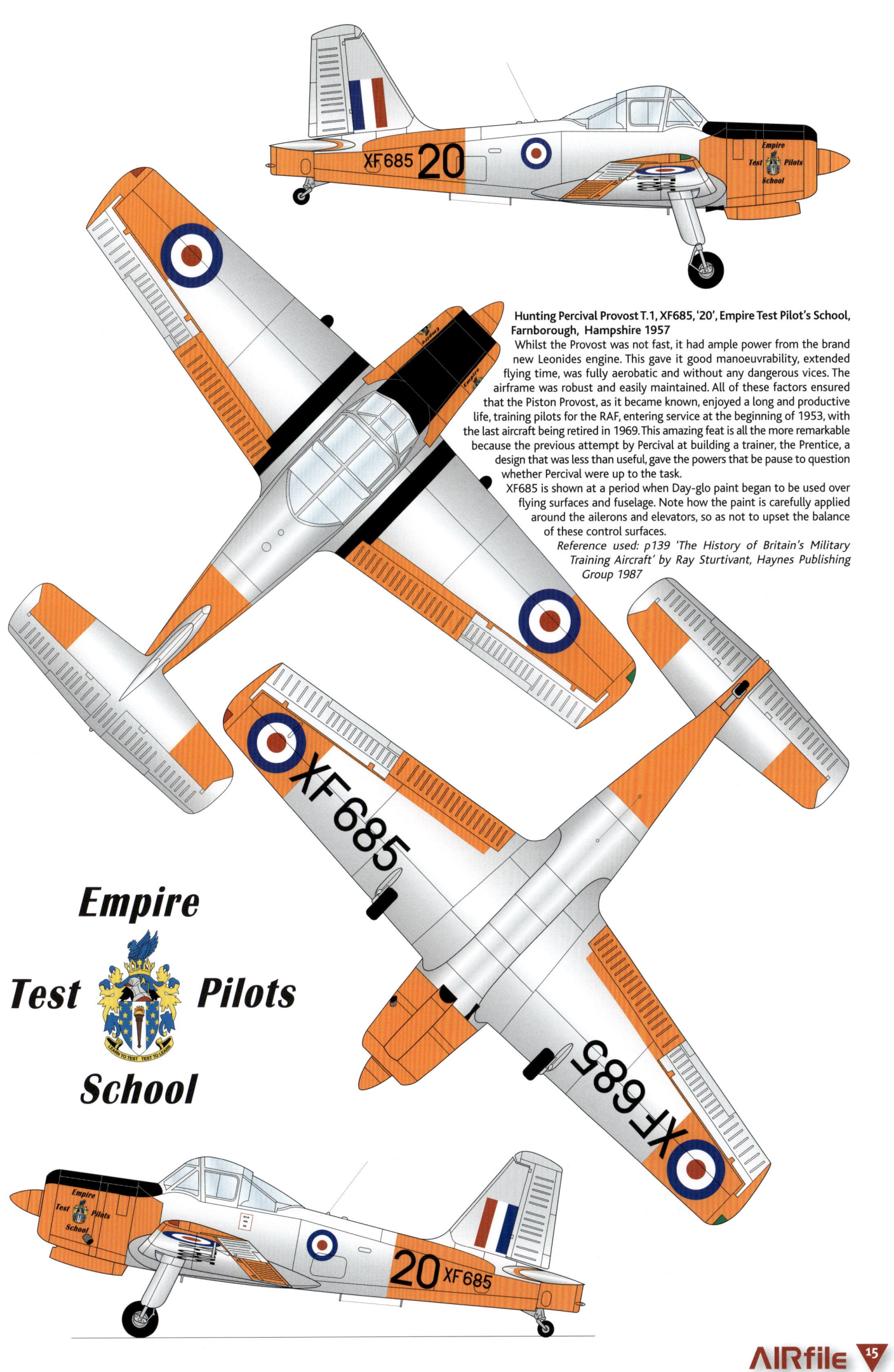

Hunting Percival Provost T.1, XF685, '20', Empire Test Pilot's School, Farnborough, Hampshire 1957

Whilst the Provost was not fast, it had ample power from the brand new Leonides engine. This gave it good manoeuvrability, extended flying time, was fully aerobatic and without any dangerous vices. The airframe was robust and easily maintained. All of these factors ensured that the Piston Provost, as it became known, enjoyed a long and productive life, training pilots for the RAF, entering service at the beginning of 1953, with the last aircraft being retired in 1969. This amazing feat is all the more remarkable because the previous attempt by Percival at building a trainer, the Prentice, a design that was less than useful, gave the powers that be pause to question whether Percival were up to the task.

XF685 is shown at a period when Day-glo paint began to be used over flying surfaces and fuselage. Note how the paint is carefully applied around the ailerons and elevators, so as not to upset the balance of these control surfaces.

Reference used: p139 'The History of Britain's Military Training Aircraft' by Ray Sturtivant, Haynes Publishing Group 1987

Empire Test Pilots School

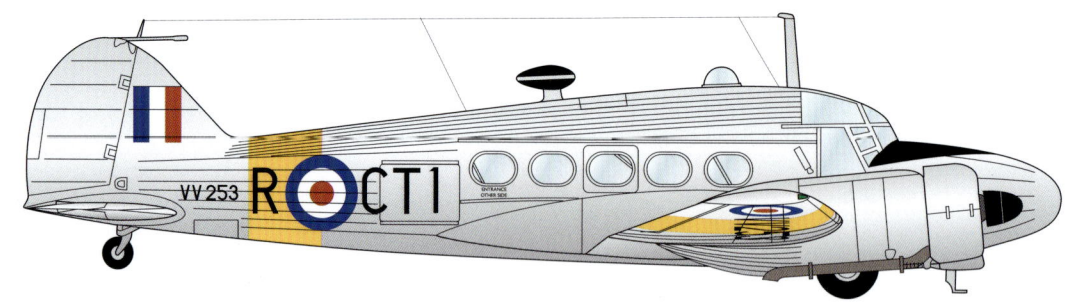

Avro Anson T.21, VV253, RCT•1, No 18 Reserve Flying School, Fairoaks, Surrey, 1950
The Anson T.21 was one of the last Marks of this useful design to be built, with the T.20 specific to South Rhodesia and used as a general trainer, and the T.22 a dedicated radio trainer. The T.21 was the navigation trainer version, of which 252 were built. No 18 RFS was created in May 1947 from what was the wartime 18 EFTS, this in turn was the offspring of the pre-war 18 ERFTS, which began operating from Fairoaks in 1937. By the time the Reserve Flying Schools were disbanded in 1953, this particular Flying School, under these three guises, stayed at Fairoaks for the entire life of the School, a period of some sixteen years, unusually never having been assigned to any other airfield.
Reference used: p87 'The History of Britain's Military Training Aircraft' by Ray Sturtivant, Haynes Publishing Group, 1987

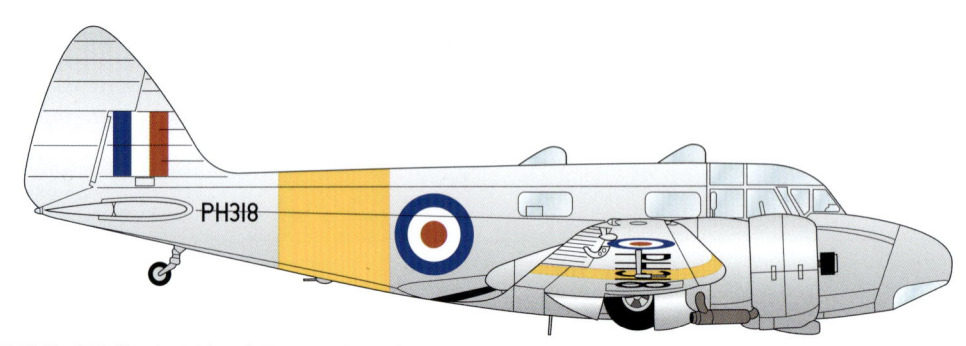

Airspeed Oxford I, PH318, No 3 Civilian Anti-Aircraft Co-operation Unit, Exeter, 1951
Production of the Oxford ceased in 1945, but despite this, many aircraft continued to be of use in various capacities up to ten years after the end of the World War Two. It also gave credence to the wood and glue construction that was initially looked upon with a certain amount of dubiousness, proving the durability of the technique, (although there are stories of Canadian 'Oxboxes' going in for service and having gallons of accumulated moisture flowing from their wings, not to mention the dry rot!). PH318 carried the post-war scheme of overall silver with yellow trainer bands. Note also the use of a second observation blister on the upper fuselage.
Reference used: p1132 'Exercising the Guns' by Keith A Saunders, Aviation News, Volume 22, Number 24, May-June 1994

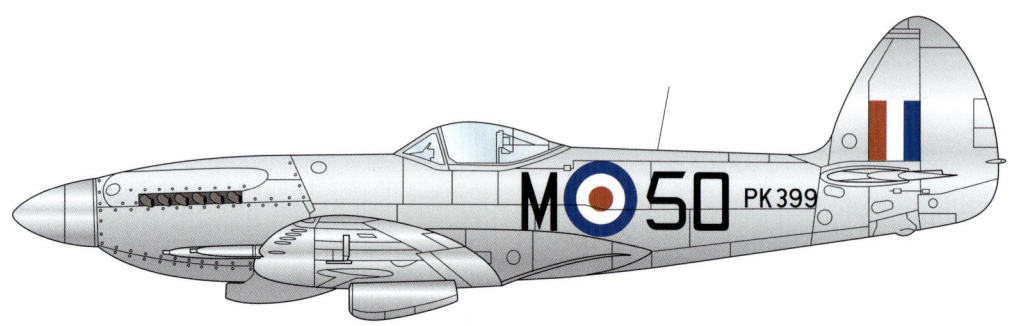

Supermarine Spitfire F.22, PK399, 'M•50', No 102 Flying Refresher School, North Luffenham, Rutland 1951
Spitfire F.22 PK399 was built towards the end of the war so by the time it entered service it never actually saw combat. In 1951 it was used as an aircraft to retrain pilots moving on to Vampires and Meteors, these pilots being part of the Royal Air Force Reserve. The Flying Refresher Schools allowed Reserve pilots the chance to fly more powerful aircraft than they were used to before transitioning to the new jets. No 102 FRS was at North Luffenham for only half a year before it disbanded. PK399 itself was sold for scrap in 1954.
Reference used: Collection of Mike Starmer

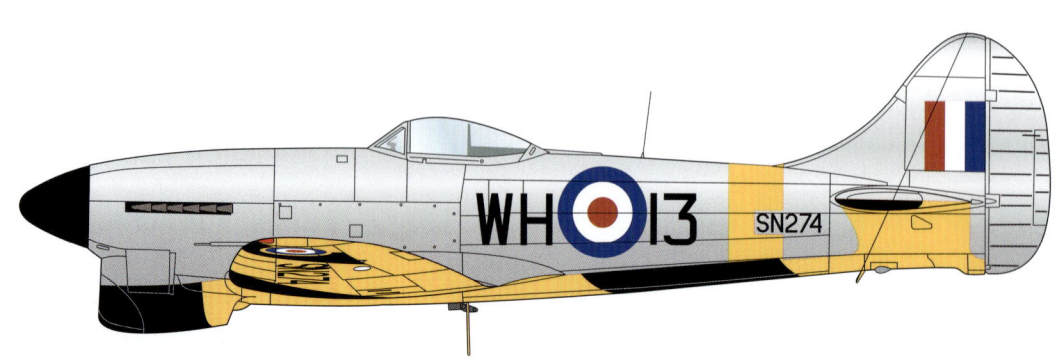

Hawker Tempest TT.5, SN274, 'WH•13', Armament Practice Station, Acklington, Northumberland 1951
By 1947 the RAF was moving towards having jet fighters exclusively, with only a few squadrons that were still flying the ultimate piston engine fighters such as the Spitfire 24 and the Tempest V. The latter was considered obsolescent and held in storage areas from where some eighty airframes were converted into Target Tugs, the high speed of these aircraft being deemed suitable for towing targets for the guns of Vampires and Meteors. Previous tugs were now considered much too slow. The one disadvantage in using Tempests was the fact that it was a one target per flight system. The wire for the target was attached to the belly of the Tempest, whilst the rest of the cable and the target itself were laid out on the runway. The Tempest would take off dragging the target into the air. After the firing exercise was over the aircraft would overfly the airfield and release the target.
Reference used: p528 'Target Tugs' by M W Payne, Aircraft in Detail, Scale Aircraft Modelling, Volume 10 Number 12 September 1988

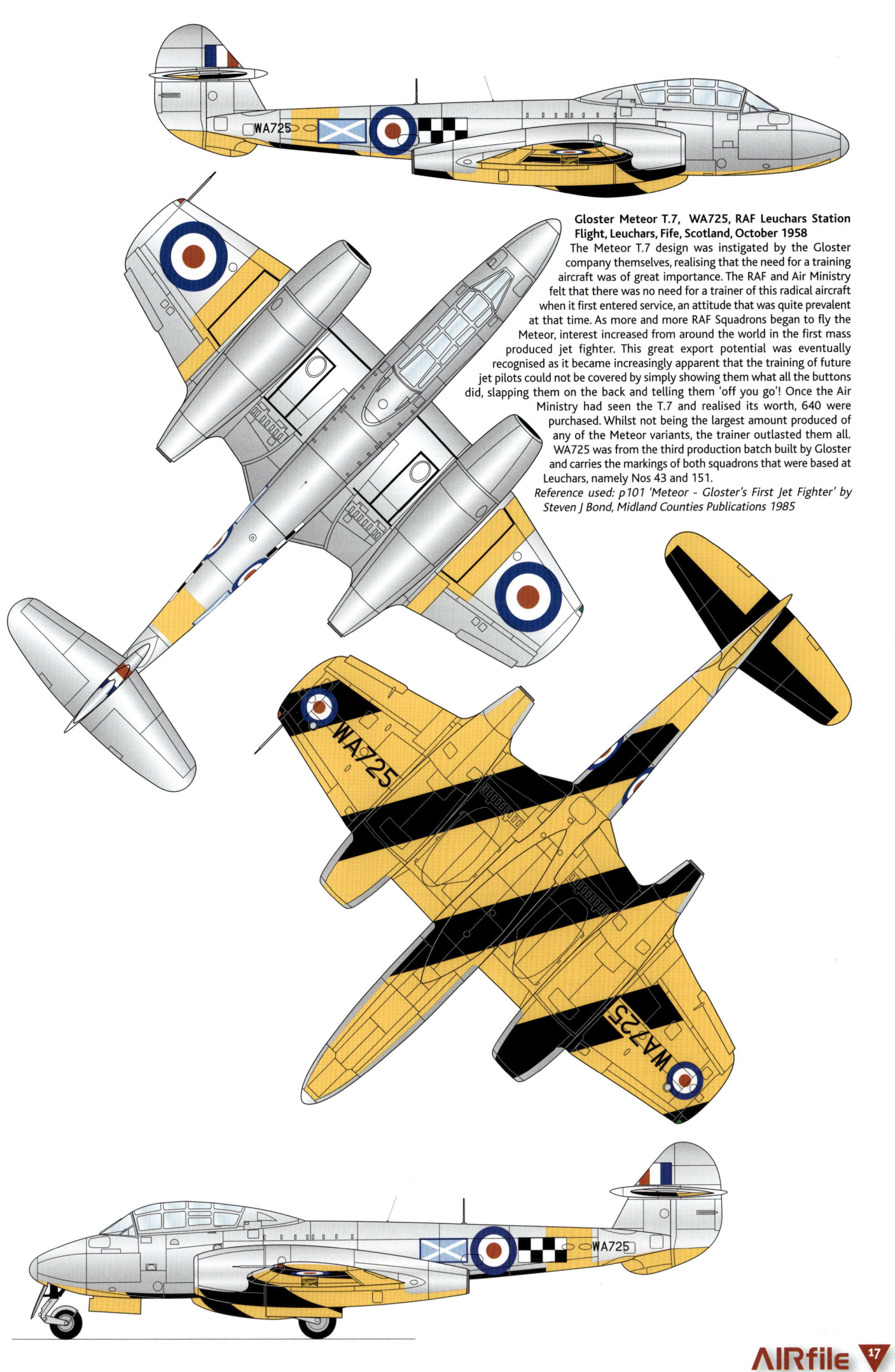

Gloster Meteor T.7, WA725, RAF Leuchars Station Flight, Leuchars, Fife, Scotland, October 1958

The Meteor T.7 design was instigated by the Gloster company themselves, realising that the need for a training aircraft was of great importance. The RAF and Air Ministry felt that there was no need for a trainer of this radical aircraft when it first entered service, an attitude that was quite prevalent at that time. As more and more RAF Squadrons began to fly the Meteor, interest increased from around the world in the first mass produced jet fighter. This great export potential was eventually recognised as it became increasingly apparent that the training of future jet pilots could not be covered by simply showing them what all the buttons did, slapping them on the back and telling them 'off you go'! Once the Air Ministry had seen the T.7 and realised its worth, 640 were purchased. Whilst not being the largest amount produced of any of the Meteor variants, the trainer outlasted them all. WA725 was from the third production batch built by Gloster and carries the markings of both squadrons that were based at Leuchars, namely Nos 43 and 151.

Reference used: *p101 'Meteor - Gloster's First Jet Fighter' by Steven J Bond, Midland Counties Publications 1985*

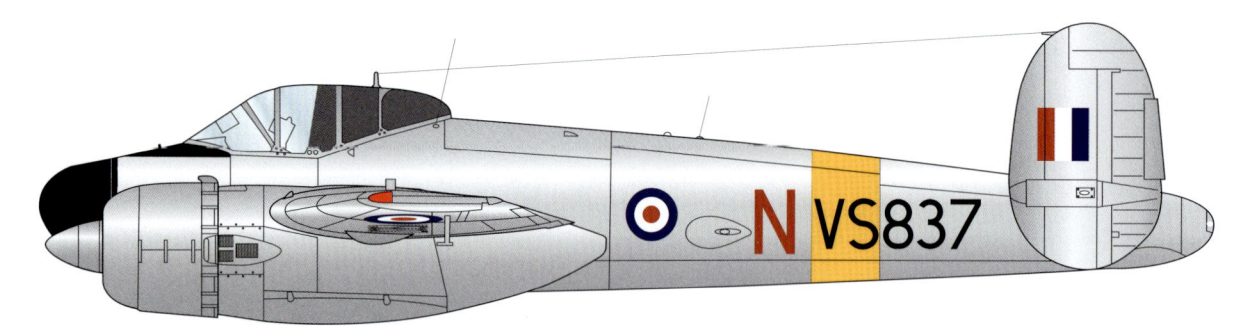

Bristol Brigand T.4, VS837, 'N', No 228 Operational Conversion Unit, RAF Leeming, Yorkshire 1951
Brigand VS837 was initially built as a bomber, the B.1 version, in 1949. In a very short period of time, it had been converted to T.4 standard and was flying with 228 OCU by 1951. This unit gave radar navigators their initial training in the use of Airborne Intercept radar. Fitted with an AI radar in an extended nose, the trainee would sit in the aft cockpit under a blacked out canopy. This large one piece moulding gave the crew (of B.Is) an unparalleled view from the high mounted cockpit. The down side to this was that the Brigand B.Is operated almost exclusively abroad, and the extensive cockpit glazing acted as a huge greenhouse, practically cooking the crews alive. The last Brigands retired from the RAF in 1958.
Reference used: p154 'Aircraft of the Royal Air Force since 1918' by Owen Thetford, Guild Publishing London, 1988

Canadair Sabre F.4, XB738, 'U', Sabre Conversion Flight, RAF(G) Wildenrath, West Germany 1954
This particular Sabre was one of the aircraft that were used by the Sabre Conversion Flight. This unit had come into existence in March 1953 at Wildenrath in Germany to retrain Vampire pilots, as Britain, at this point, had no high speed fighter aircraft, with both the Swift and the Hunter yet to enter service. It was because of this fact that the British Government had to go 'cap in hand' to the Americans for the only suitable aircraft, namely the Sabre. The North American Company, unable to fulfill the needs of both the USAF and Britain, passed the request on to Canadair, who were building Sabres under licence. The F.4 Sabres supplied to Britain were used for a mere three years before being replaced by the Hunter. The Sabre Conversion Flight was dis-banded in June 1954, whereupon all Sabre training was undertaken by 229 OCU.
Reference used: http://www.rafjever.org/4sqnpic277.htm & p43 'Flying on the Sharp Edge' by Charles Keil, Scale Aircraft Modelling, September 2012

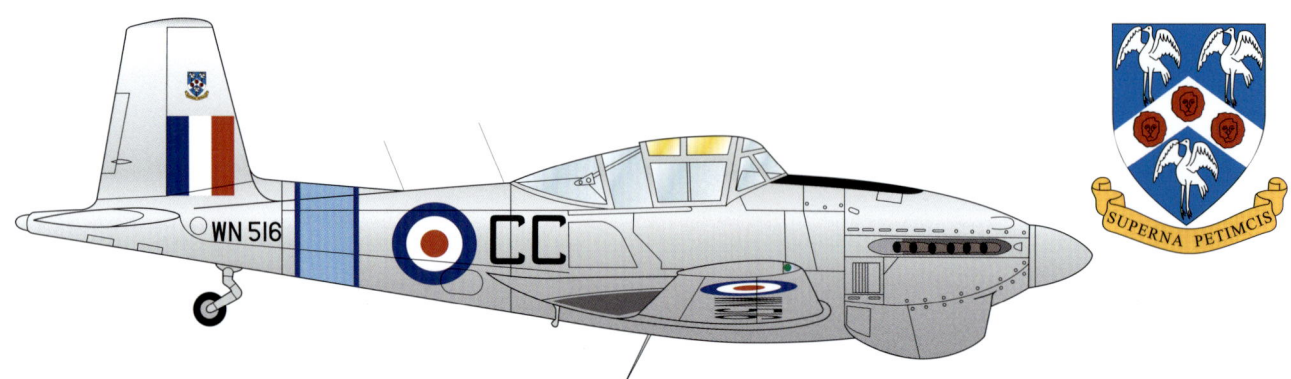

Boulton Paul Balliol T.2, WN516, 'CC', RAF College, Cranwell, Lincolnshire 1955
After a very limited service life with No 7 FTS, a mere two years, most Balliols were passed on to the RAF College at Cranwell. It was here that pilots got their last chance to fly an aircraft that was as close to a wartime fighter as it was possible to get, with a Merlin engine up front and a fighter-like appearance. A pilot had to be careful though, as the Merlin engine could bite back if the throttle was opened too quickly, the resulting torque spinning the airframe in the opposite direction to the propeller. Notwithstanding the small numbers built, Cranwell became the recipient of the largest amount, approximately one third of all Balliols built passing through the College. Even so, their tenure there was short lived, being replaced by the Vampire T.11 in 1956. WN516 was one of the batch of thirty airframes constructed under license at Blackburns. The forward fuselage of this aircraft still exists at the North East Aircraft Museum in Sunderland.
Reference used: p151 'The History of Britain's Military Training Aircraft' by Ray Sturtivant, Haynes Publishing Group 1987

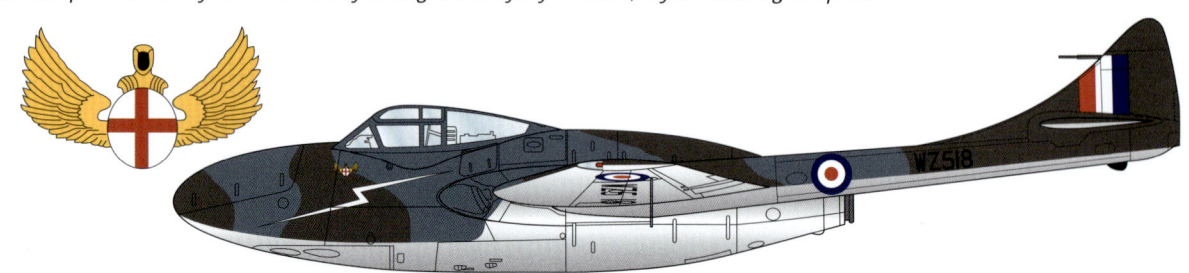

De Havilland Vampire T.11, WZ518, No 14 Squadron, 2nd TAF Communication Flight and Station Flight, Oldenburg, Germany 1955
There were three main criticisms levelled at the Vampire T.11 when it first entered service. Certain traits of the aircraft, when in a spin, were considered less that satisfactory. So the familiar 'bullets' at the bases of the fins were replaced with enlarged surfaces that extended along the booms. The initial canopy was inherited from the Night Fighter version, the heavy framing restricting the view and the perspex causing distortion. The ingress and egress of the pilots through the top of this canopy was also considered poor, dangerously so, as the lack of ejection seats made exiting the aircraft in flight almost impossible. All of these problems were addressed later in the production run, and early T.11s were retrofitted with fin extensions, ejection seats and an improved canopy. WZ518 has the altered tail fins but retains the early canopy and bucket seats.
Reference used: p29 'de Havilland Vampire' by WA Harrison, Warpaint Series No.27, Hall Park Books Ltd

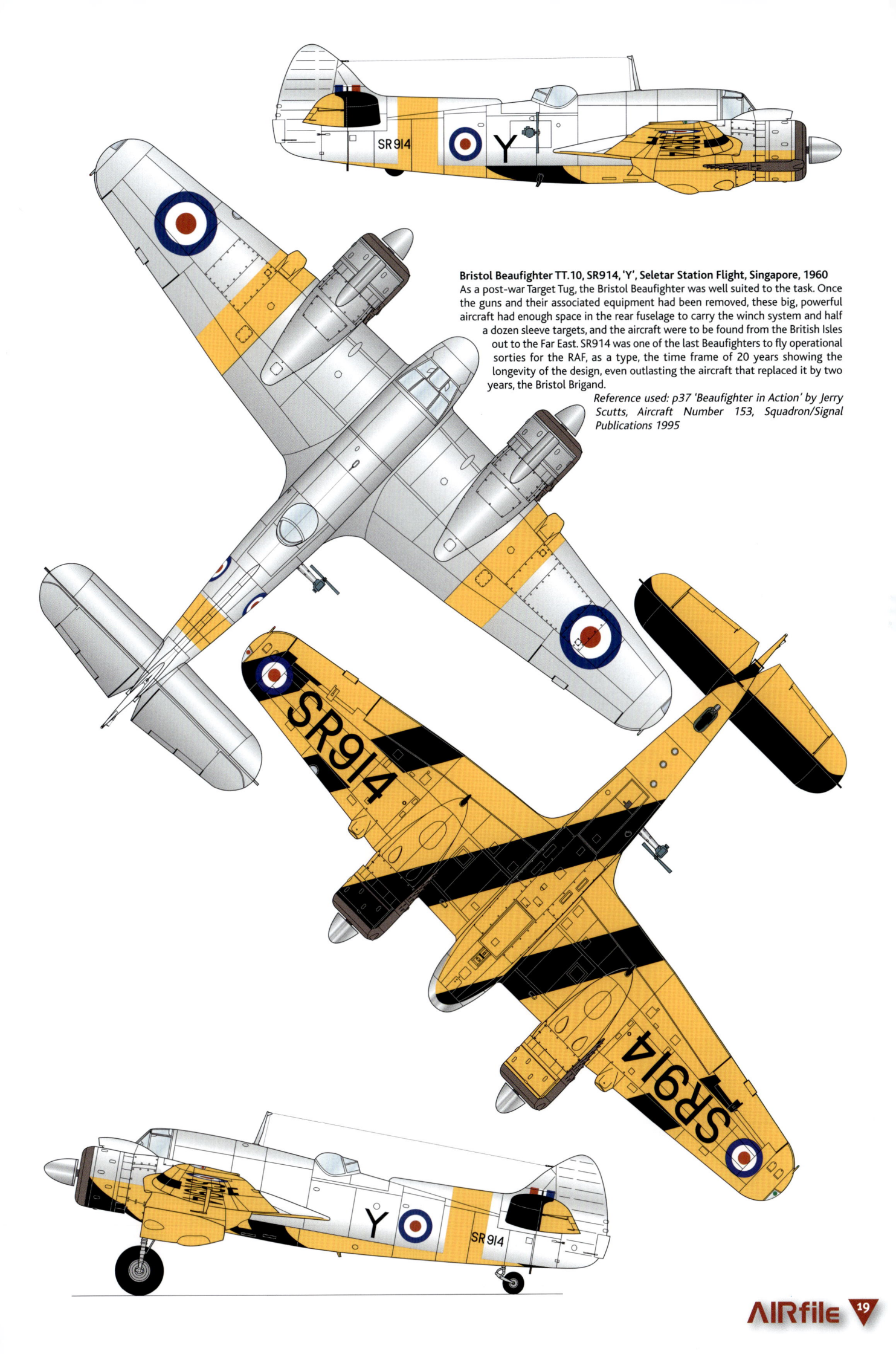

Bristol Beaufighter TT.10, SR914, 'Y', Seletar Station Flight, Singapore, 1960
As a post-war Target Tug, the Bristol Beaufighter was well suited to the task. Once the guns and their associated equipment had been removed, these big, powerful aircraft had enough space in the rear fuselage to carry the winch system and half a dozen sleeve targets, and the aircraft were to be found from the British Isles out to the Far East. SR914 was one of the last Beaufighters to fly operational sorties for the RAF, as a type, the time frame of 20 years showing the longevity of the design, even outlasting the aircraft that replaced it by two years, the Bristol Brigand.

Reference used: p37 'Beaufighter in Action' by Jerry Scutts, Aircraft Number 153, Squadron/Signal Publications 1995

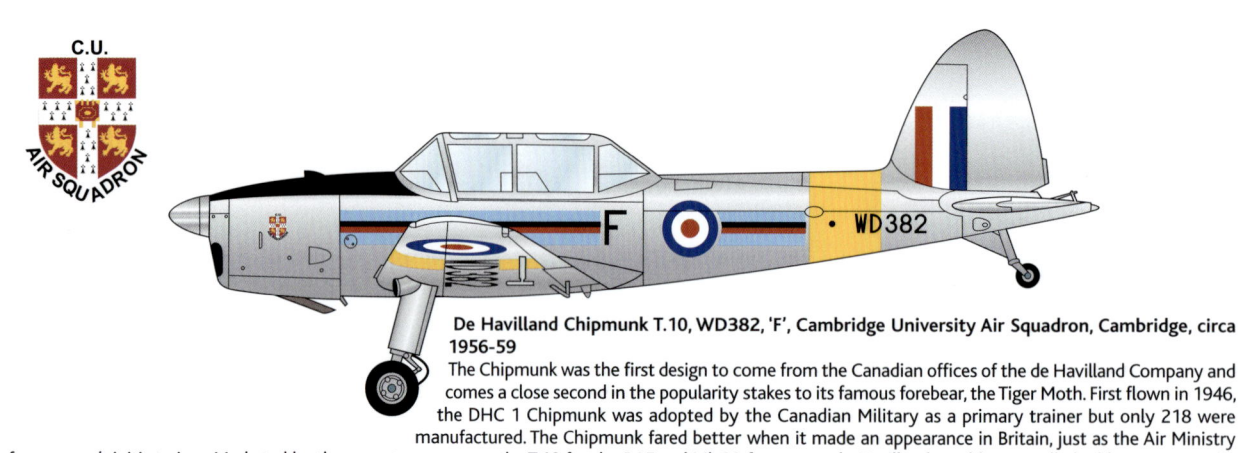

De Havilland Chipmunk T.10, WD382, 'F', Cambridge University Air Squadron, Cambridge, circa 1956-59

The Chipmunk was the first design to come from the Canadian offices of the de Havilland Company and comes a close second in the popularity stakes to its famous forebear, the Tiger Moth. First flown in 1946, the DHC 1 Chipmunk was adopted by the Canadian Military as a primary trainer but only 218 were manufactured. The Chipmunk fared better when it made an appearance in Britain, just as the Air Ministry were looking for a new *ab initio* trainer. Marketed by the parent company as the T.10 for the RAF and Mk.20 for export, de Havilland would eventually build over 1,000. The first examples went to the University Air Squadrons and WD382 is shown in the early silver scheme. Note the lack of anti-spin strakes forward of the tailplane.
Reference used: p282 'RAF Flying Training and Support Units since 1912' by Ray Sturtivant with John Hamlin, Air Britain Publications 2007

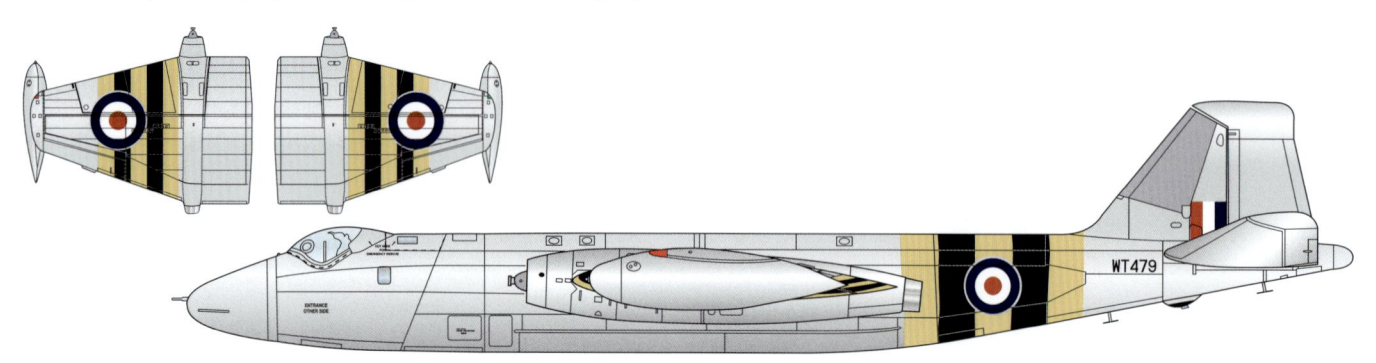

English Electric Canberra T.4, WT479, Upwood Station Flight, RAF Upwood, Cambridgeshire, (detachment to Nicosia, Cyprus), December 1956

When President Nasser of Egypt declared he would nationalise the Suez Canal, which was a 'tit-for-tat' political response to the removal of finance for the Aswan Dam, he set in motion events that would lead Britain and France, then owners of the Suez Canal, to retaliate with military force. The joint Anglo-French operation was to be known as Operation 'Musketeer', and the aim was to forcibly regain control of the Canal. Over a dozen Canberra squadrons took part, flying from the dubious safe haven of Cyprus, and WT479, detached to Nicosia, was caught up in the action, to the extent that cream and black 'invasion' stripes were applied.
Reference used: p254 'English Electric Canberra, by Ken Delve, Peter Green & John Clemons, Midland Counties Publications, 1992

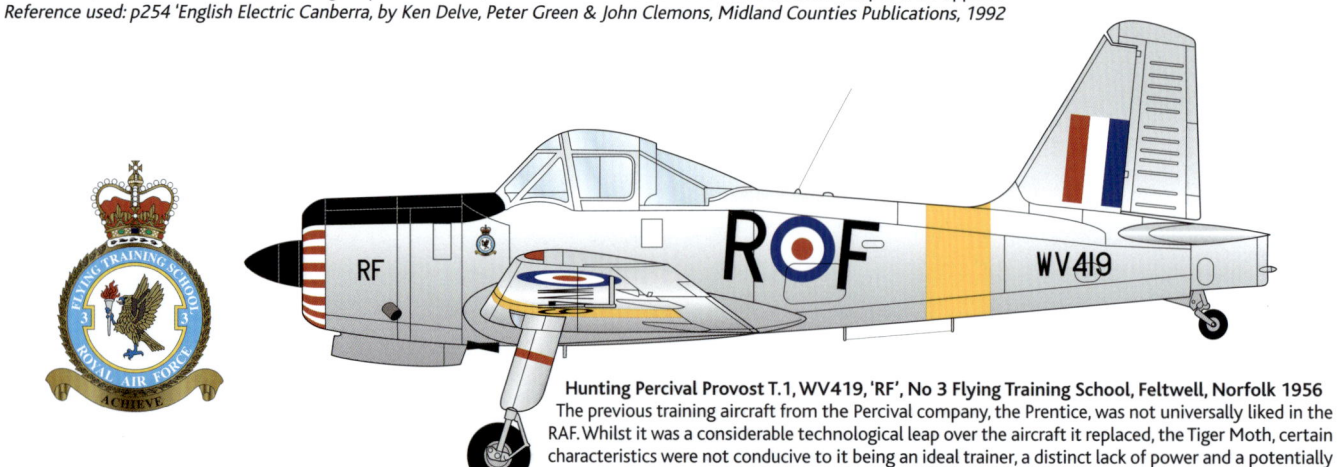

Hunting Percival Provost T.1, WV419, 'RF', No 3 Flying Training School, Feltwell, Norfolk 1956

The previous training aircraft from the Percival company, the Prentice, was not universally liked in the RAF. Whilst it was a considerable technological leap over the aircraft it replaced, the Tiger Moth, certain characteristics were not conducive to it being an ideal trainer, a distinct lack of power and a potentially fatal flat spinning tendancy were the main problems. Percival took on board the criticisms levelled at their product and produced the Provost, which was everything the Prentice was not. Produced as a private venture, the Provost pre-empted to a certain extent the RAF specification that called for the Prentice replacement, and was accepted as the next basic trainer for the RAF.
Reference used: p200 'Hunting Percival Provost' by Alan W Hall, Aircraft in Detail, Scale Aircraft Modelling, Volume 10, Number 5, February 1988

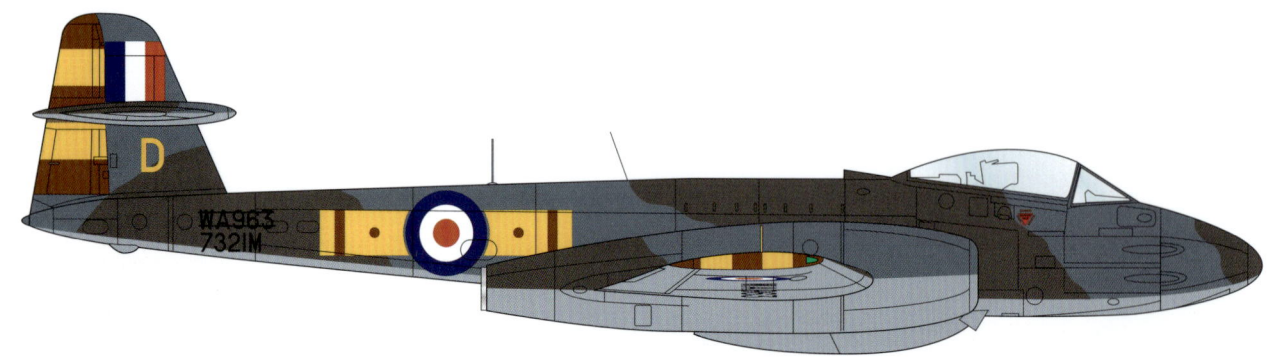

Gloster Meteor F.8, WA963, 'D', No 1 School of Technical Training, Halton, Buckinghamshire, March 1956

Like many redundant airframes, WA963 was to become a resident at one of the many Schools of Technical Training. With the original serial number crossed out and substituted with the ground instructional airframe number 7321M (some sources quote 7821M), this aircraft would end its days being picked over by various armourers, fitters, electricians and apprentices. Originally built by the parent company, Glosters, in the early 1950s, this F.8 served with No 65 Squadron and No 34 Squadron before going to the Armament Practice Station at Acklington, whose colours it continued to wear until its final demise. The design either side of the fuselage roundel are not squadron bars, but a representation of the target flag itself, and the dark red and yellow (black and yellow?) colours are repeated on the rudder and wingtips.
Reference used: p108 'Meteor - Gloster's First Jet Fighter' by Steven J Bond, Midland Counties Publications 1985

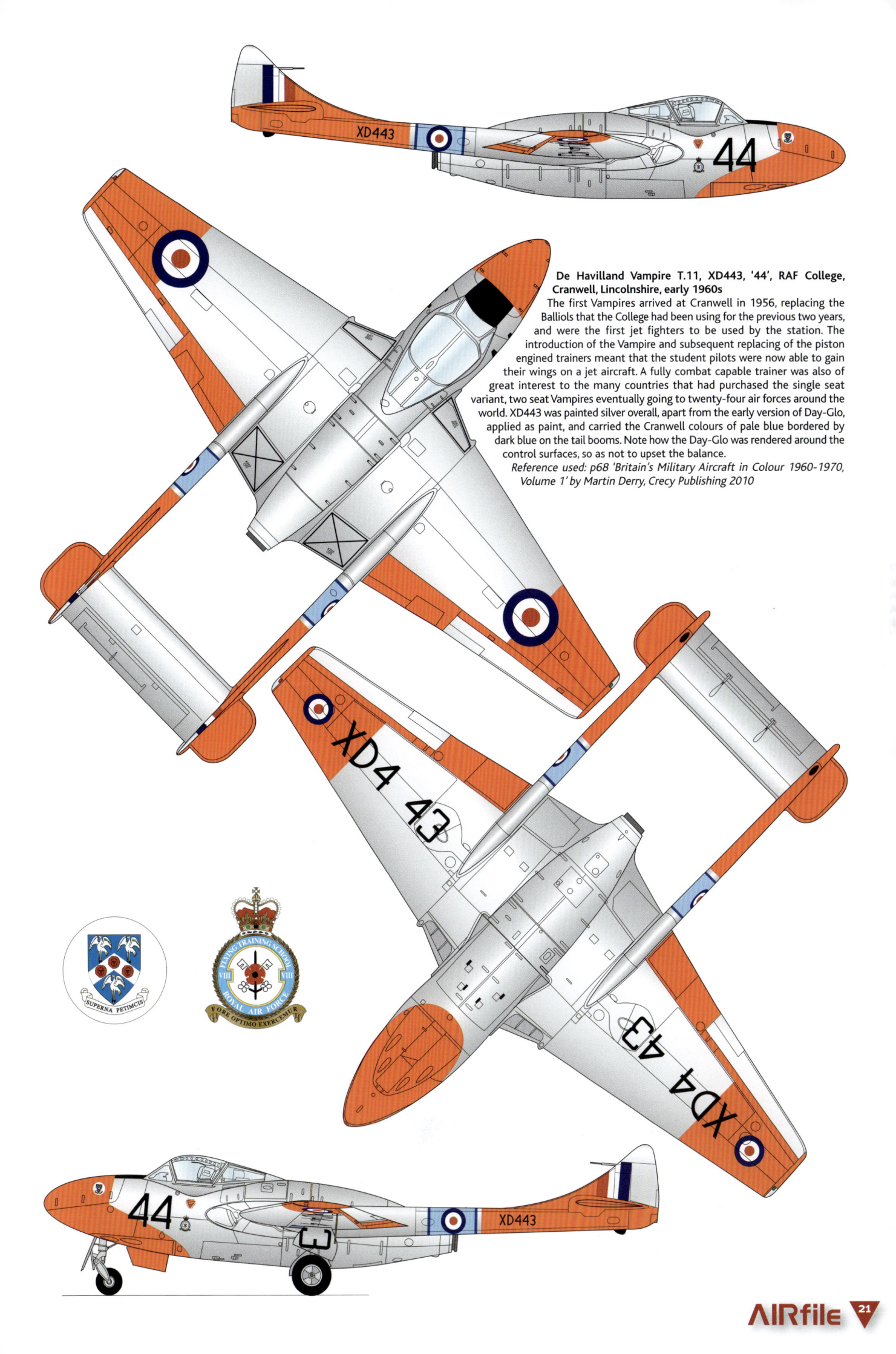

De Havilland Vampire T.11, XD443, '44', RAF College, Cranwell, Lincolnshire, early 1960s

The first Vampires arrived at Cranwell in 1956, replacing the Balliols that the College had been using for the previous two years, and were the first jet fighters to be used by the station. The introduction of the Vampire and subsequent replacing of the piston engined trainers meant that the student pilots were now able to gain their wings on a jet aircraft. A fully combat capable trainer was also of great interest to the many countries that had purchased the single seat variant, two seat Vampires eventually going to twenty-four air forces around the world. XD443 was painted silver overall, apart from the early version of Day-Glo, applied as paint, and carried the Cranwell colours of pale blue bordered by dark blue on the tail booms. Note how the Day-Glo was rendered around the control surfaces, so as not to upset the balance.

Reference used: p68 'Britain's Military Aircraft in Colour 1960-1970, Volume 1' by Martin Derry, Crecy Publishing 2010

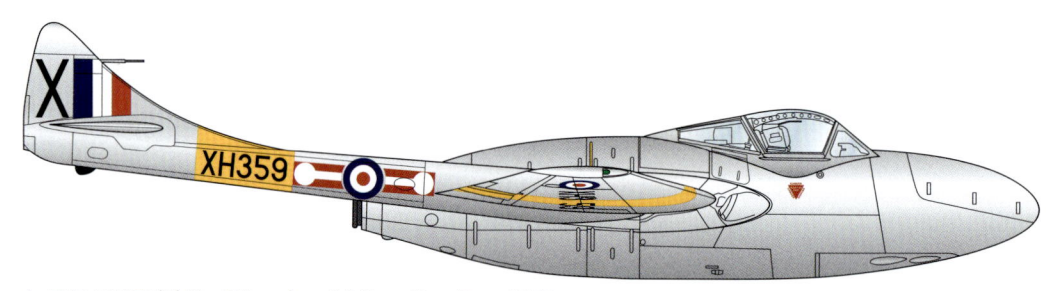

De Havilland Vampire T.11, XH359, 'X', No 45 Squadron, Sek Kong, Hong Kong, 1957
The similarity between the Vampire trainer and the Venom series of fighter bombers meant that any Venom Squadron would more than likely have a Vampire T.11 (or two) close to hand for refresher and training flights. No 45 Squadron used Vampire fighters for only a few months during 1955, alongside some Meteors. Both of these aircraft types were exchanged for Venoms in October of 1955, flying from Hong Kong on frontier patrol duties until the Squadron was disbanded in November 1957. XH359 was retained by the squadron, as mentioned, for training, and carries the unit marking of a white dumbell either side of the tail boom roundel. This insignia dates all the way back to World War One, when the Camels of the squadron were so marked.
Reference used: p247 'De Havilland Vampire - the complete history' by David Watkins, Sutton Publishing Ltd., 1996

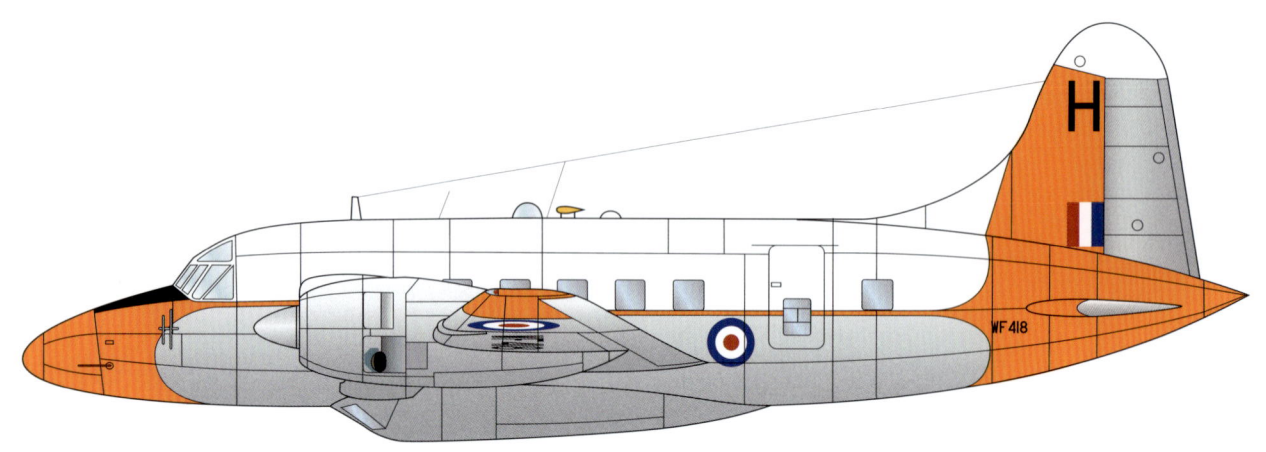

Vickers Varsity T.1, WF418, 'H', No 1 Air Navigation School, Topcliffe, North Yorkshire, August 1958
The Varsity was the logical next step in the Viking/Valetta family. Increased engine power, tricycle undercarriage and an overall increase in size gave the RAF a modern advanced multi-engined trainer to replace the Wellington T.10. The belly gondola allowed for the training of bomb aimers, the area just behind them capable of carrying up to 600lb of practice bombs. WF418 served with No. 2 Air Navigation School, and was probably part of the complement of aircraft that went to supply No 1 Air Navigation School at Topcliffe. This aircraft is also known to have served with the Air Electronics School.
Reference used: http://www.abpic.co.uk/photo/1224814/

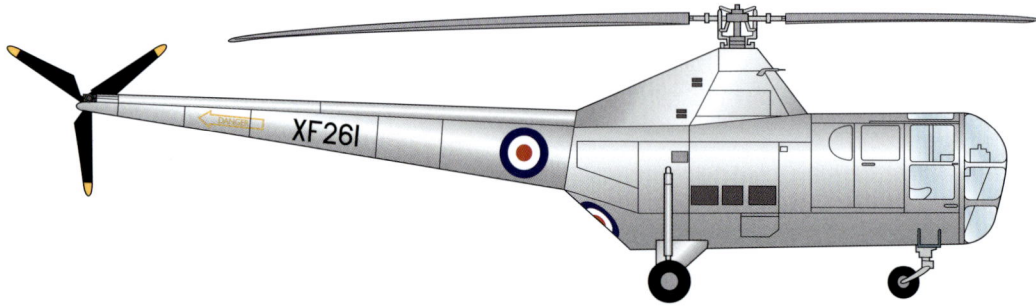

Westland Dragonfly HC.4, XF261, Central Flying School, RAF South Cerney, Gloucestershire, 1959
The Dragonfly was the first foray into helicopters for the Westland company, a design that was a license built copy of the Sikorsky S-51. It was also the first British built helicopter to go into service with the RAF, this particular Mark, the HC.4, serving from 1952. A small batch of just twelve HC.4 aircraft were constructed, and used for casualty evacuation. XF261 was the last of these to be built, and was part of the Central Flying School's Helicopter Squadron. Formed in 1954, it was the first unit to train instructors on the helicopter. Although the initial production run amounted to just 149 aircraft of all Marks, both Westland and the RAF realised the potential of this new form of transport, with Westland becoming world leaders in helicopter building, and the RAF adopting and adapting the helicopter in great numbers.
Reference used: www.abpic.co.uk/photo/1168614/

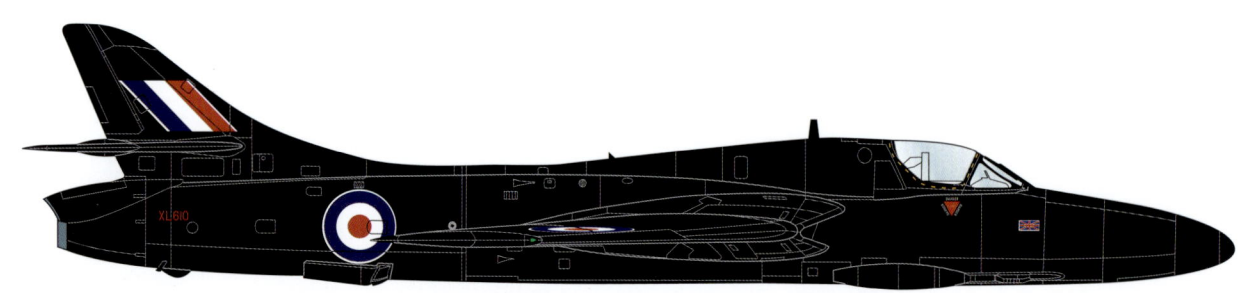

Hawker Hunter T.7, XL610, No 111 Squadron, 'Black Arrows' Aerobatic Display Team, RAF Wattisham, Suffolk 1959
By the time 'Treble One Squadron' were using this T.7, the trainer had been in RAF service for about half a year, service entry being with 229 OCU in August 1958. XL610 became the team leader's aircraft, and was coded 'Z' on the nose gear door. From 1957 until 1960, No 111 Squadron was the leading aerobatic team in the RAF, renowned for their mass formation manoeuvres, especially the looping of twenty-two Hunters, and only disbanded when the squadron went on to be re-equipped with the English Electric Lightning. XL610 stayed at Wattisham to become part of the Station Flight, but was to crash fatally in 1962.
Reference used: p23 'Hawker Hunter' by Alan W Hall, Warpaint Series No.8, Hall Park Books Ltd

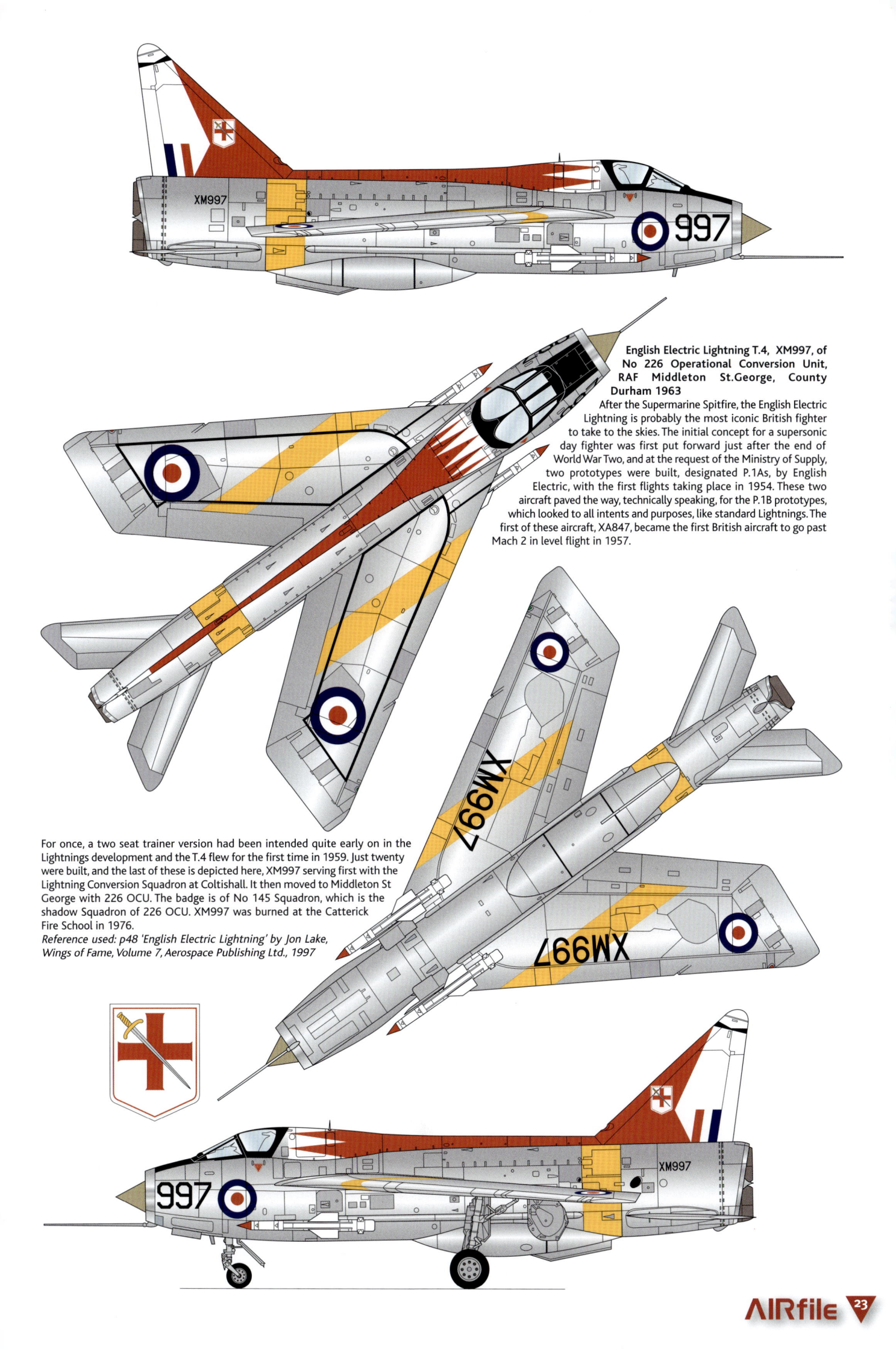

English Electric Lightning T.4, XM997, of No 226 Operational Conversion Unit, RAF Middleton St.George, County Durham 1963

After the Supermarine Spitfire, the English Electric Lightning is probably the most iconic British fighter to take to the skies. The initial concept for a supersonic day fighter was first put forward just after the end of World War Two, and at the request of the Ministry of Supply, two prototypes were built, designated P.1As, by English Electric, with the first flights taking place in 1954. These two aircraft paved the way, technically speaking, for the P.1B prototypes, which looked to all intents and purposes, like standard Lightnings. The first of these aircraft, XA847, became the first British aircraft to go past Mach 2 in level flight in 1957.

For once, a two seat trainer version had been intended quite early on in the Lightnings development and the T.4 flew for the first time in 1959. Just twenty were built, and the last of these is depicted here, XM997 serving first with the Lightning Conversion Squadron at Coltishall. It then moved to Middleton St George with 226 OCU. The badge is of No 145 Squadron, which is the shadow Squadron of 226 OCU. XM997 was burned at the Catterick Fire School in 1976.

Reference used: p48 'English Electric Lightning' by Jon Lake, Wings of Fame, Volume 7, Aerospace Publishing Ltd., 1997

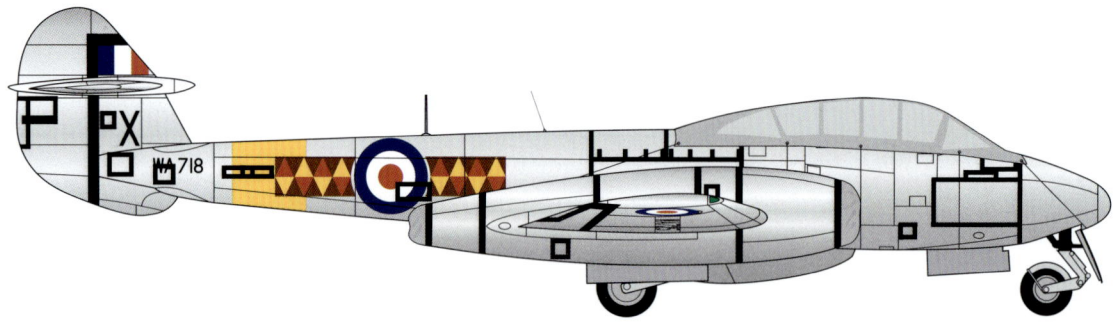

Gloster Meteor T.7, WA718 'X', ex-611 Squadron, No.12 Maintenance Unit, Kirkbride, Scotland, late 1950s
WA718 is depicted as it appeared sealed for storage at Kirkbride. The aircraft was initially based at No 205 Advanced Flying School before service with No 612 Squadron, then No 611 Squadron whose markings it displays. No 611 Squadron disbanded in 1957, and so it is assumed that WA718 was put into storage during that period. However, and unlike many of its squadron's aircraft, WA718 returned to active service and spent periods with the RAF Flying College and College of Air Warfare. It was finally struck off charge in August 1968 and scrapped in November 1978.
Reference used: p98 'Meteor - Gloster's First Jet Fighter' by Steven J Bond, Midland Counties Publications 1985

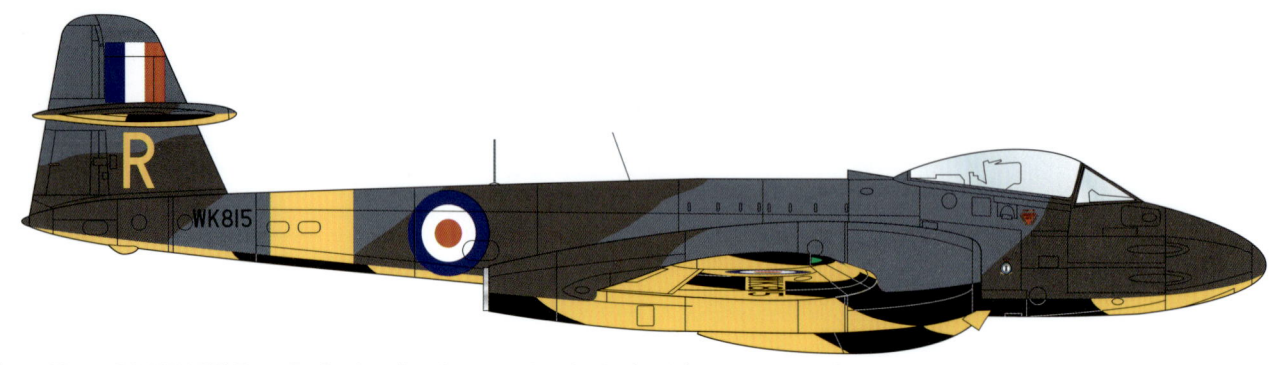

Gloster Meteor F.8, WK815 'R', Target Towing Squadron, Armament Practice Station, Sylt, Germany 1959
This Meteor was never assigned to any particular front-line squadron, going straight to the Central Fighter Establishment. While at the CFE it was re-assigned or borrowed (a not uncommon occurence) and spent time with the All Weather Development Squadron. It was then used by the Air Attache to Paris as his personal aircraft. WK815 is shown here as it appeared as part of the Target Towing Squadron at the Sylt Armament Practice Station. The standard colour scheme has now been adorned with black and yellow undersides, and broad yellow bands to the aft fuselage and to the upper wings just outboard of the engine nacelles. Unlike many contemporary F.8s that were scrapped in the late 1950s, WK815 managed to survive into the 1960s, being scrapped in May of 1962.
Reference used: p44 'RAF Hunters in Germany' by Gunther Kipp and Roger Lindsay, Published by Gunther Kipp & Roger LIndsay, 2003

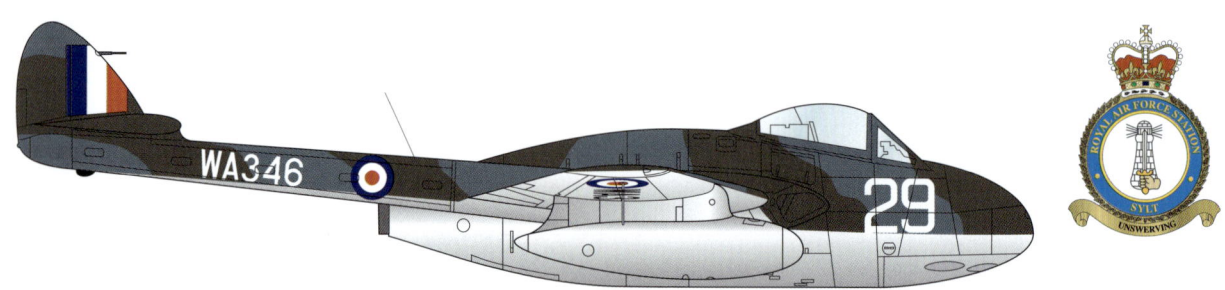

De Havilland Vampire FB.5, WA346 '29', No 3/4 Civilian Anti-Aircraft Co-operation Unit, Exeter, Devon, 1960
When the RAF decided to concentrate on the Meteor as the main interceptor aircraft, de Havilland developed the Vampire into a ground attack aircraft, a role then filled by the ageing Tempest, which the RAF were looking to replace. With good load carrying abilities and capable of switching to a fighter role once the ordnance had been used, the FB.5 was seen as a good interim fighter/bomber design, and served for several years (especially in Germany) with the tactical squadrons of the RAF. WA346 served with several units, the final one being 3/4 CAACU, a civilian run operation, and the last unit to fly FB.5s. A good number of these aircraft were used, and large nose numbers were standard, white numbers used on camouflaged aircraft, and black numbers on overall silver aircraft.
Reference used: p18 'de Havilland Vampire' by WA Harrison, Warpaint Series No.27, Hall Park Books Ltd

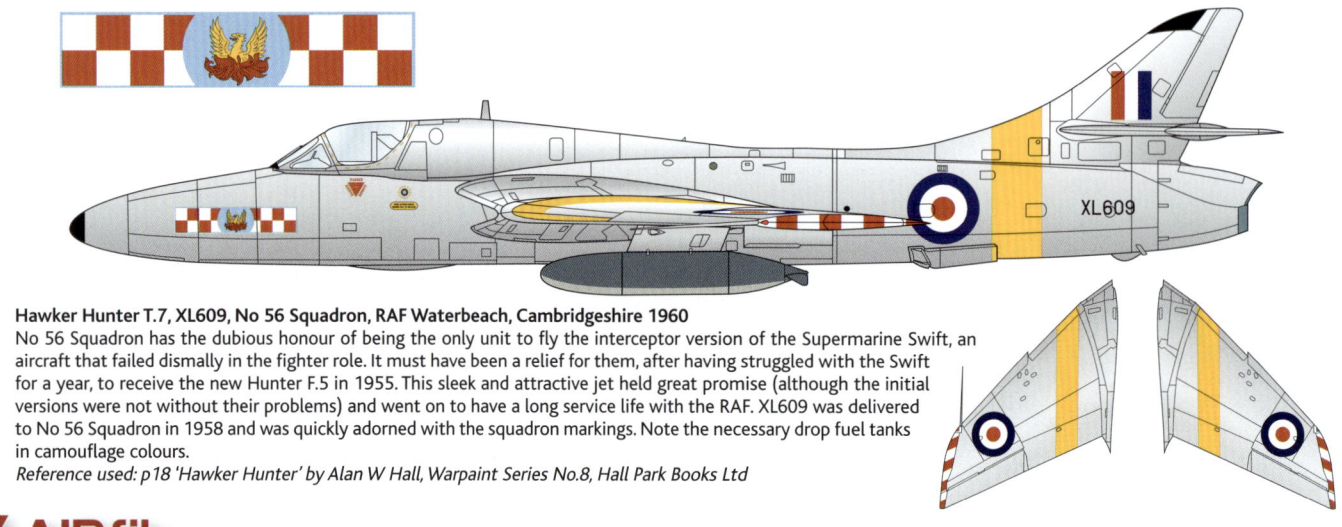

Hawker Hunter T.7, XL609, No 56 Squadron, RAF Waterbeach, Cambridgeshire 1960
No 56 Squadron has the dubious honour of being the only unit to fly the interceptor version of the Supermarine Swift, an aircraft that failed dismally in the fighter role. It must have been a relief for them, after having struggled with the Swift for a year, to receive the new Hunter F.5 in 1955. This sleek and attractive jet held great promise (although the initial versions were not without their problems) and went on to have a long service life with the RAF. XL609 was delivered to No 56 Squadron in 1958 and was quickly adorned with the squadron markings. Note the necessary drop fuel tanks in camouflage colours.
Reference used: p18 'Hawker Hunter' by Alan W Hall, Warpaint Series No.8, Hall Park Books Ltd

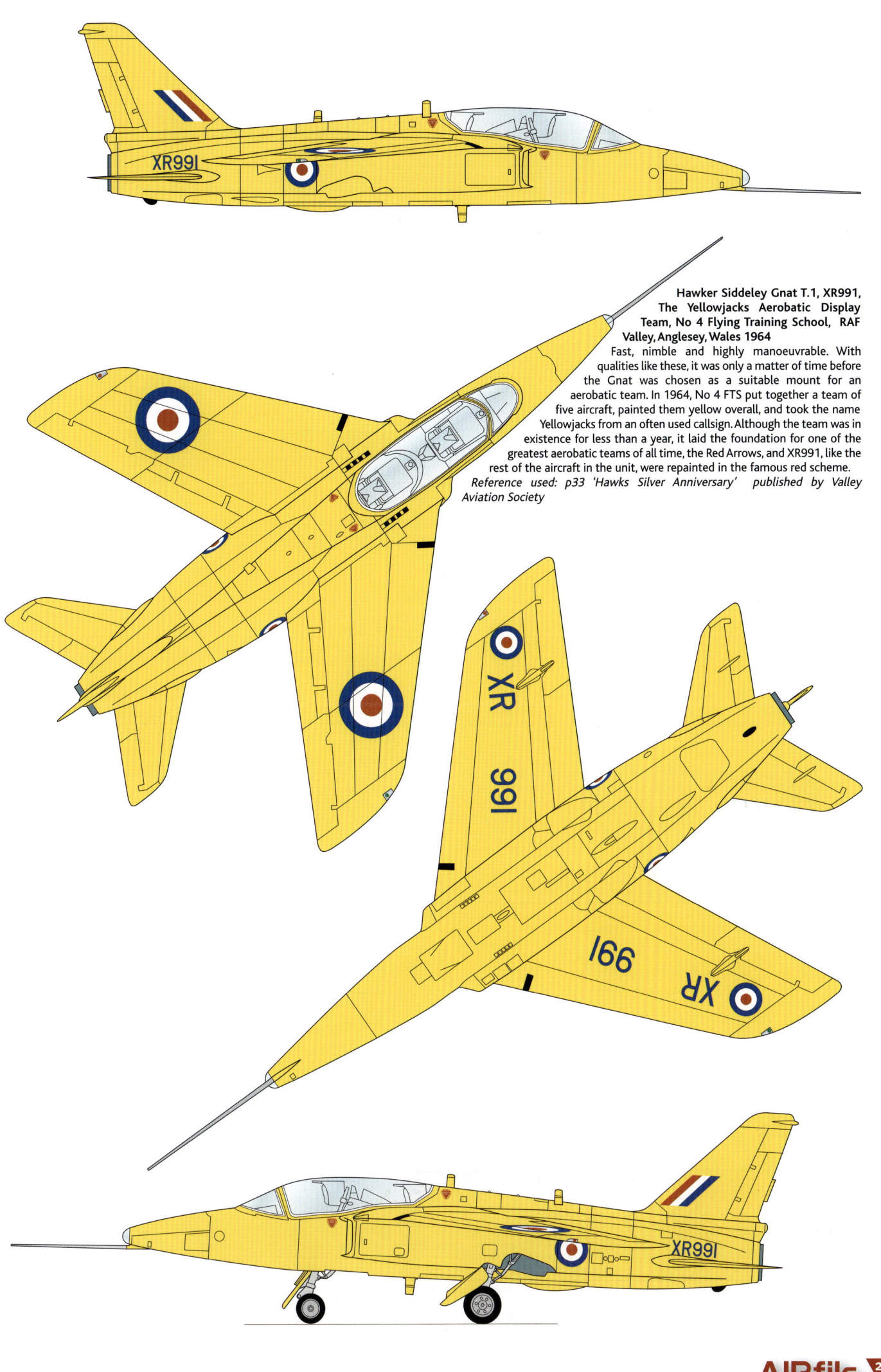

Hawker Siddeley Gnat T.1, XR991, The Yellowjacks Aerobatic Display Team, No 4 Flying Training School, RAF Valley, Anglesey, Wales 1964

Fast, nimble and highly manoeuvrable. With qualities like these, it was only a matter of time before the Gnat was chosen as a suitable mount for an aerobatic team. In 1964, No 4 FTS put together a team of five aircraft, painted them yellow overall, and took the name Yellowjacks from an often used callsign. Although the team was in existence for less than a year, it laid the foundation for one of the greatest aerobatic teams of all time, the Red Arrows, and XR991, like the rest of the aircraft in the unit, were repainted in the famous red scheme.

Reference used: p33 'Hawks Silver Anniversary' published by Valley Aviation Society

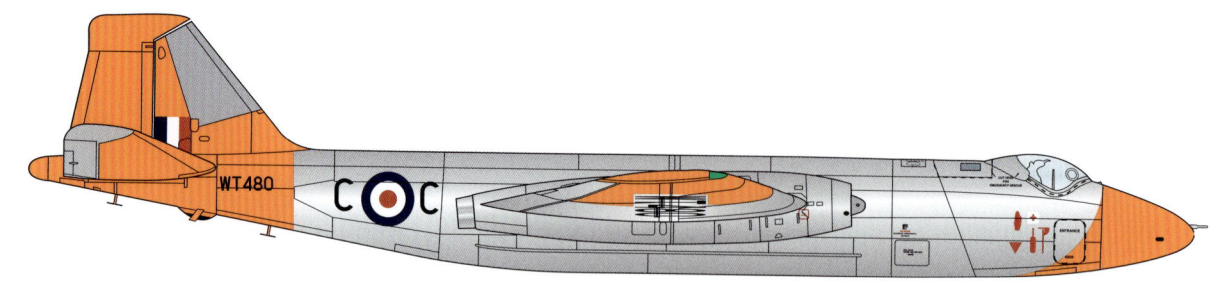

English Electric Canberra T.4, WT480 'C-C, Central Flying School, Little Rissington, Gloucestershire, May 1960
The dual control Canberra T.4 took to the skies for the first time in June of 1952, with slightly more than sixty of this version being built, out of a total of 925 aircraft constructed on home soil. Seven T.4 trainer aircraft went to 231 OCU, which had the honour of being not only the longest serving OCU in the RAF and the longest jet conversion unit in existence, they were one of the first to have a bomber aerobatic team. WT480 is the second of three that were delivered to the CFS in the late 1950s. Day-glo orange paint was still prevalent at this time.
Reference used: p126 'English Electric Canberra, by Ken Delve, Peter Green & John Clemons, Midland Counties Publications, 1992

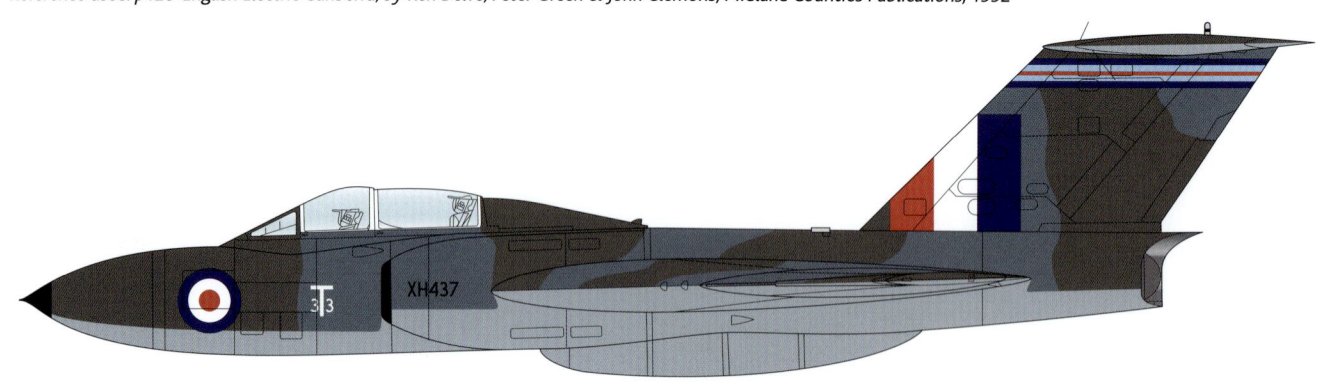

Gloster Javelin T.3, XH437 '3T3', No 33 Squadron, RAF Middleton St. George, County Durham, 1961
Deliveries of FAW.1s began in February 1956 and FAW.2s in 1957. The need for a trainer variant was recognised early in the aircraft's development but delays and necessary changes saw the first of twenty-two T.3 aircraft start to fly in January 1958. Prior to this, to remedy the lack of a trainer variant, a special training unit had to be established called the Javelin Mobile Conversion Unit. Based at RAF Leeming the unit toured Europe stopping off at Javelin unit stations in order to give instruction on the type. The JMCU had a Vickers Valetta transport aircraft fitted out with an AI.17 radar in order to train navigators, whilst pilots were trained on ground-based procedure trainers and actual flying training by sitting in the Navigator's seat and receiving instruction from a qualified Javelin pilot. Besides 228 OCU, most operational squadrons received one or two T.3s for in-service training and instrument checks. XH437 was allocated to No 33 Squadron aquiring its unusual '3T3' code.
Reference used: p9 'Gloster Javelin' by Tony Butler AMRAeS, Warpaint Series No.17, Hall Park Books Ltd

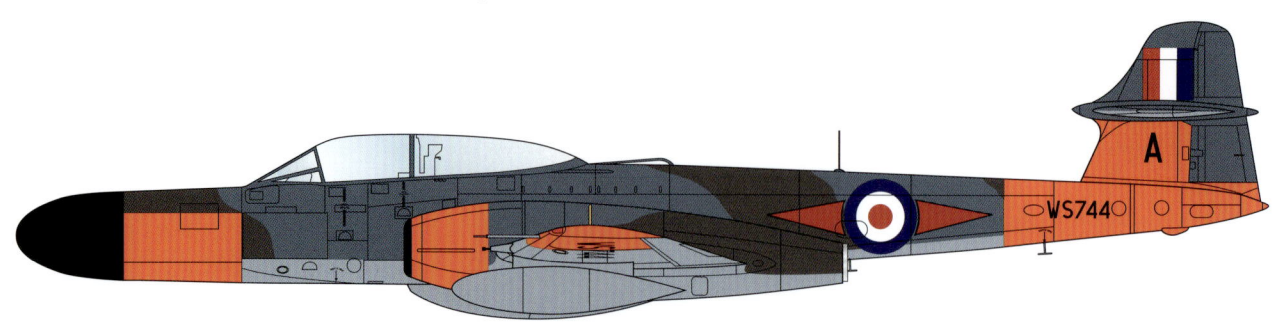

Gloster Meteor NF(T).14, WS744 'A', No 2 Air Navigation School, Thorney Island, Sussex, August 1961
The Night Fighter versions of the Meteor were an interim solution, as the post-war RAF was keen to convert practically all types of aircraft, and most especially the fighters, into jets. This applied also to the Night Fighter force, the Mosquito aircraft patently unable to catch any jet propelled night intruder. The Meteor series of Night Fighters were exclusively built by Armstrong Whitworth Aircraft, as Glosters themselves were busy building F.8 Meteors for the RAF and the air forces of the world, and also deeply ensconced in the development of the Javelin. WS744 was an NF.14, the last of the versions built, and considered by pilots as the best of the Night Fighters. It initially served with No 85 Squadron, and was passed to 2 ANS as these aircraft became redundant in front line service, being converted to train navigators, thereby becoming an NF(T).14. After 2 ANS this aircraft went to 1 ANS and eventually ended up as an instructional airframe at RAF Leeming.
Reference used: p47 'Meteor - Gloster's First Jet Fighter' by Steven J Bond, Midland Counties Publications 1985

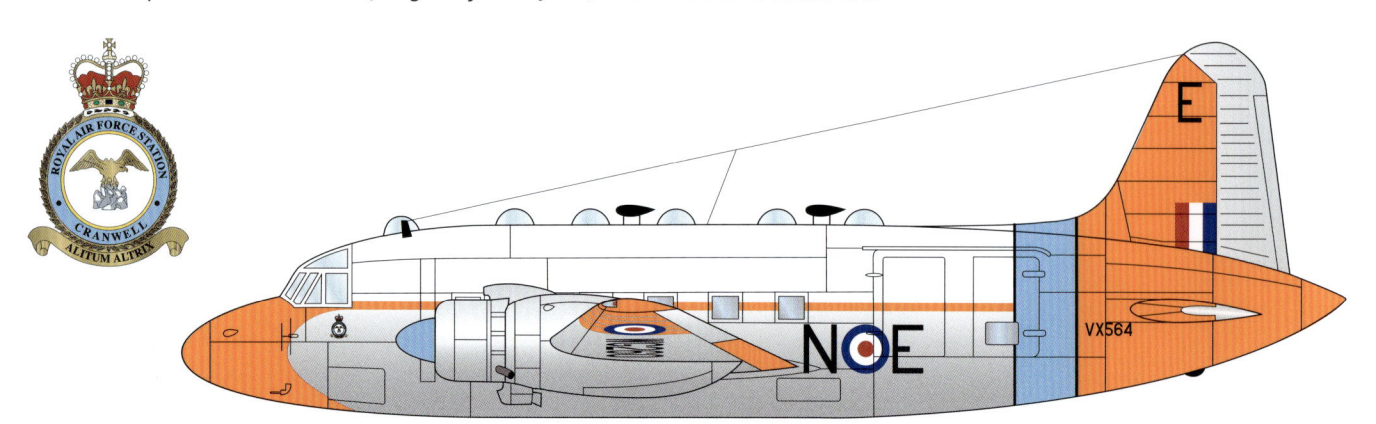

Vickers Valetta T.3, VX564 'N-E', RAF College, Cranwell, Lincolnshire, May 1962
The Valetta was developed from the extremely successful Viking, and replaced the ageing Dakota transport aircraft. The Valetta quickly established a reputation for adaptability to a variety of roles within Transport Command, the basic airframe being used for troop carrying, supply drops, ambulance aircraft, glider tug, parachute dropping, as well as the primary role of military freighter. The T.3 version first flew in 1950, and forty were eventually in service with the Air Navigation Schools. The serial number of this aircraft, VX564, shows that it was to have been built as a C.1 version, but was finished as (possibly) the first T.3. The light blue fuselage band and single letter coding of Cranwell (N, which was particular to Valettas and Varsities), is accompanied by large areas of Day-Glo orange paint and the individual aircraft letter 'E'.
Reference used: http://www.abpic.co.uk/photo/1000710/

**Gloster Javelin FAW.7 XH754,
Royal Aircraft Establishment, Farnborough, 1964**

The FAW.7 was the most common of the Javelin variants with 142 being produced. With the FAW.5 as its basis, the FAW.7 had uprated engines, different jet nozzles and extended rear fuselage to help reduce drag. Service squadrons started receiving the FAW.7 in 1958, but a few were held back for trials and research. Amongst these was XH754 which was used from January 1960 on the development of an effective rain dispersal system for the windscreen of the TSR.2. Continuing the TSR.2 development, the aircraft was flown to RAF Changi, Singapore in 1961, for a series of high speed trials in the heavy tropical rain. Capable of speeds up to 565 knots in the heaviest rain, XH 754 was given additional protection by the addition of yellow-brown plastic sheathing to the leading edges of the wings, fin and tailplanes. Whilst at RAF Changi, XH754 aquired a red kiwi 'zap' from RNZAF personnel in recognition of its pilot, Sqn Ldr. Daryl Stinton's New Zealand origin.

On its return to the UK, the aircraft was given the colourful and conspicuous markings illustrated here when it was used to drop various parachute test devices over the weapons test range at Larkhill, Sailsbury Plain. XH754 was retired from service in 1964. In 1965 it was moved to the National Gas Turbine Establishment, and later supported research at the Blue Streak rocket engine test base at Spadeadam in Cumberland.

Reference used: 'Service History of the Gloster Javelin Marks 7 to 9R' by Roger Lindsay & 'Gloster Javelin' by Tony Butler AMRAeS, Warpaint Series No.17, Hall Park Books Ltd

Gloster Meteor F.8, WL166, No 2 Squadron, RAF Flying College, Strubby, Lincolnshire 1962
When WL166 first entered service, it was with No 616 Squadron, who were the first to use the Meteor, and was coded 'B' by that squadron. When No 616 gave up their Meteors in 1957, WL166 went to the RAF Flying College at Manby. Part of the curriculum was to teach high ranking officers different aspects of air operations. When it was realised that some of these officers were not up to current standards, the School of Refresher Flying was established at the satellite field of Strubby. It was here that WL166 found itself training RAF (and foreign air force) officers that had previously 'flown' desks. In 1962 the RAF Flying College was re-named the College of Air Warfare.
Reference used: p110 'Meteor - Gloster's First Jet Fighter' by Steven J Bond, Midland Counties Publications 1985

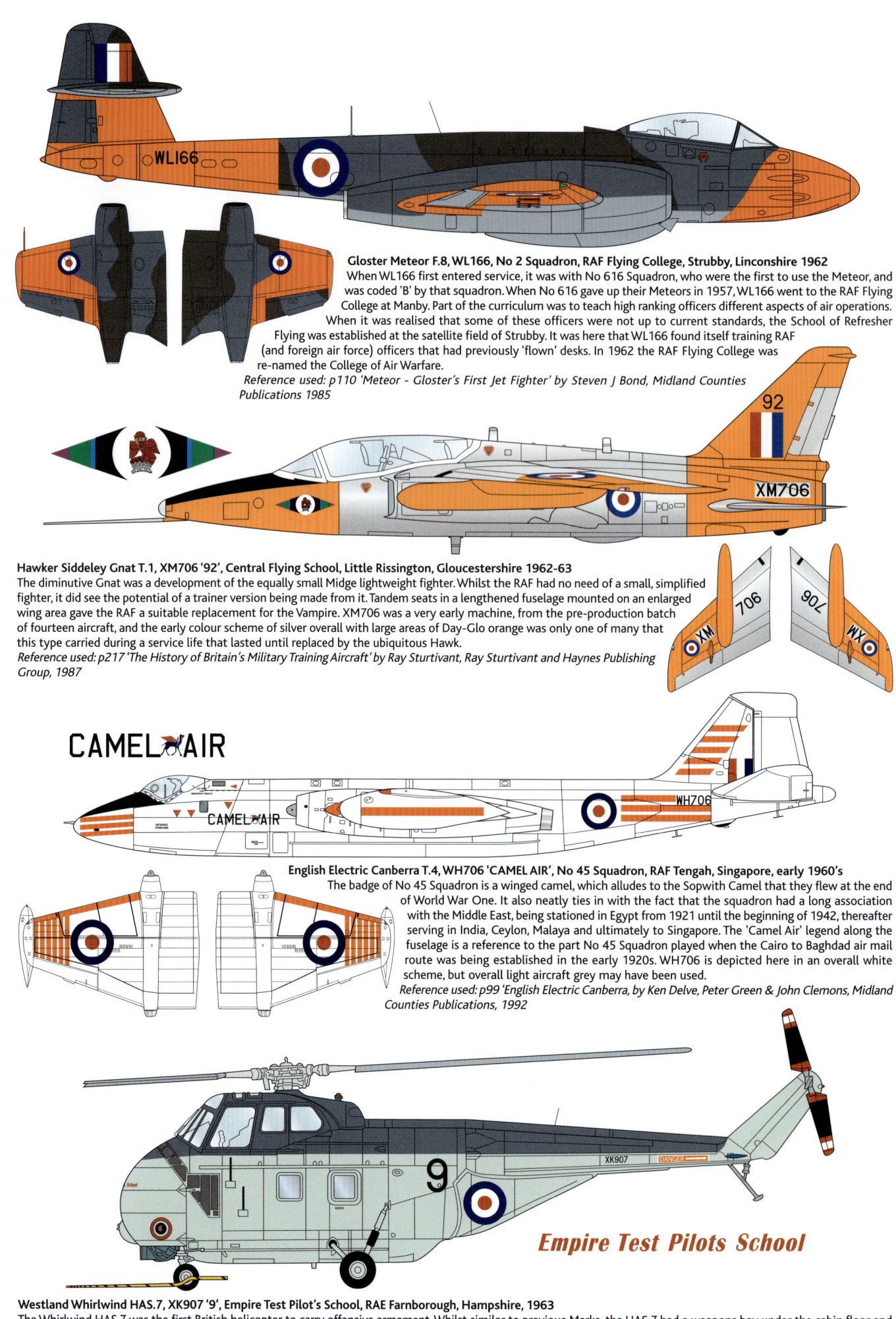

Hawker Siddeley Gnat T.1, XM706 '92', Central Flying School, Little Rissington, Gloucestershire 1962-63
The diminutive Gnat was a development of the equally small Midge lightweight fighter. Whilst the RAF had no need of a small, simplified fighter, it did see the potential of a trainer version being made from it. Tandem seats in a lengthened fuselage mounted on an enlarged wing area gave the RAF a suitable replacement for the Vampire. XM706 was a very early machine, from the pre-production batch of fourteen aircraft, and the early colour scheme of silver overall with large areas of Day-Glo orange was only one of many that this type carried during a service life that lasted until replaced by the ubiquitous Hawk.
Reference used: p217 'The History of Britain's Military Training Aircraft' by Ray Sturtivant, Ray Sturtivant and Haynes Publishing Group, 1987

English Electric Canberra T.4, WH706 'CAMEL AIR', No 45 Squadron, RAF Tengah, Singapore, early 1960's
The badge of No 45 Squadron is a winged camel, which alludes to the Sopwith Camel that they flew at the end of World War One. It also neatly ties in with the fact that the squadron had a long association with the Middle East, being stationed in Egypt from 1921 until the beginning of 1942, thereafter serving in India, Ceylon, Malaya and ultimately to Singapore. The 'Camel Air' legend along the fuselage is a reference to the part No 45 Squadron played when the Cairo to Baghdad air mail route was being established in the early 1920s. WH706 is depicted here in an overall white scheme, but overall light aircraft grey may have been used.
Reference used: p99 'English Electric Canberra, by Ken Delve, Peter Green & John Clemons, Midland Counties Publications, 1992

Westland Whirlwind HAS.7, XK907 '9', Empire Test Pilot's School, RAE Farnborough, Hampshire, 1963
The Whirlwind HAS.7 was the first British helicopter to carry offensive armament. Whilst similar to previous Marks, the HAS.7 had a weapons bay under the cabin floor and could carry a single torpedo or depth charges or bombs for the anti-submarine role. This version was also the most produced of all the variants built, a total of 129 HAS.7 aircraft going into service with the Royal Navy. XK907 somehow found itself at the ETPS, and despite the lack of 'Royal Navy' titling along the tail boom, the retention of Extra Dark Sea Grey over Sky colours show where it initially had a home. The instrumentation boom is distinctly non-standard.
Reference used: www.abpic.co.uk/photo/1046950

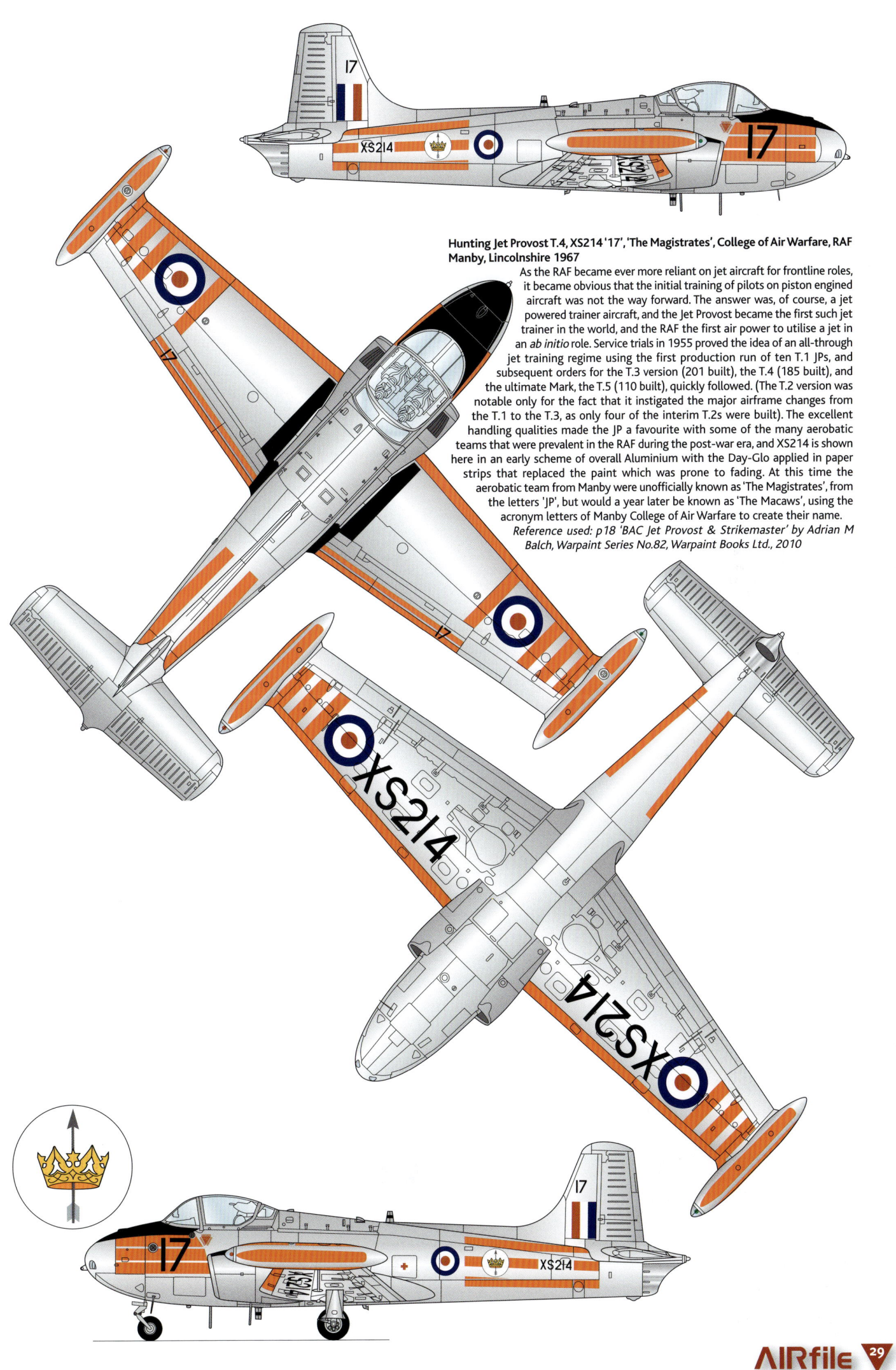

Hunting Jet Provost T.4, XS214 '17', 'The Magistrates', College of Air Warfare, RAF Manby, Lincolnshire 1967

As the RAF became ever more reliant on jet aircraft for frontline roles, it became obvious that the initial training of pilots on piston engined aircraft was not the way forward. The answer was, of course, a jet powered trainer aircraft, and the Jet Provost became the first such jet trainer in the world, and the RAF the first air power to utilise a jet in an *ab initio* role. Service trials in 1955 proved the idea of an all-through jet training regime using the first production run of ten T.1 JPs, and subsequent orders for the T.3 version (201 built), the T.4 (185 built), and the ultimate Mark, the T.5 (110 built), quickly followed. (The T.2 version was notable only for the fact that it instigated the major airframe changes from the T.1 to the T.3, as only four of the interim T.2s were built). The excellent handling qualities made the JP a favourite with some of the many aerobatic teams that were prevalent in the RAF during the post-war era, and XS214 is shown here in an early scheme of overall Aluminium with the Day-Glo applied in paper strips that replaced the paint which was prone to fading. At this time the aerobatic team from Manby were unofficially known as 'The Magistrates', from the letters 'JP', but would a year later be known as 'The Macaws', using the acronym letters of Manby College of Air Warfare to create their name.
Reference used: p18 'BAC Jet Provost & Strikemaster' by Adrian M Balch, Warpaint Series No.82, Warpaint Books Ltd., 2010

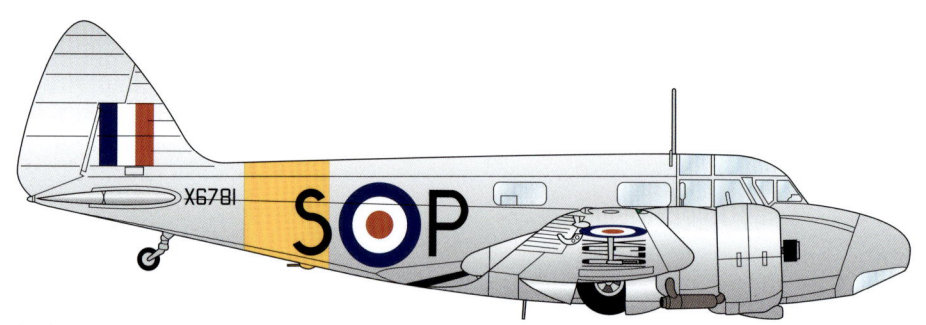

Airspeed Oxford I, X6781, 'S•P', No 8 Advanced Flying Training Squadron, Dalcross, Highlands, Scotland 1963
With the end of World War Two came the inevitable reduction in pilots and aircraft, no longer needed in the peaceful post-war world. This trend was reversed, however, when the Iron Curtain was raised and Berlin became a city under siege, and North Korea attacked a woefully ill-prepared South Korea. As a consequence, pilot training once again became a priority, with an emphasis on twin engined aircraft, such as the new de Havilland Hornet, the Meteor and the still useful Mosquito, many wartime single engine pilots transitioning onto twins by way of aircraft such as the Oxford. X6781 was one of the aircraft used at Dalcross to cope with this new expansion of the RAF and managed to survive a full span of fourteen years service life with the RAF. Just one year later all Oxfords were struck off charge.
Reference used: p389 'Airspeed Oxford' by Alan W Hall, Aircraft in Detail, Volume 15, Number 9/10, June/July 1993

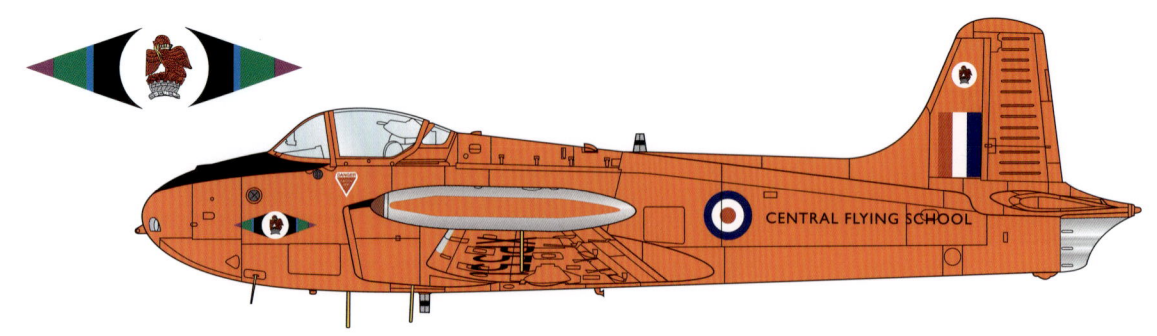

Hunting Jet Provost T.4, XP551, 'Red Pelicans' Aerobatic Display Team, Central Flying School, RAF Little Rissington, Gloucestershire, July 1964
The T.4 Jet Provost was an up-engined version of the preceding T.3, the airframe differences between the two being minimal. The more powerful Viper engine gave the T.4 a speed increase of 90mph, which was actually beneficial to the student pilots, as higher standards were achieved. Unfortunately the airframe life was not as long as the RAF had hoped, and T.4 aircraft started to be retired in the mid 1970s, some being replaced by the earlier T.3 versions. The 'Red Pelicans' flew the T.4 initially in a Day-Glo Red scheme, as shown here, but this was a difficult colour to maintain, fading badly, so a gloss red was used from 1966 until the team re-equipped with the T.5 in 1969.
Reference used: p22 'BAC Jet Provost & Strikemaster' by Adrian M Balch, Warpaint Series No.82, Warpaint Books Ltd., 2010

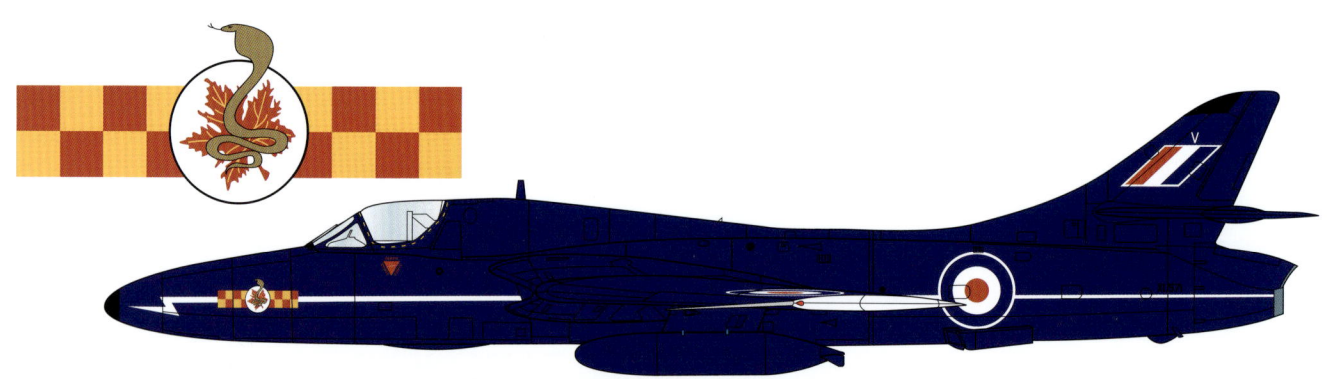

Hawker Hunter T.7, XL571 'V', No 92 Squadron, 'Blue Diamonds' Aerobatic Display Team, RAF Leconfield, Yorkshire East Riding, 1964
The role of the premier display team of the RAF passed from No 111 Squadron to No 92 Squadron in 1961, when the former unit began to re-equip with Lightnings. Like the 'Black Arrows', the Blue Diamonds' displayed in a single overall colour, which has variously been described as Roundel Blue, Aircraft Blue and even as a special Blue Diamonds Blue. 1962 was the last display season for No 92 Squadron, as they, like No 111 Squadron, re-equipped with Lightnings. XL571 was delivered to 229 OCU in 1958, then spent some time with the Fighter Command Instrument Rating Squadron before becoming one of two T.7s used by No 92 Squadron. The aircraft was eventually used by No 1 Tactical Weapons Unit at Brawdy in the mid 1970s.
Reference used: www.abpic.co.uk/photo/1001097/

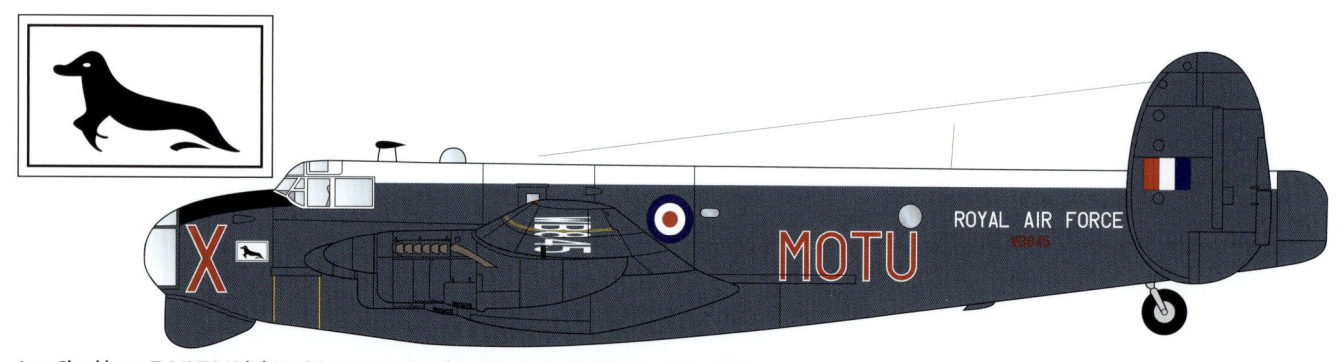

Avro Shackleton T.4, WB845 'X', Maritime Operational Training Unit, St Mawgan, Wales 1965
With the end of World War Two, all equipment acquired by Britain under the Lend-Lease scheme was returned. This meant that Coastal Command was no longer able to use shore-based, long range aircraft, like the Flying Fortress and Liberator. The Sunderland flying boat would soldier on for a while, and the service introduction of the LIncoln allowed Lancasters to temporarily fill the maritime role, but it was seen that a dedicated aircraft was needed for this role. The Shackleton was developed using parts from the Lincoln and the Tudor airliner and went into service in 1950. The MOTU was an amalgamation of 236 OCU and the School of Maritime Reconnaissance and was in existence from 1956 until 1970. WB845 was one of seventeen MRI/MRIA aircraft converted to T.4 standard.
Reference used: p26 'Avro Shackleton' by John Chartres, Postwar Military Aircraft:3, Book Club Associates 1985

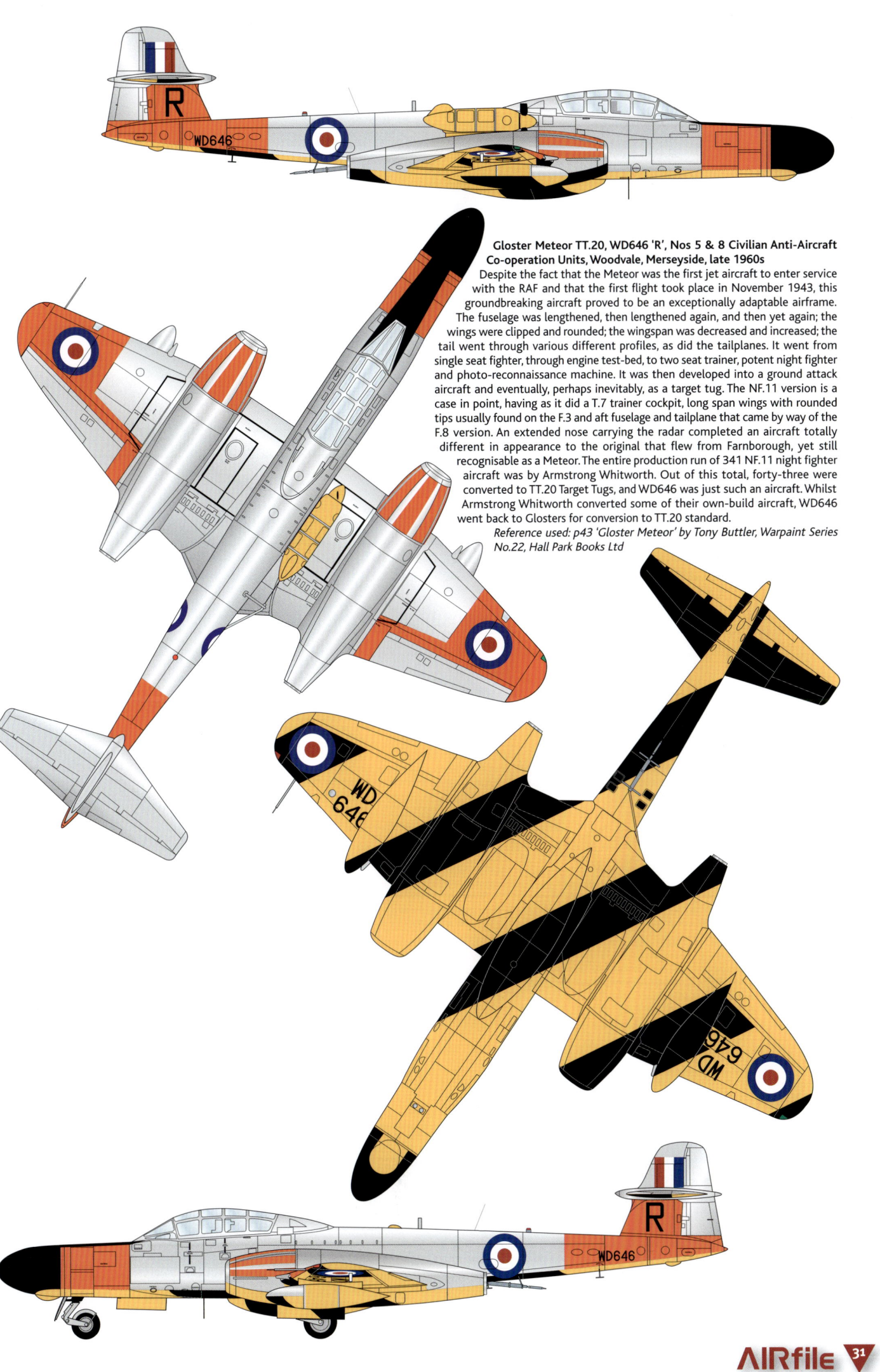

Gloster Meteor TT.20, WD646 'R', Nos 5 & 8 Civilian Anti-Aircraft Co-operation Units, Woodvale, Merseyside, late 1960s

Despite the fact that the Meteor was the first jet aircraft to enter service with the RAF and that the first flight took place in November 1943, this groundbreaking aircraft proved to be an exceptionally adaptable airframe. The fuselage was lengthened, then lengthened again, and then yet again; the wings were clipped and rounded; the wingspan was decreased and increased; the tail went through various different profiles, as did the tailplanes. It went from single seat fighter, through engine test-bed, to two seat trainer, potent night fighter and photo-reconnaissance machine. It was then developed into a ground attack aircraft and eventually, perhaps inevitably, as a target tug. The NF.11 version is a case in point, having as it did a T.7 trainer cockpit, long span wings with rounded tips usually found on the F.3 and aft fuselage and tailplane that came by way of the F.8 version. An extended nose carrying the radar completed an aircraft totally different in appearance to the original that flew from Farnborough, yet still recognisable as a Meteor. The entire production run of 341 NF.11 night fighter aircraft was by Armstrong Whitworth. Out of this total, forty-three were converted to TT.20 Target Tugs, and WD646 was just such an aircraft. Whilst Armstrong Whitworth converted some of their own-build aircraft, WD646 went back to Glosters for conversion to TT.20 standard.

Reference used: p43 'Gloster Meteor' by Tony Buttler, Warpaint Series No.22, Hall Park Books Ltd

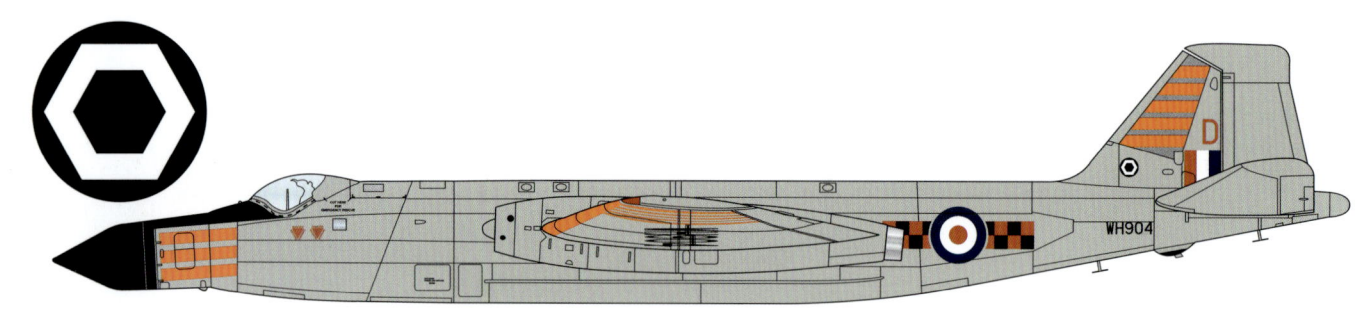

English Electric Canberra T.11, WH904 'D', No 85 Squadron, RAF Binbrook, Lincolnshire, mid-1960s
The T.11 version of the Canberra first flew in March of 1958, and was used for the training of Airborne Intercept radar operators. WH904 did not start life as a T.11, it was actually built four years earlier in February of 1954 as a standard B.2. Once converted it went to serve with 228 OCU, and from there to West Raynham as part of the Target Facilities Squadron. It then became part of No 85 Squadron at Binbrook, the only Canberra unit in Fighter Command, as illustrated here. WH904 was converted again to T.19 configuration before being sold in 1980. This aircraft is still in existence and can be seen at Newark Air Museum.
Reference used: p85 'Britain's Military Aircraft in Colour 1960-1970. Volume 1' by Martin Derry, Crecy Publishing 2010

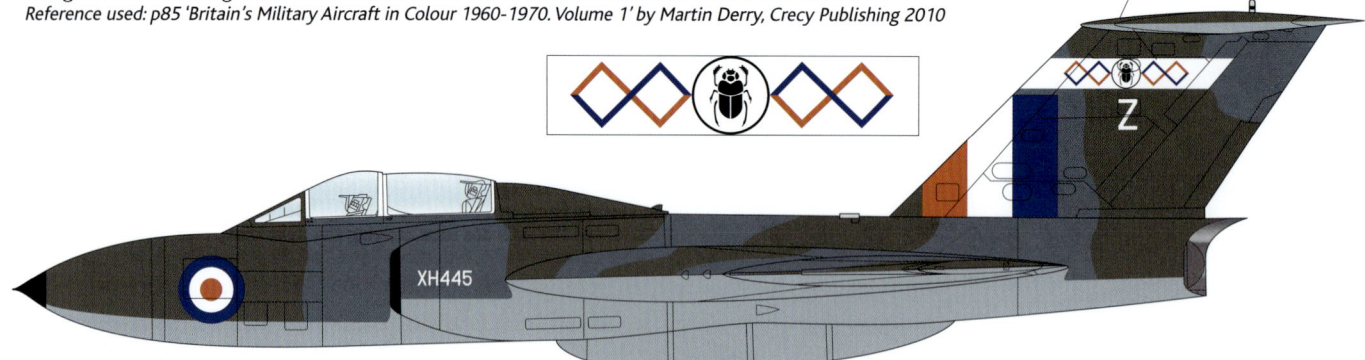

Gloster Javelin T.3, XH445 'Z', No 64 Squadron, RAF Tengah, Singapore, 1966
Perhaps the only Javelins to see any armed conflict were those of Nos 60 and 64 Squadrons. These operated out of RAF Tengah, Singapore during the Malaysian Confrontation with Indonesia from September 1963 until August 1966, flying combat patrols over the jungles of Malaysia. The visual appearance of the T.3 differs very little from its FAW brethren, apart from an increase of 3.67 feet in length, an enlarged cockpit and the removal of the nose AI radar. The rear seat was raised to give the instuctor a clear view forward. The 30mm cannon were retained for instructional purposes and twin periscopes each side of the fuselage permitted the instructor to assist with aiming. XH445 is depicted a year before the squadron was disbanded, wearing the distinctive scarab beetle badge adopted by the squadron when based in Egypt during the 1930s.
Reference used: p28 'Gloster Javelin' by Tony Butler AMRAeS, Warpaint Series No.17, Hall Park Books Ltd

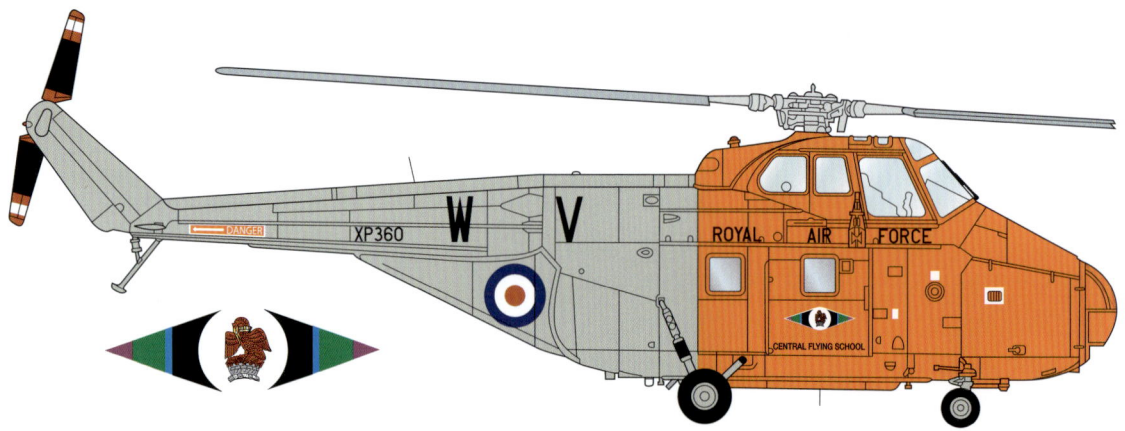

Westland Whirlwind HAR.10, XP360 'W-V', Central Flying School (Helicopter) Squadron, RAF Ternhill, Shropshire, 1968
By the late 1950s/early 1960s the basic airframe of the Whirlwind was showing it still had potential, but the original piston engine was failing to keep up with the weight demands, especially in hot and high conditions. The installation of the new Gnome turboshaft engine increased power by almost half, despite being smaller and lighter than the original engine, allowing the aircraft to continue in service for longer. Earlier Marks were also converted to take the Gnome engine, and these aircraft were re-classified as Mark 10s. The code letters of XP360 show the simplified version used by the CFS, with the 'V' being the aircraft letter (repeated on the front of the nose), while the 'W' is type specific, obviously denoting Whirlwinds.
Reference used: www.abpic.co.uk/photo/1037921

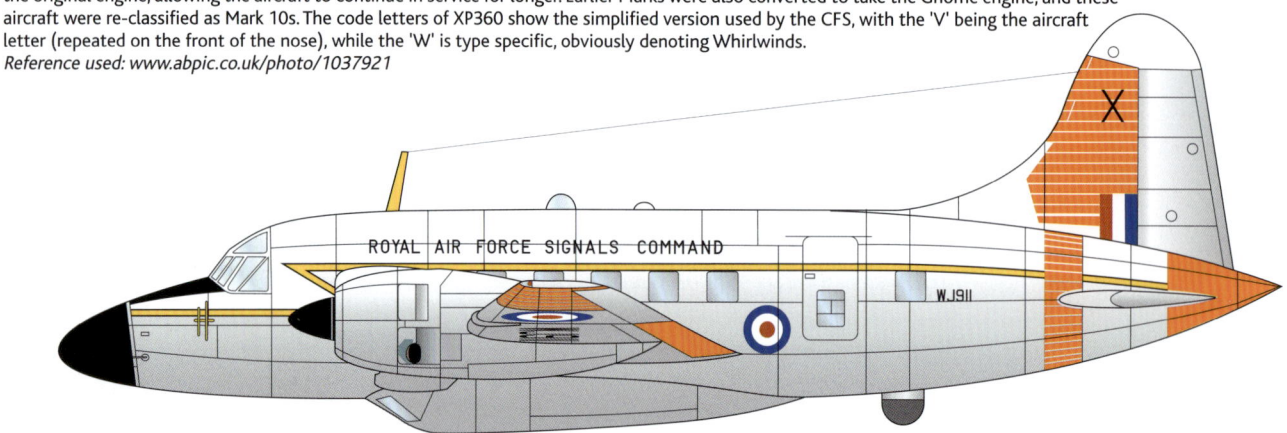

Vickers Varsity T.1, WJ911 'X', No 115 Squadron, RAF Cottesmore, Rutland, July 1968
In August 1958, No 116 Squadron at Watton was re-numbered No 115 Squadron. It was part of No 90 Signals Group and its task was that of calibrating from the air all radio and radar installations at RAF airfields. Later in the year it moved to Tangmere, where it remained for five years on this task and also took part in calibrating ships' installations. It later returned to Watton and in 1968 the squadron re-equipped with Hawker Siddeley Argosy E.1s and with these it moved to Cottesmore, retaining some Vickers Varsities for another 18 months. It was one of these latter that flew the last 'Gee' checking sortie, so the squadron claims to be the first and last operator of 'Gee'. Now the calibration duties were extended as far as the Far East Air Force, and No 115 Squadron's aircraft were to be seen wherever there were RAF bases.
Reference used: http://www.abpic.co.uk/photo/1027921/

AIRfile

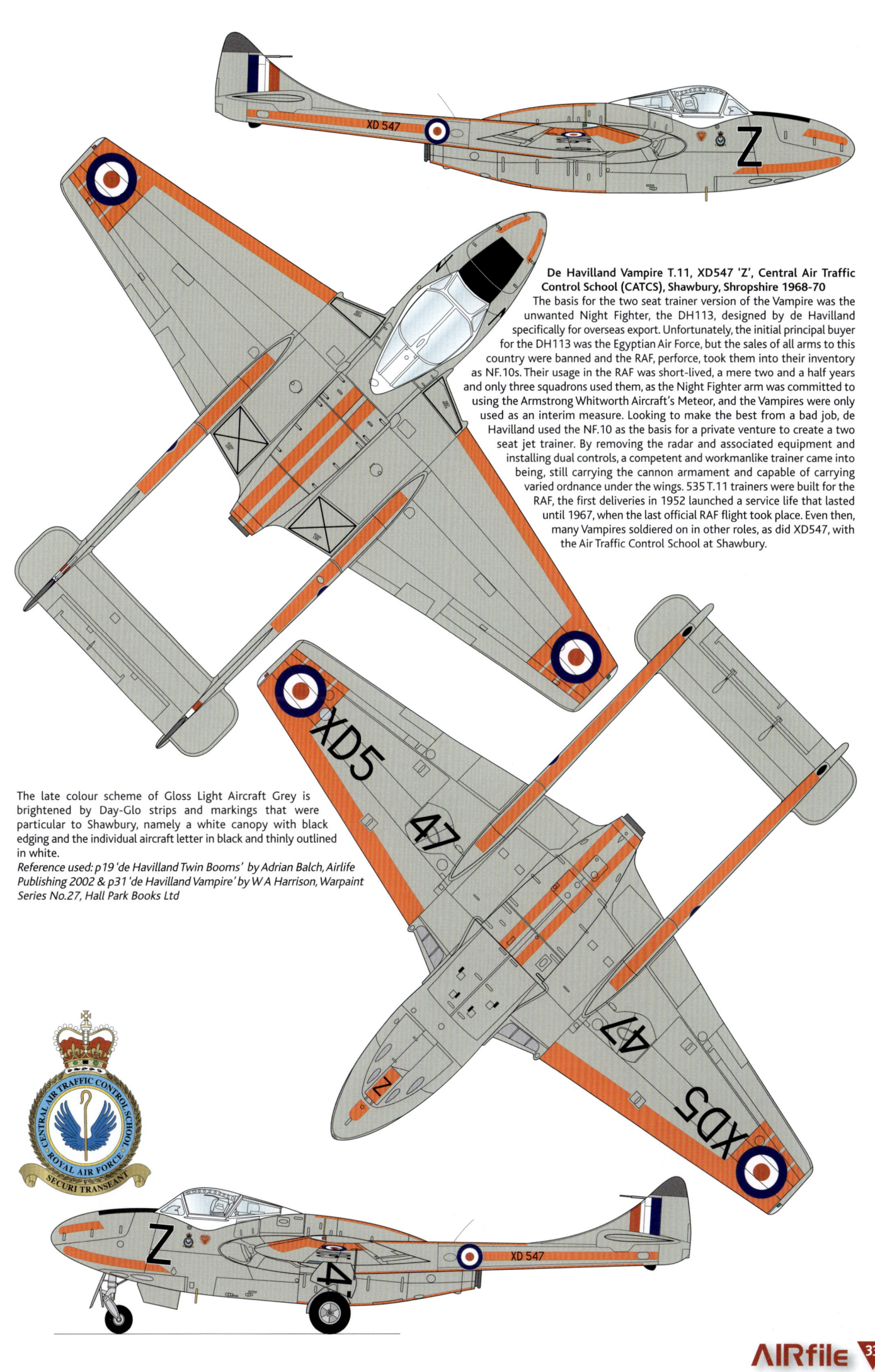

De Havilland Vampire T.11, XD547 'Z', Central Air Traffic Control School (CATCS), Shawbury, Shropshire 1968-70

The basis for the two seat trainer version of the Vampire was the unwanted Night Fighter, the DH113, designed by de Havilland specifically for overseas export. Unfortunately, the initial principal buyer for the DH113 was the Egyptian Air Force, but the sales of all arms to this country were banned and the RAF, perforce, took them into their inventory as NF.10s. Their usage in the RAF was short-lived, a mere two and a half years and only three squadrons used them, as the Night Fighter arm was committed to using the Armstrong Whitworth Aircraft's Meteor, and the Vampires were only used as an interim measure. Looking to make the best from a bad job, de Havilland used the NF.10 as the basis for a private venture to create a two seat jet trainer. By removing the radar and associated equipment and installing dual controls, a competent and workmanlike trainer came into being, still carrying the cannon armament and capable of carrying varied ordnance under the wings. 535 T.11 trainers were built for the RAF, the first deliveries in 1952 launched a service life that lasted until 1967, when the last official RAF flight took place. Even then, many Vampires soldiered on in other roles, as did XD547, with the Air Traffic Control School at Shawbury.

The late colour scheme of Gloss Light Aircraft Grey is brightened by Day-Glo strips and markings that were particular to Shawbury, namely a white canopy with black edging and the individual aircraft letter in black and thinly outlined in white.

Reference used: p19 'de Havilland Twin Booms' by Adrian Balch, Airlife Publishing 2002 & p31 'de Havilland Vampire' by W A Harrison, Warpaint Series No.27, Hall Park Books Ltd

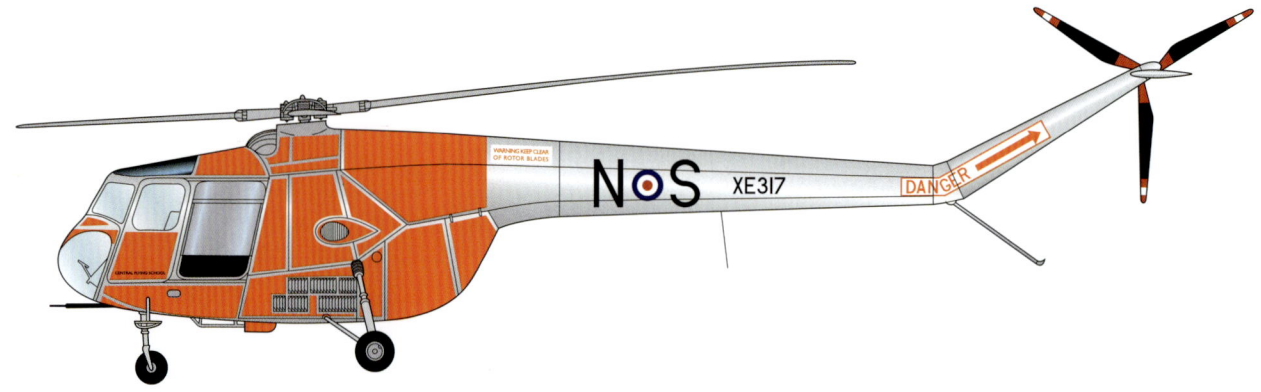

Bristol Sycamore HR.14, XE317 'N-S', Central Flying School, RAF Ternhill, Shropshire, late 1960s
The HR.14 variant of the Sycamore was the most produced of the series with ninety entering service with the Royal Air Force in 1953. Their main purpose was for Search and Rescue duties with their distinguishing feature being the large rear access panels for winching. XE317 was retired from CFS duties late in 1960, and transferred to the Royal Navy for instructional use at HMS Vernon in Portsmouth. Here it was regularly 'ditched' in a large water tank, for the purposes of escape training. Note the use of adhesive day-glo patches on the forward fuselage.
Reference used: www.airport-data.com/aircraft/photo/386573.html

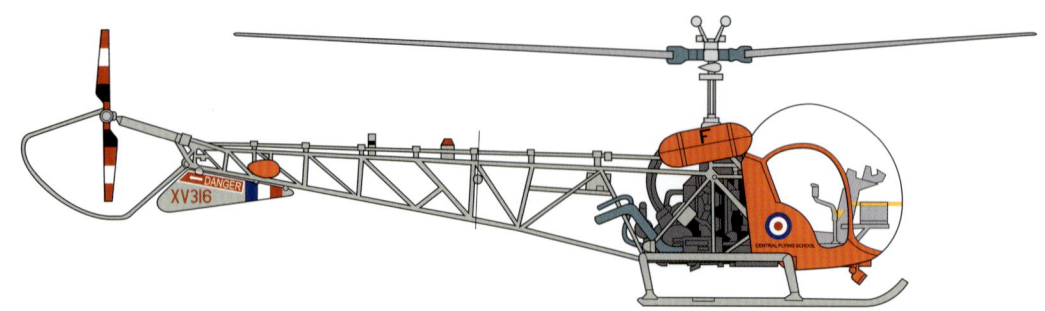

Westland Sioux HT.2, XV316 'F', 'Tomahawks' Aerobatic Display Team, Central Flying School, Helicopter Wing, RAF Little Rissington, Gloucestershire, June 1969
The manufacturing license for the Bell 47G Sioux came from the Augusta Company in Italy, and not, as you would expect, from Bell in America. Chosen in 1963 to be the standard helicopter for the British Army, Westland began manufacture in 1964, to add to the aircraft supplied by Augusta. A small number also went to the Central Flying School for the initial training of helicopter instructor pilots, and XV316 flew with the CFS in this bright day-glo red scheme for the 1969 Royal Review of the CFS at Little Rissington as one of the 'Tomahawks' Display Team. It was one of eight that the three display aircraft could be drawn from. The team were usually based at RAF Ternhill in Shropshire.
Reference used: http://www.airliners.net/photo/UK---Air/Westland-Sioux-HT2/1210950/M/

De Havilland DHC-1 Chipmunk T.10, WP790 'T', University of Birmingham Air Squadron, DCAE Cosford, Shropshire 1970
When the Chipmunk was first procured for the RAF, the initial recipients of the aircraft were the University Air Squadrons. Oxford being the first, early in 1950. As was the norm at that time, all trainers were coloured silver with yellow training bands and the Chipmunks were painted accordingly. From the late 1950s onwards, day-glo paint started to be used, at first sparingly, and then more and more, until large swathes of this colour were being applied to fuselages and flying surfaces. A quicker method of application came about when day-glo was supplied in tape form, resulting in strips of colour rather than whole panels. After service with the University of Birmingham Air Squadron, WP790 became part of the static display at the Mosquito Aircraft Museum, Salisbury Hall.
Reference used: p129 'Mosquito Aircraft Museum' by Philip Birtles, Aircraft Annual 1977, Ian Allen Ltd 1976 & http://www.abpic.co.uk/photo/1029408/

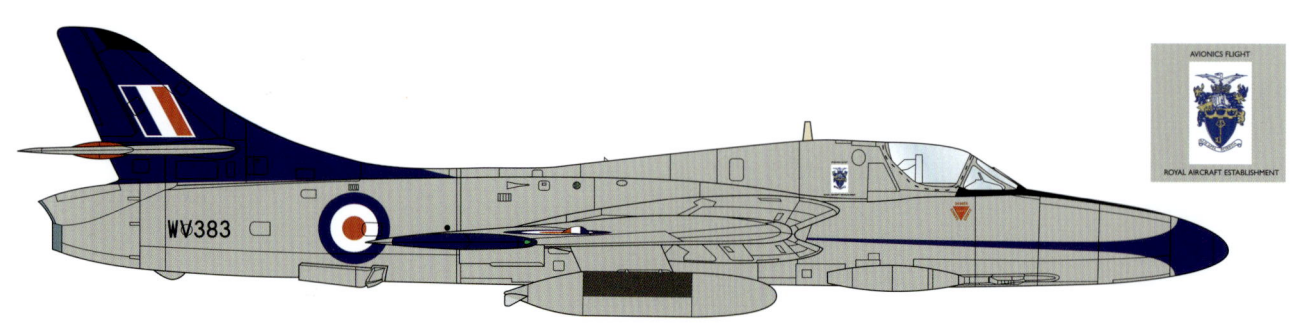

Hawker Hunter T.7, WV383, Avionics Flight, Royal Aircraft Establishment, Farnborough, Hampshire, early 1970s
This particular Hunter started life as an F.4 aircraft, in 1955, and was used by the RAF College at Manby during that year. Twelve months later it was involved in a wheels-up landing and was returned to Hawkers for conversion to T.7 standard, one of six to be so converted, as evidenced by the serial number, as all new build T.7s were in the XL range, whereas the converts carried their original F.4 WV and XF prefix serials. It then spent time in Germany with the Station Flights at Gutersloh and Jever before going to No 28 Squadron at Kai Tak. WV383 joined the RAE in July 1971. Portrayed here in a smart gloss Light Aircraft Grey with Blue trim scheme, it was eventually painted in the even more attractive Raspberry Ripple colours. It was used by the RAE to develop Head Up displays and night flying instrumentation, well into the 1980's.
Reference used: p36 'Hunter Squadrons of the Royal Air Force and Fleet Air Arm' by Richard L Ward, Linewrights Ltd., 1985

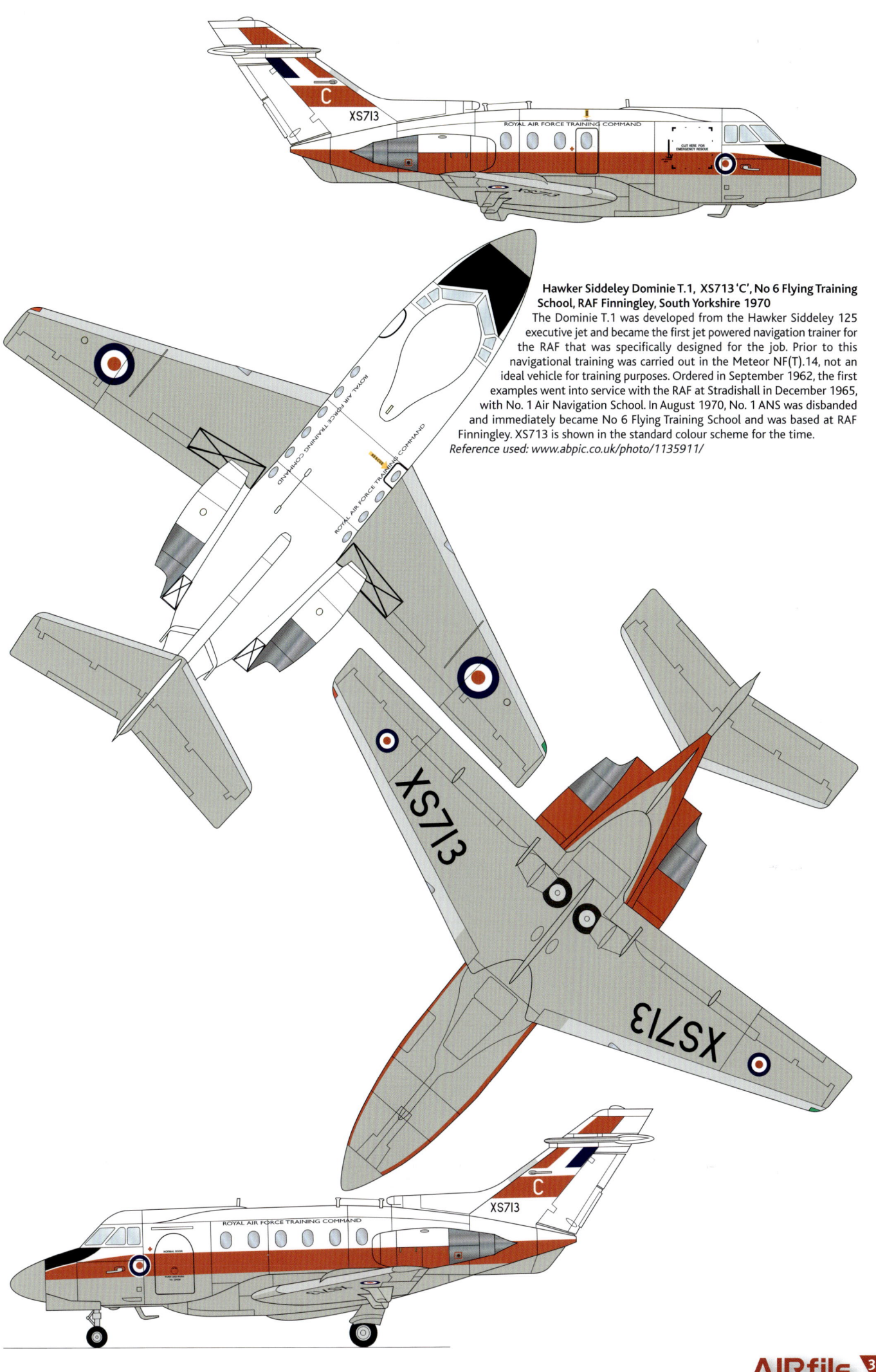

Hawker Siddeley Dominie T.1, XS713 'C', No 6 Flying Training School, RAF Finningley, South Yorkshire 1970

The Dominie T.1 was developed from the Hawker Siddeley 125 executive jet and became the first jet powered navigation trainer for the RAF that was specifically designed for the job. Prior to this navigational training was carried out in the Meteor NF(T).14, not an ideal vehicle for training purposes. Ordered in September 1962, the first examples went into service with the RAF at Stradishall in December 1965, with No. 1 Air Navigation School. In August 1970, No. 1 ANS was disbanded and immediately became No 6 Flying Training School and was based at RAF Finningley. XS713 is shown in the standard colour scheme for the time.
Reference used: www.abpic.co.uk/photo/1135911/

R Scrap view of WV372 nose wheel door

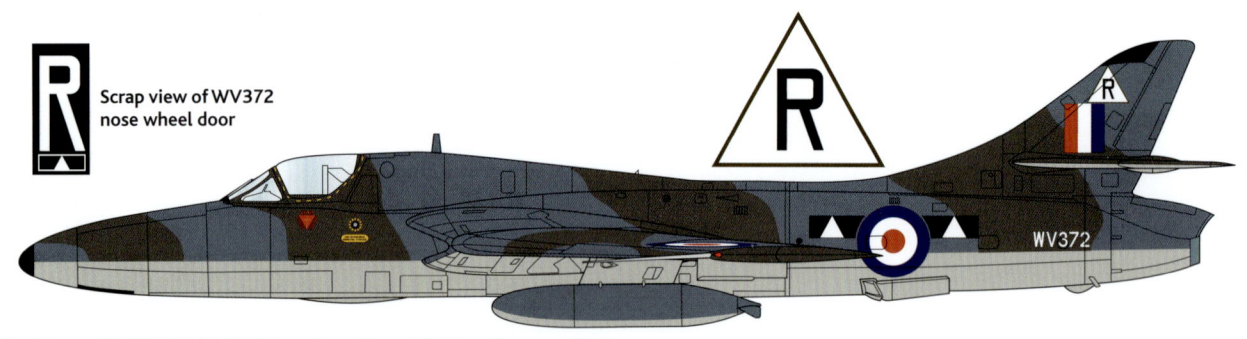

Hawker Hunter T.7, WV372, 'R', No 2 Squadron, Gutersloh, West Germany 1970
No 2 Squadron was one of only two squadrons to fly the ill-fated Supermarine Swift in the fighter/reconnaissance role (the other being No 79 Squadron). As a fighter, the Swift was poor, but was developed into a moderately good tactical fighter/recon aircraft. Despite this, the RAF were looking to get rid of the trouble prone aircraft, so the Hunter was developed into the FR.10, which No 2 Squadron began flying in Germany in 1961 and continued to use it for the next decade. Originally an F.4 aircraft, WV372 suffered an in-flight fire and was converted to a T.7 soon after. It then spent a period of time with the Station Flights at Jever and Gutersloh, after which it was used by No 2 Squadron as a training and check aircraft.
Reference used: p24 'Hawker Hunter' by Alan W Hall, Warpaint Series No.8, Hall Park Books Ltd

Slingsby T.38 Grasshopper TX.1, WZ778, Collyers School CCF, Horsham, West Sussex 1970
The Slingsby T.38 Grasshopper's lineage can be traced back to 1938 and the German built SG 38 Schulgleiter which played a key part in the training of *Luftwaffe* pilots prior to World War Two. Being cheap to manufacture and easy to store, Slingsby Sailplanes modified the design for the RAF into the Grasshopper TX.1 in the early 1950s. Over 100 of the basic gliders were delivered to RAF ATC and CCF units around the UK. The Grasshopper was launched by a vee-shaped elastic rope pulled by groups of cadets, and once airborne it could float for short distances. The glider could also be mounted on a tripod for demonstrating the use of the control surfaces. Most of these aircraft were subsequently handed over to various RAF contingencies of the Combined Cadet Force (CCF) at public and grammar schools during the 1970s and 80s.
Reference used: www.abpic.co.uk/photo/1034308/

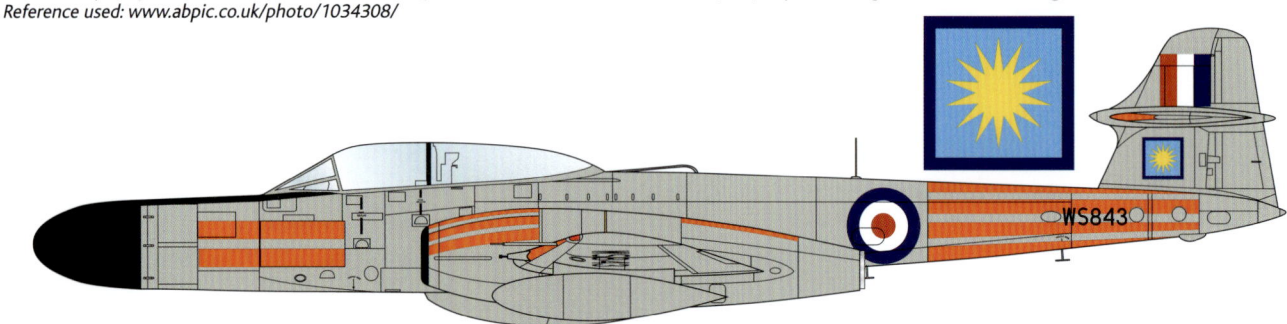

Gloster Meteor NF.14, WS843, No 4 School of Technical Training, St Athan, Wales, September 1971
By the time this Meteor was photographed, it had been retired from active service and was being used as an instructional airframe, but still with full serials under the wings and on the aft fuselage and not the Airframe Instructural 'M' number it should have carried. The over-large 'zap' on the tailfin of the Malaysian star would not have been carried on an in-service aircraft and the non-standard overall gloss Light Aircraft Grey was probably for durability in this ground instructional role. Points to note about all the versions of the Night Fighter Meteors are the belly and drop fuel tanks, de rigeuer for Night Fighters, as the radar operator's position took up the space usually used by the fuel tank, and the fact that none of the NF Marks seemed to carry underwing roundels, only serials.
WS843 was originally assigned to No 64 Squadron.
Reference used: p134 'Gloster Meteor, Britain's Celebrated First-Generation Jet' by Phil Butler and Tony Buttler, Midland Publishing 2006

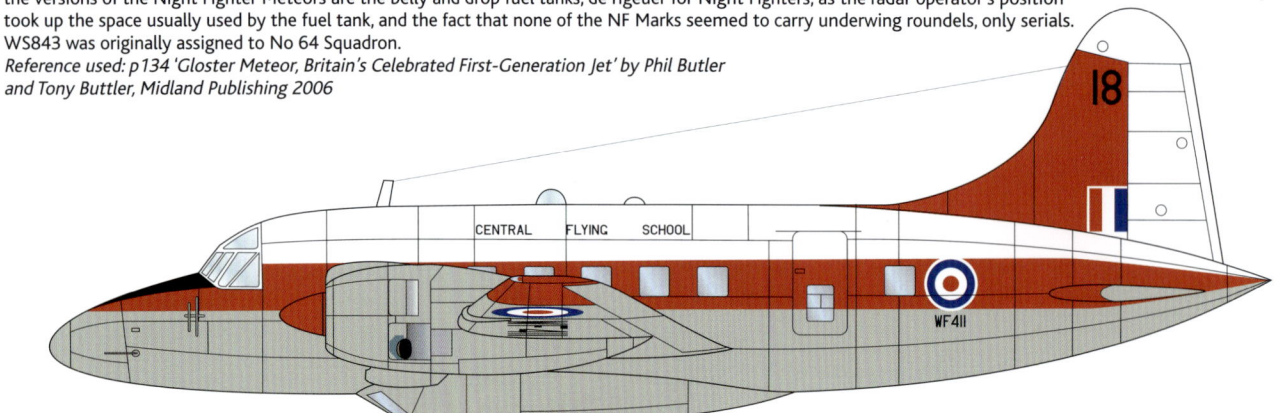

Vickers Varsity T.1, WF411 '18', Central Flying School, Little Rissington, Gloucestershire 1971
Varsities continued to serve the RAF until the mid 1970s, when they started to be replaced by the Jetstream. As well as the Air Navigation Schools, Varsities could be found in units as diverse as the School of Air Warfare, Bomber Command Bombing School, the Blind Landing Experimental Unit, the Electrical Wireless School, and continued into the 1980s and 1990s with the Empire Test Pilots School and the Royal Aircraft Establishment. WF411 had a colour scheme that was standard for the time, apart from having Roundel Red for the high visibility areas, as opposed to the normal Day-Glo finish.
Reference used: http://www.abpic.co.uk/photo/1246726/

AIRfile

De Havilland DHC-1 Chipmunk T.10, WD347, 'Skylarks' Aerobatic Team, Central Flying School, Little Rissington 1970-71

The 'Skylarks Aerobatic Team' were formed in 1967 and lasted until 1971. The team was one of several which flew representing the Central Flying School throughout its history. WD347 is depicted as it appeared in the last two seasons of the team, with day-glo strips applied to an overall gloss Light Aircraft Grey. This scheme started to be introduced in 1966, but did not last long, as the Red, White and Light Aircraft Grey scheme began to be applied to trainers from 1969. The Skylarks colour scheme is completed with a dark green flash down the fuselage side, incorporating the CFS crest, a dark green spinner and a skylark motif above the fin flash.

Reference used: http://aerobaticteams.net/raf-skylarks.html

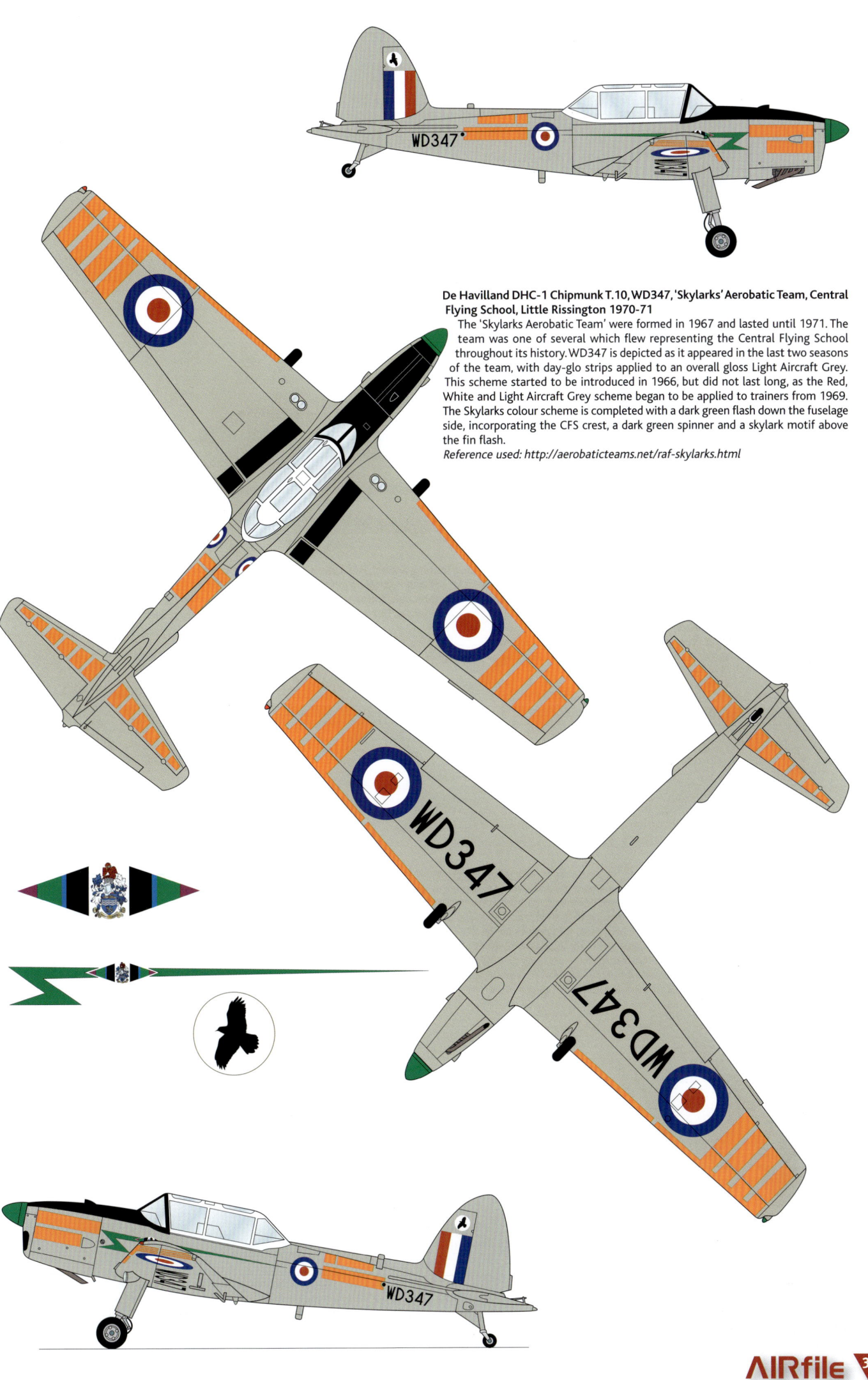

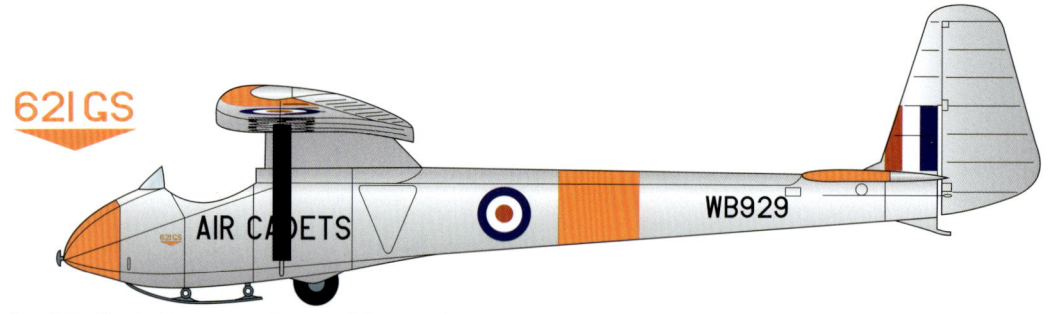

Slingsby T.21 (Sedbergh TX.1), WB929, No.621 Volunteer Gliding Squadron, Weston-super-Mare, Somerset, June 1972
The Slingsby T.21 is an open-cockpit, side-by-side two-seat glider, built by Slingsby Sailplanes Ltd and first flown in 1944. It was of wooden construction covered with fabric, and was in most respects a scaled-up development of the single-seat German Grunau Baby, which Slingsby had built under licence before the war. The T.21 first flew in December 1947 and went into quantity production both for the RAF (named the Sedbergh TX.1 after the public school of that name) and for civilian clubs. The RAF received ninety-five Sedberghs, and the type remained in service until the mid-1980s, when all their wooden gliders were replaced by Grob Vikings. Known affectionately as 'the Barge', because of its boat-like fuselage, the Sedbergh provided flying experience for thousands of cadets during its service life and is still used by many private clubs to this day.
Reference used: http://www.612vgs.co.uk/history.html

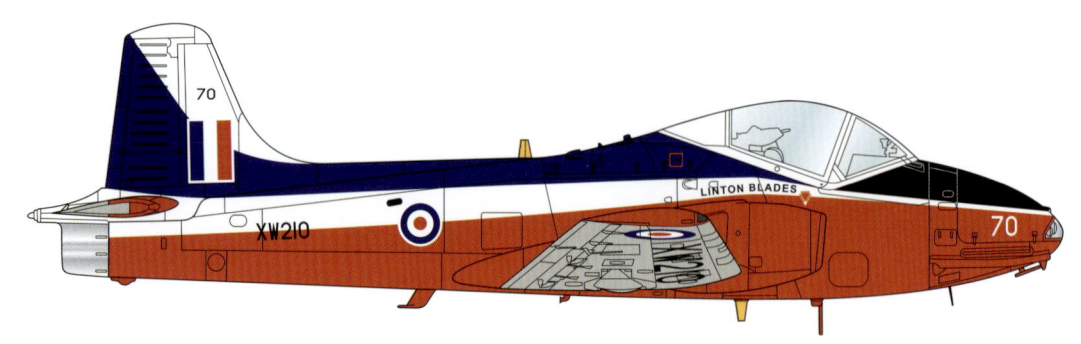

BAC Jet Provost T.5, XW210 '70', 'Linton Blades Aerobatic Team', No 1 Flying Training School, RAF Linton-on-Ouse, North Yorkshire February 1973
By the time the T.5 Jet Provost began to be introduced into service with the RAF, Hunting Percival no longer existed as an independent company, having been amalgamated into the British Aircraft Corporation in the 1960s. It was still an internal part of BAC though, and was given the task of up-grading the T.4 into a pressurized version for the RAF to train pilots in high altitude work. XW210 is shown here as part of the Linton Blades Team, in their last season before disbanding, with the standard training colours altered to include the upper fuselage painted in Roundel Blue.
Reference used: p28 'BAC Jet Provost & Strikemaster' by Adrian M Balch, Warpaint Series No.82, Warpaint Books Ltd., 2010

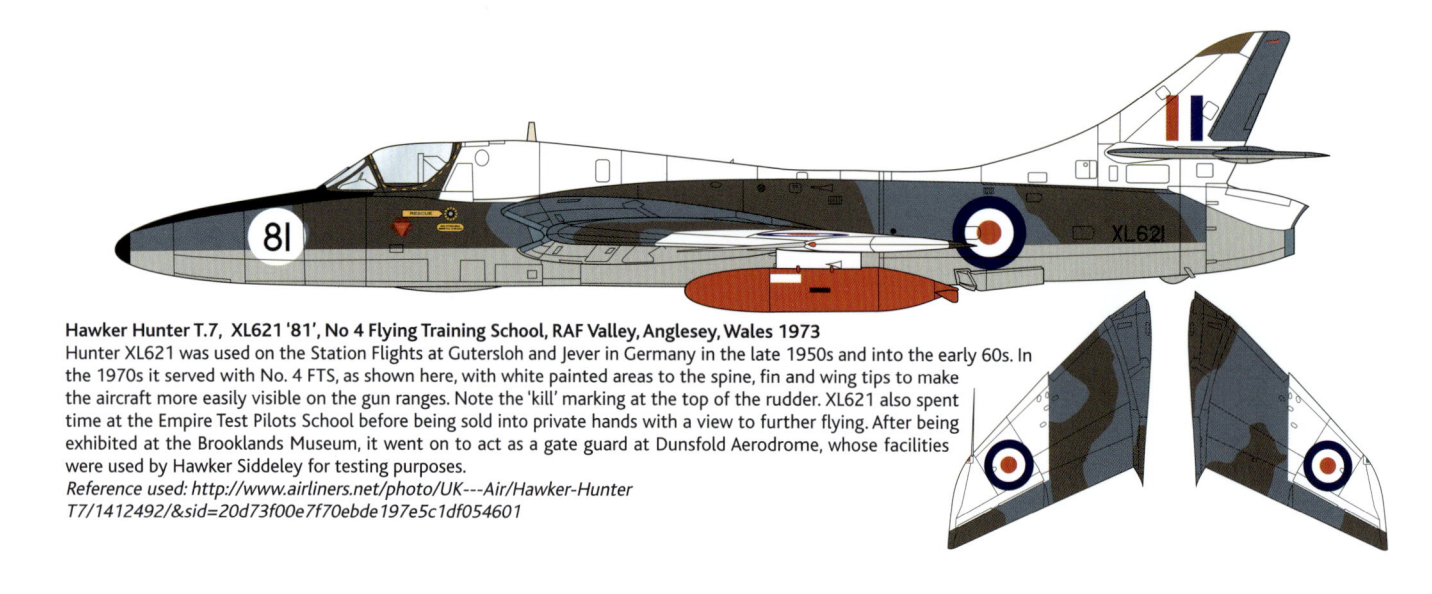

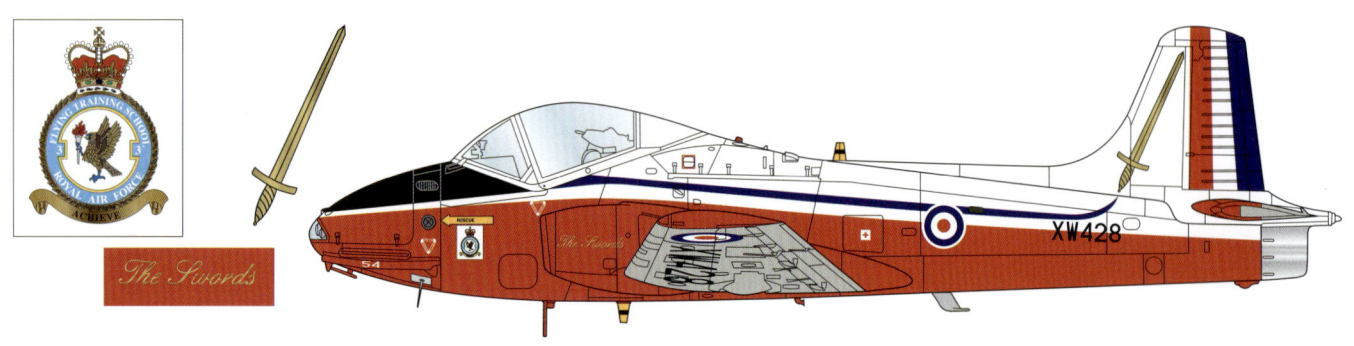

Hawker Hunter T.7, XL621 '81', No 4 Flying Training School, RAF Valley, Anglesey, Wales 1973
Hunter XL621 was used on the Station Flights at Gutersloh and Jever in Germany in the late 1950s and into the early 60s. In the 1970s it served with No. 4 FTS, as shown here, with white painted areas to the spine, fin and wing tips to make the aircraft more easily visible on the gun ranges. Note the 'kill' marking at the top of the rudder. XL621 also spent time at the Empire Test Pilots School before being sold into private hands with a view to further flying. After being exhibited at the Brooklands Museum, it went on to act as a gate guard at Dunsfold Aerodrome, whose facilities were used by Hawker Siddeley for testing purposes.
Reference used: http://www.airliners.net/photo/UK---Air/Hawker-Hunter T7/1412492/&sid=20d73f00e7f70ebde197e5c1df054601

BAC Jet Provost T.5, XW428 '54', The Swords Aerobatic Team, No 3 Flying Training School, RAF Leeming, North Yorkshire 1974
The Swords was one of the more ephemeral Aerobatic Teams of the RAF, lasting for just a single year and operating out of RAF Leeming, whose station crest included a sword in the design, and from which the team took its name and tail logo. The only deviations from the standard training scheme of Red/Light Aircraft Grey/White was a Roundel Blue cheat line along the fuselage side to the hilt of the sword on the fin, the fin flash consequently being dis-placed to the rudder, taking in the full height and width.
Reference used: p29 'BAC Jet Provost & Strikemaster' by Adrian M Balch, Warpaint Series No.82, Warpaint Books Ltd., 2010

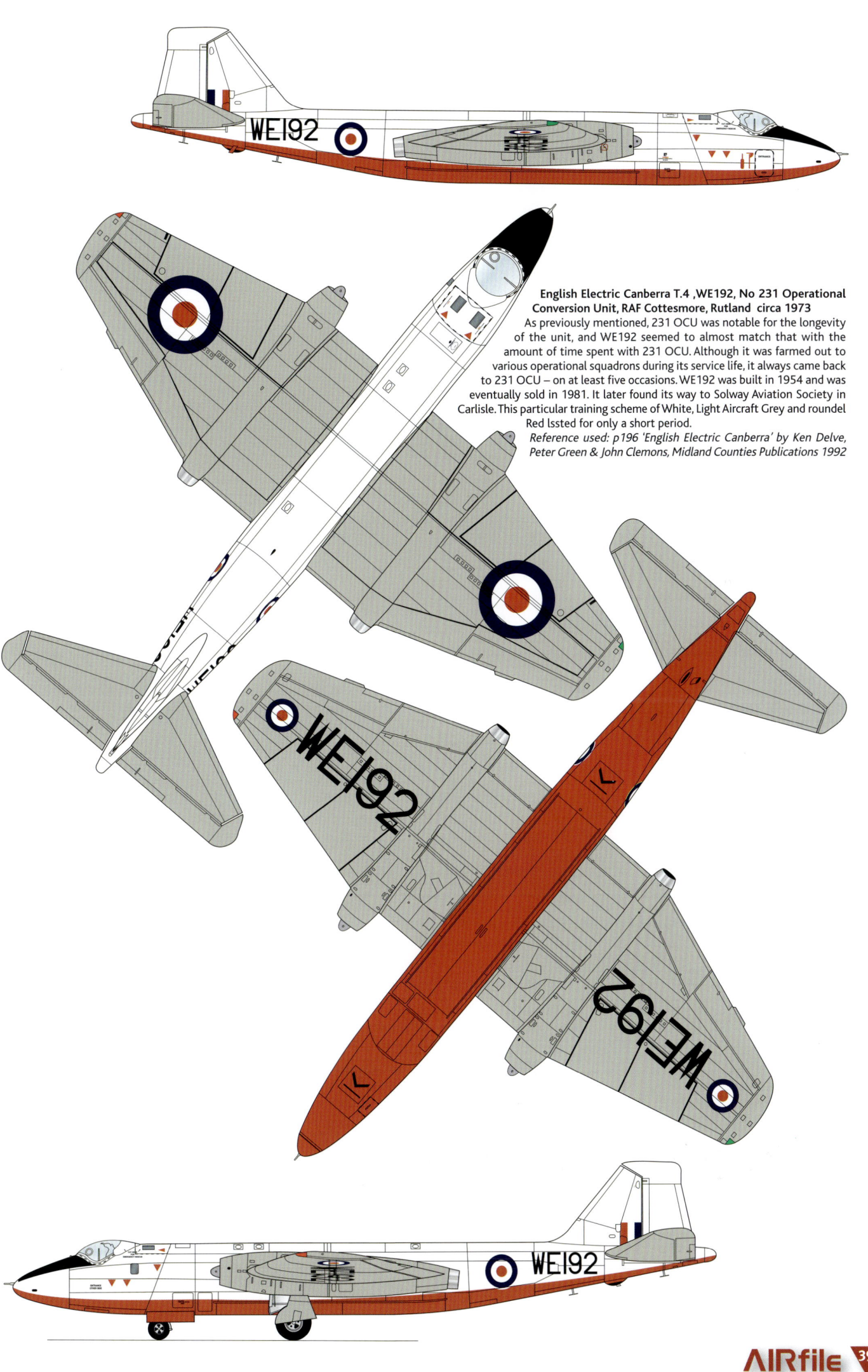

English Electric Canberra T.4, WE192, No 231 Operational Conversion Unit, RAF Cottesmore, Rutland circa 1973

As previously mentioned, 231 OCU was notable for the longevity of the unit, and WE192 seemed to almost match that with the amount of time spent with 231 OCU. Although it was farmed out to various operational squadrons during its service life, it always came back to 231 OCU – on at least five occasions. WE192 was built in 1954 and was eventually sold in 1981. It later found its way to Solway Aviation Society in Carlisle. This particular training scheme of White, Light Aircraft Grey and roundel Red lssted for only a short period.

Reference used: p196 'English Electric Canberra' by Ken Delve, Peter Green & John Clemons, Midland Counties Publications 1992

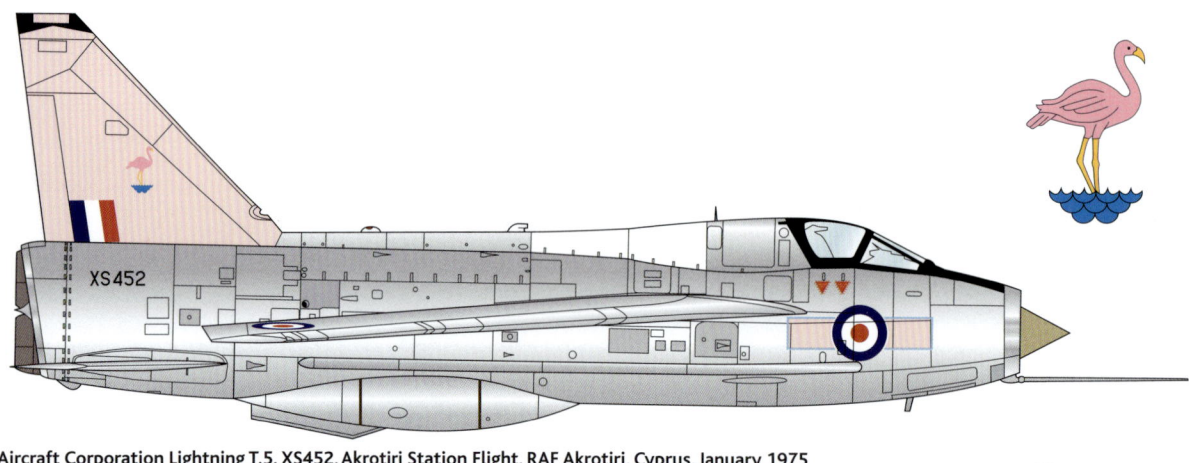

British Aircraft Corporation Lightning T.5, XS452, Akrotiri Station Flight, RAF Akrotiri, Cyprus, January 1975
XS452 appeared briefly in the pink fin and roundel rectangles of the Akrotiri Station Flight in January 1975. Initially part of No 56 Squadron, the aircraft was assigned to the Station Flight when the squadron left Cyprus to return to the UK. While at Akrotiri XS452 was mainly used by visiting UK Lightning squadrons while attending Armament Practice Camps on the island. After 6 months it was re-assigned to No 11 Squadron and repainted in an experimental all-over dark green scheme.
Reference used: p99 'English Electric Lightning' by Jon Lake, Wings of Fame, Volume 7, Aerospace Publishing Ltd., 1997

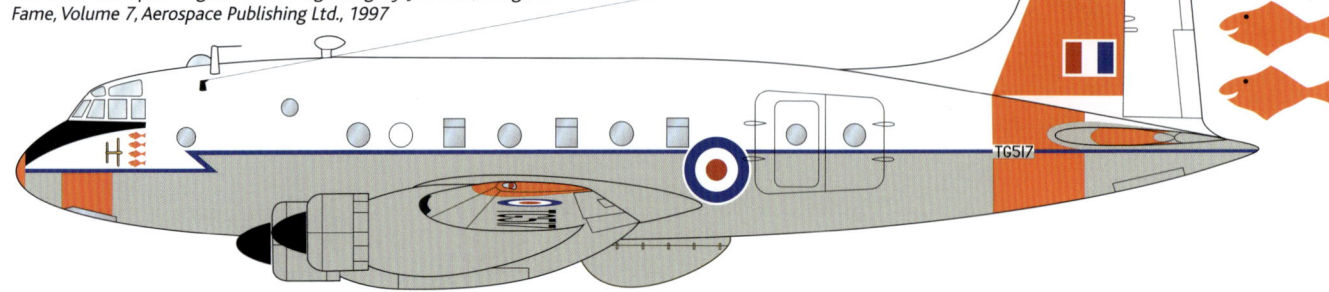

Handley Page Hastings T.5, TG517 '517', No 230 Operational Conversion Unit, Scampton, Lincolnshire 1975-76
TG517 had a long and chequered service history being the ninteenth Hastings C.1 to be produced and delivered to No 5 Maintenance Unit, Kemble in July 1948. It then went to serve with Nos 47 and 53 Squadrons, participating in the Berlin Airlift in 1948 while with No 47 Squadron. In October 1950 it was converted to the Hastings MET.1 variant. Now fitted with special weather reconnaissance equipment TG517 served with No 202 Squadron at RAF Aldergrove, Northern Ireland, until 1958. It was finally one of eight Hastings converted to T.5 standard in 1959, with a large ventral dome containing radar bomb-sight equipment. The RAF Bombing School, at RAF Lindholme, was its base until 1968. The last operations flown by TG517 were from RAF Scampton with 230 Operational Conversion Unit, this including four fishery protection sorties during the Icelandic "Cod War" of 1975-76. *Reference used: www.abpic.co.uk/photo/1142396/*

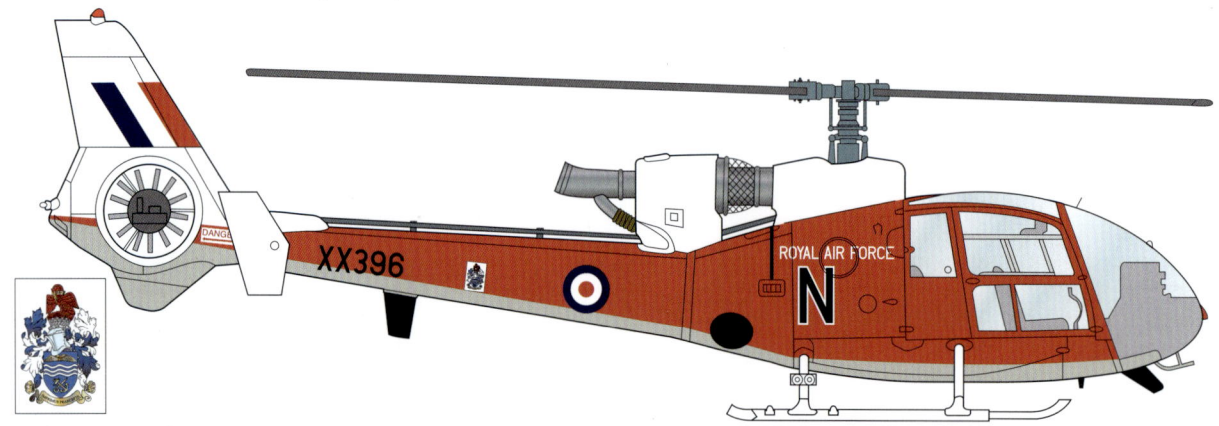

Aerospatiale SA.341 Gazelle HT.3, XX396 'N', Central Flying School, RAF Little Rissington, Gloucestershire, 1976
Although part of the agreement signed by the French and British Governments, the Gazelle was essentially an all French design. Both Governments had, prior to the agreement, been looking for replacement helicopters in the light observation category, the French to replace the Alouette series and the British the Sioux HT.2 used by the RAF and the Hiller HT.2 used by the Royal Navy. By the time of the agreement, the Gazelle prototype was almost ready to take to the air for the first time, effectively eliminating all other designs that were being considered, for example the Hughes OH-6. The type entered service with the RAF in 1973. XX396 is shown as it appeared during the last year that Little Rissington functioned as an operational airfield. The CFS then moved to Cranwell.
Reference used: http://www.abpic.co.uk/photo/1336108/

HSA Hawk T.1, XX163 '163', No 4 Flying Training School, RAF Valley, Wales, November 1976
The jet training aircraft of the RAF, through the 1960s and into the early 70s, consisted of the basic Jet Provost, the Hunter (a 1950's design with the technology to match), and the Gnat, a diminutive tandem two seater that was complicated in certain respects, but more importantly, had no facility for weapons training. These latter two aircraft needed urgent replacement. The aircraft originally slated as their successor was the Jaguar T.2, but it quickly became apparent that this was practically a full on combat aircraft, suitable only for pilot conversion. A new trainer was needed, incorporating the then much coveted traits of adaptability, cost efficiency and longevity. Hawker Siddeley Aviation were already ahead of the game, having initiated a series of designs, so when Air Staff Target 397 was issued, HSA were in a good position with a design that would eventually become the Hawk. XX163 was one of the two Hawks that were the first to be officially delivered to the RAF in November 1976. It later became the Solo Hawk Display aircraft at RAF Valley in 1992. Unfortunately, it crashed a year later attempting to turn back to the airfield.
Reference used: p19 'Hawk Comes of Age' by Peter R March, The RAF Benevolent Fund Enterprises 1995

AIRfile

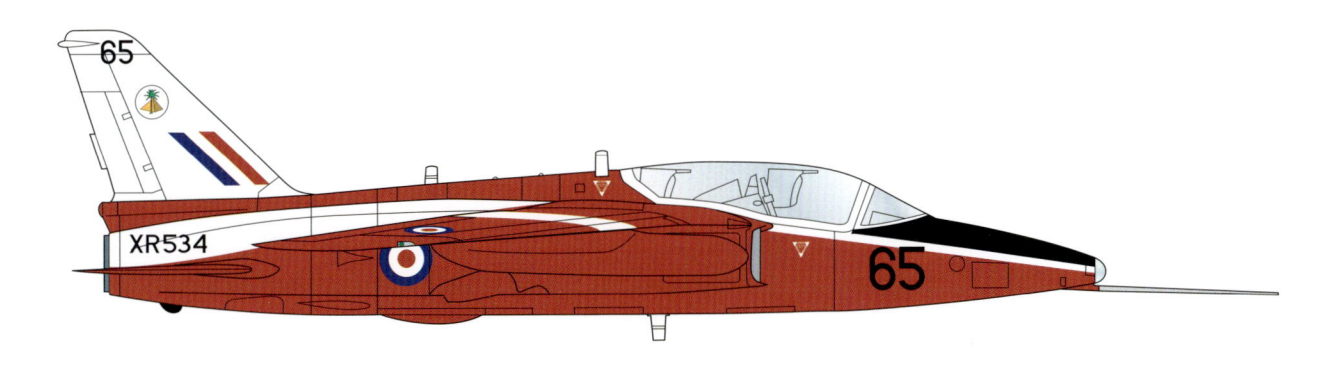

Hawker Siddeley Gnat T.1, XR534 '65', No 4 Flying Training School, RAF Valley, Anglesey, Wales circa mid 1970's

The original concept from which the Gnat was developed, the Midge light weight fighter, was an attempt by the designer, 'Teddy' Petter, to simplify and bring down the escalating costs and complexities of the then current fighters. This idea was not taken up by the RAF (although Finland and India were more receptive), but the thought of a cheap, and at the same time fast and moderately complicated trainer, was appealing. The return to tandem seating allowed the trainee a view of the fast jets to come, and a taste of the speed, as the Gnat was not quite supersonic (but this could be achieved in a shallow dive). Paradoxically, the Gnat became the aircraft that Petter was trying to move away from, a complex piece of engineering, this internal complexity leading to an external difficulty in flying the aircraft. If the hydraulics in the aircraft failed, then it could be flown in a mechanical fashion, but to do this the pilot had to go through a long, complicated sequence. It was also the same if electrical power was lost, and the pilot then had to rely on limited battery power. Trainees spent many hours learning the relevant drills for these eventualities. XR534 is depicted in one of the many colour schemes the Gnat wore, this one being applied from approximately 1972 onwards.
Reference used:
www.abpic.co.uk/photo/1083180/

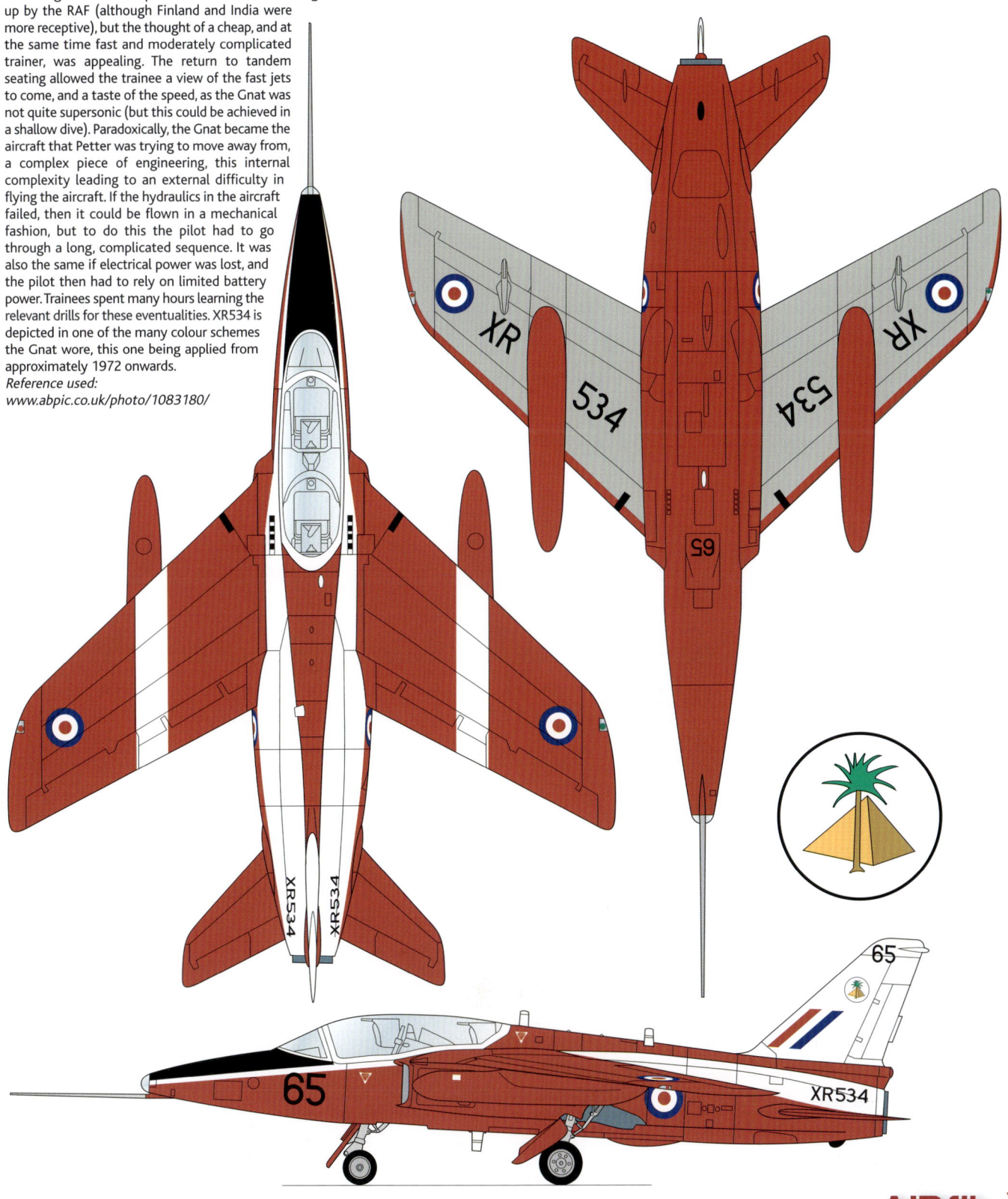

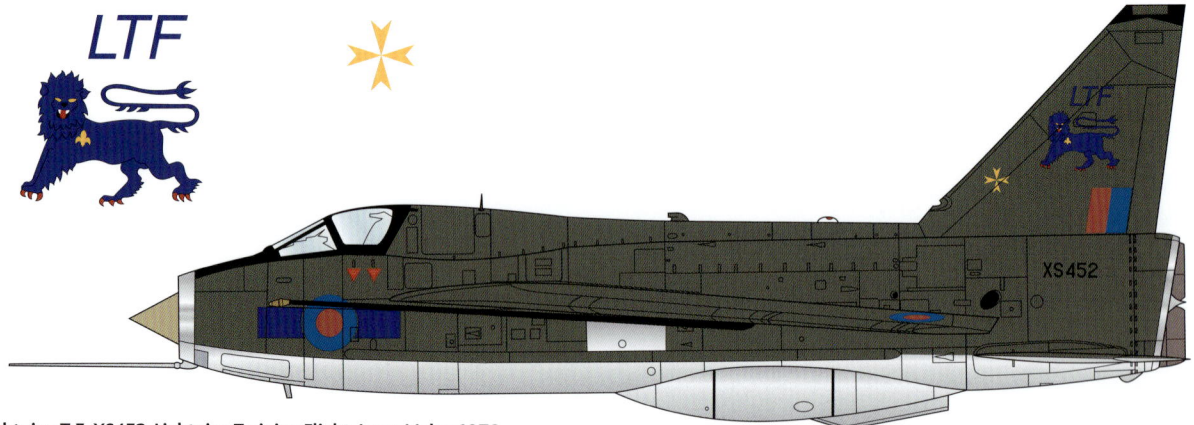

BAC Lightning T.5, XS452, Lightning Training Flight, Luqa, Malta 1976
When 226 OCU were disbanded in September 1974, (although a month later it was re-formed to train Jaguar pilots), the RAF had no facility to train and maintain the hours of Lightning pilots. A temporary stop-gap unit was created from 'C' Flight of No 11 Squadron, but it soon became apparent that a dedicated unit was needed. So 'C' Flight became the fully autonomous Lightning Training Flight in October 1975. The LTF was also only supposed to be temporary, but even so, still managed to last until April 1987. XS452 had a long and productive life, from the first flight in 1965 to the last flight with the RAF in 1988, and during that time several colour schemes were worn, from natural metal (with pink fin and flamingo), to Dark Green over natural metal (the first to carry this scheme), tactical grey and green, right up to the final Barley Grey scheme. Reference used: p439 'Later Lightnings' by Alan W Hall, Aircraft in Detail, Scale Aircraft Modelling, Volume 9 Number 10, July 1987

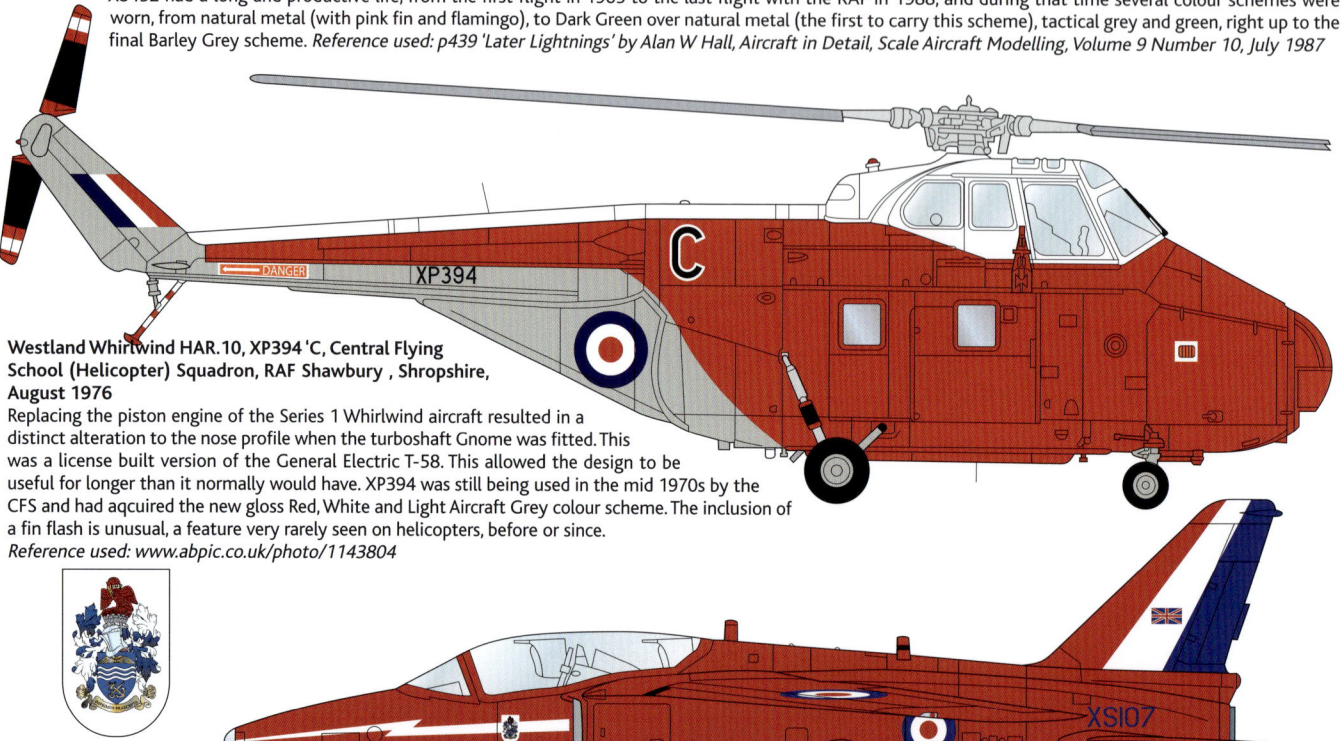

Westland Whirlwind HAR.10, XP394 'C', Central Flying School (Helicopter) Squadron, RAF Shawbury, Shropshire, August 1976
Replacing the piston engine of the Series 1 Whirlwind aircraft resulted in a distinct alteration to the nose profile when the turboshaft Gnome was fitted. This was a license built version of the General Electric T-58. This allowed the design to be useful for longer than it normally would have. XP394 was still being used in the mid 1970s by the CFS and had aqcuired the new gloss Red, White and Light Aircraft Grey colour scheme. The inclusion of a fin flash is unusual, a feature very rarely seen on helicopters, before or since.
Reference used: www.abpic.co.uk/photo/1143804

Hawker Siddeley Gnat T.1, XS107, Red Arrows Aerobatic Team, Central Flying School, Little Rissington, Gloucestershire 1977
Despite a short life in the limelight, the Yellowjacks' single season had convinced the RAF that a permanent display team would not only be good for morale but would also be good public relations. As a result, the yellow Gnats were repainted overall red and given the name 'Red Arrows', The Red Arrows flew their aircraft with great effect all around the world, until replacing their mounts in 1979 with the BAe Hawk. The heyday of the Gnat was over, and despite the seeming proliferation of the aircraft, only 105 of the type were built. Out of this total, an amazing one third of all Gnats were eventually to pass through the hands of Red Arrow pilots!
Reference used: www.airport-data.com/aircraft/photo/603616.html

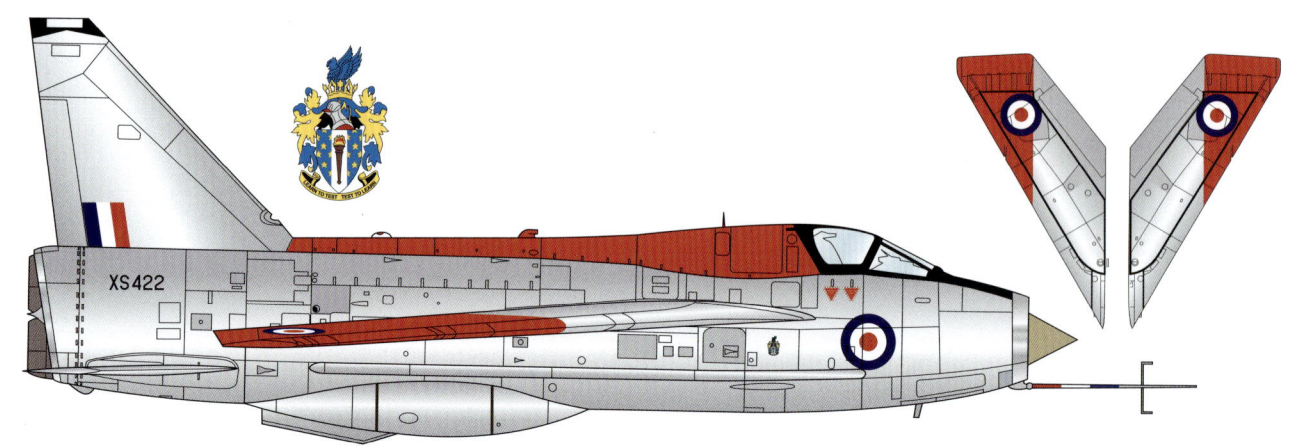

BAC Lightning T.5, XS422, Empire Test Pilots School, Boscombe Down, Wiltshire, late 1970s
The T.5 trainer is equivalent to the single seat F.3 and can be distinguished from the T.4 by the squared-off fin tip. Twenty-two of this later version were built. The Empire Test Pilots School used the Lightning for quite a few years, even if only making use of two aircraft. The first being T.4 XL629, which was used from May 1966 until November 1975. The second is shown here, taking over from XL629, and serving up until being retired in 1987. The red spine and wing tips were applied to XS422 fairly early in its career, when it joined the ETPS in 1976.
Reference used: p84 'English Electric Lightning' by Jon Lake, Wings of Fame, Volume 7, Aerospace Publishing Ltd., 1997

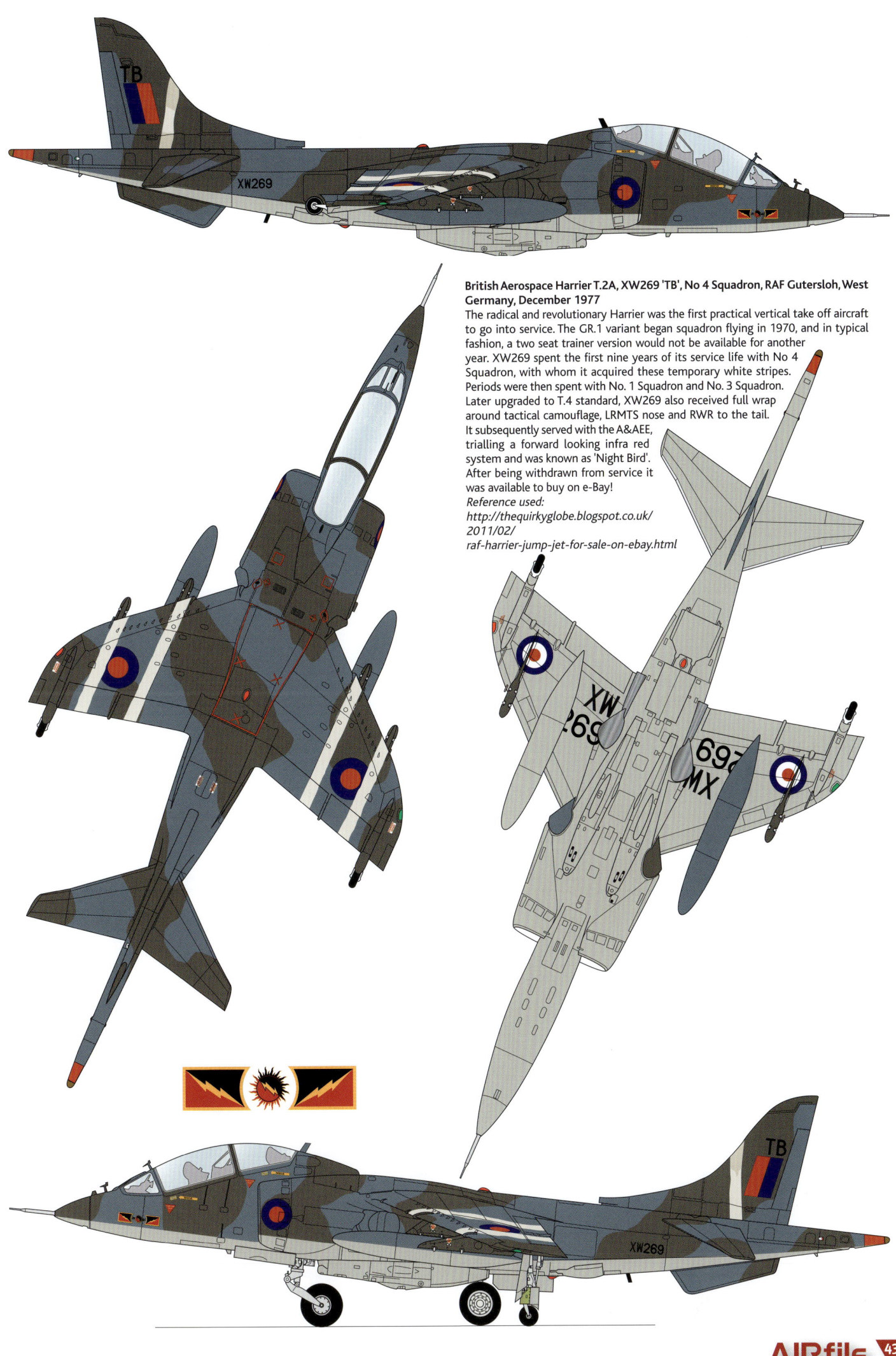

British Aerospace Harrier T.2A, XW269 'TB', No 4 Squadron, RAF Gutersloh, West Germany, December 1977

The radical and revolutionary Harrier was the first practical vertical take off aircraft to go into service. The GR.1 variant began squadron flying in 1970, and in typical fashion, a two seat trainer version would not be available for another year. XW269 spent the first nine years of its service life with No 4 Squadron, with whom it acquired these temporary white stripes. Periods were then spent with No. 1 Squadron and No. 3 Squadron. Later upgraded to T.4 standard, XW269 also received full wrap around tactical camouflage, LRMTS nose and RWR to the tail. It subsequently served with the A&AEE, trialling a forward looking infra red system and was known as 'Night Bird'. After being withdrawn from service it was available to buy on e-Bay!

Reference used:
http://thequirkyglobe.blogspot.co.uk/2011/02/raf-harrier-jump-jet-for-sale-on-ebay.html

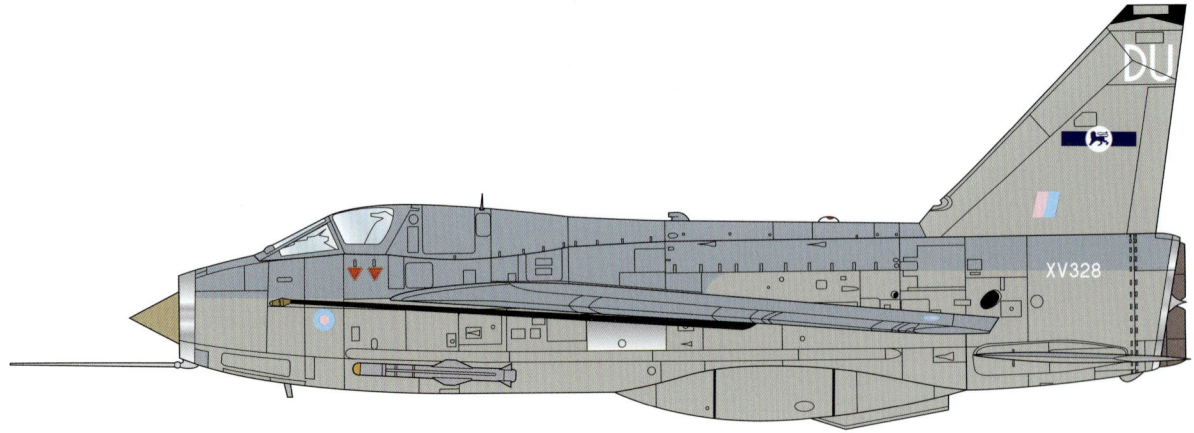

BAC Lightning T.5, XV328 'DU', Lightning Training Flight, RAF Binbrook, Lincolnshire, early 1980s
After 40 years of service, the final refuge for the Lightning was RAF Binbrook. As the RAF re-equipped with the Phantom, RAF squadrons gave up the best point defence fighter they ever had. Even so, the Lightning almost saw out its successor, as the Phantom itself was retired just five years after the 'Last, Last Lightning Show', to make way for the Tornado. When BAe needed an aircraft to be used as targets for the Tornado radar, the aircraft they chose was... the Lightning, in which role it served until 1993, close to four decades of service. XV328 is shown here in the Barley Grey scheme adopted by some aircraft towards the end, and even this final scheme could be seen with variations.
Reference used: p83 'English Electric Lightning' by Jon Lake, Wings of Fame, Volume 7, Aerospace Publishing Ltd., 1997

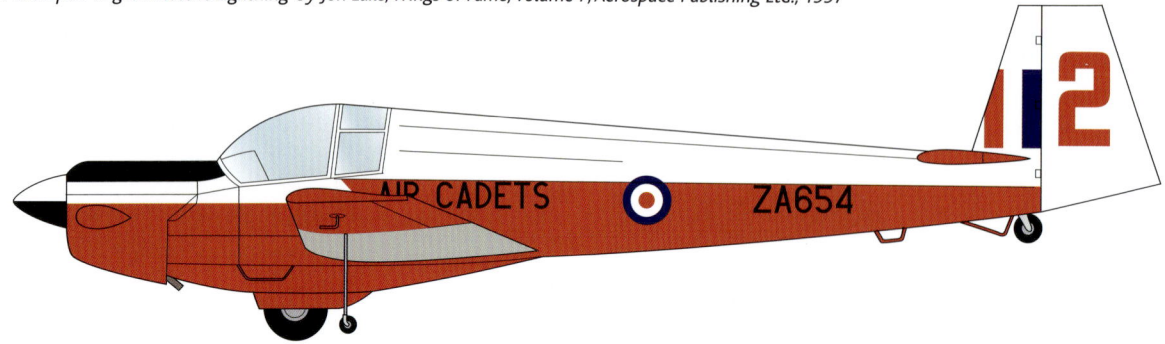

Slingsby Venture T.2, ZA654 '2', No 612 Volunteer Gliding Squadron, RAF Benson, Oxfordshire, early 1980s
The Slingsby Venture was the military version of the Slingsby Type 61 Falke, which in turn was a license-built version of the Scheibe SF 25B, a German touring motor glider. It first flew in February 1971 and provided good service to the ATC until replaced by the Grob Vigilant T1 in the 1990s. The Venture was a marked improvement on previous ATC equipment. As a motorised glider with two-seat, side-by-side layout, training and sortie times increased tremendously. 612 VGS was formed in 1945 under the title of Eastern Command 104 Elementary Gliding School, In 1978 gliding schools were renamed Volunteer Gliding Squadrons. There are currently twenty-seven VGS which operate under No 3 Flying Training School and are validated by the RAF Central Flying School.
Reference used: http://www.612vgs.co.uk/history.html

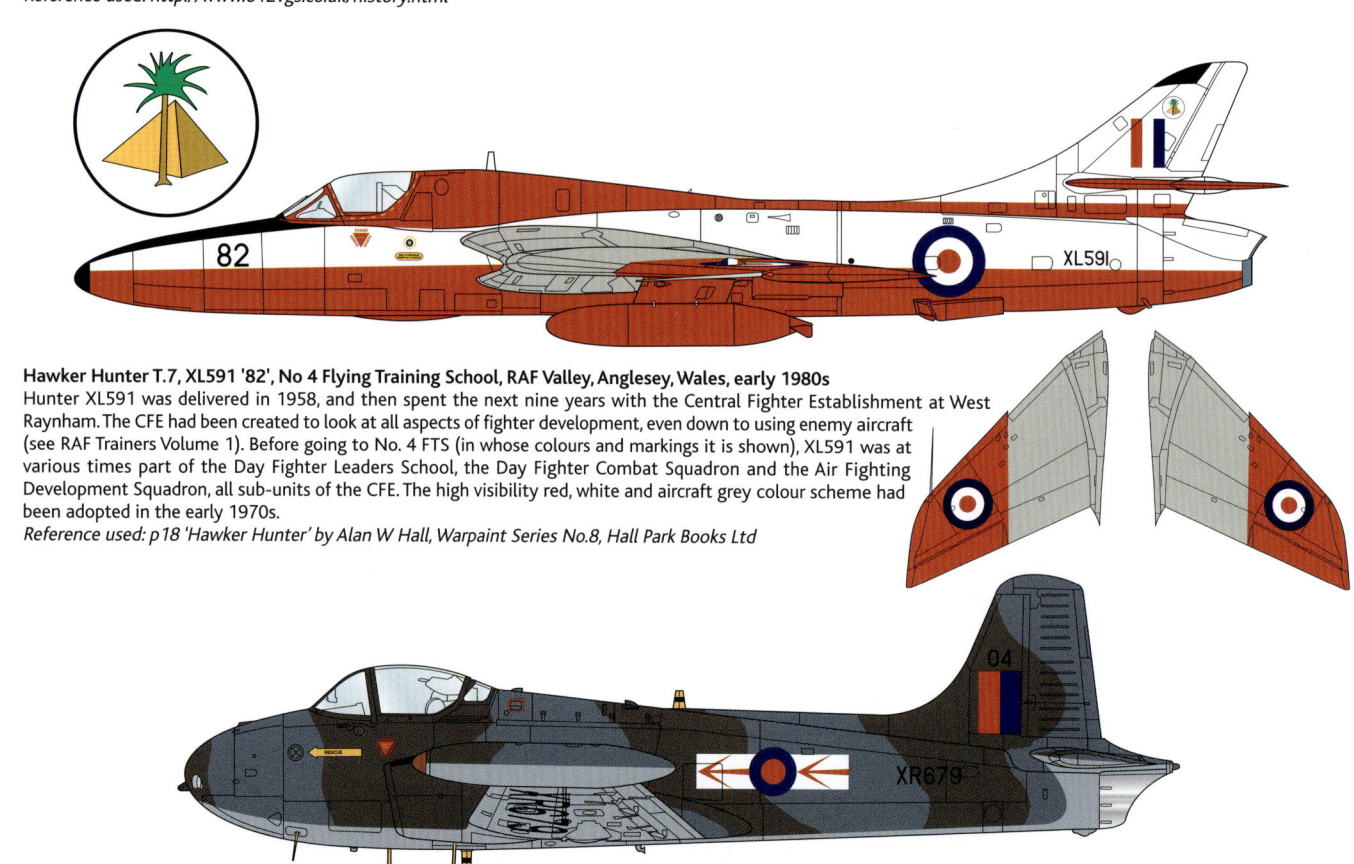

Hawker Hunter T.7, XL591 '82', No 4 Flying Training School, RAF Valley, Anglesey, Wales, early 1980s
Hunter XL591 was delivered in 1958, and then spent the next nine years with the Central Fighter Establishment at West Raynham. The CFE had been created to look at all aspects of fighter development, even down to using enemy aircraft (see RAF Trainers Volume 1). Before going to No. 4 FTS (in whose colours and markings it is shown), XL591 was at various times part of the Day Fighter Leaders School, the Day Fighter Combat Squadron and the Air Fighting Development Squadron, all sub-units of the CFE. The high visibility red, white and aircraft grey colour scheme had been adopted in the early 1970s.
Reference used: p18 'Hawker Hunter' by Alan W Hall, Warpaint Series No.8, Hall Park Books Ltd

Hunting Jet Provost T.4, XR679 '04', No 79 (R) Squadron, No 1 Tactical Weapons Unit, RAF Brawdy, Pembrokeshire, Wales 1984
The Tactical Weapons Unit had been formed in 1974, and in 1978 was split to become No. 1 TWU and No. 2 TWU. 1 TWU absorbed the TWU's Jet Provost T.4s and eventually had four T.4 aircraft on strength – XP547, XR679, XS178 and XS219. The aircraft were camouflaged and used for the initial training of Army Forward Air Controllers. The Army officers were given air experience in them and the aircraft were used as 'ground attack' aircraft for the controllers initial exercises. The last example was phased out in 1990.
Reference used: p19 'BAC Jet Provost & Strikemaster' by Adrian M Balch, Warpaint Series No.82, Warpaint Books Ltd., 2010

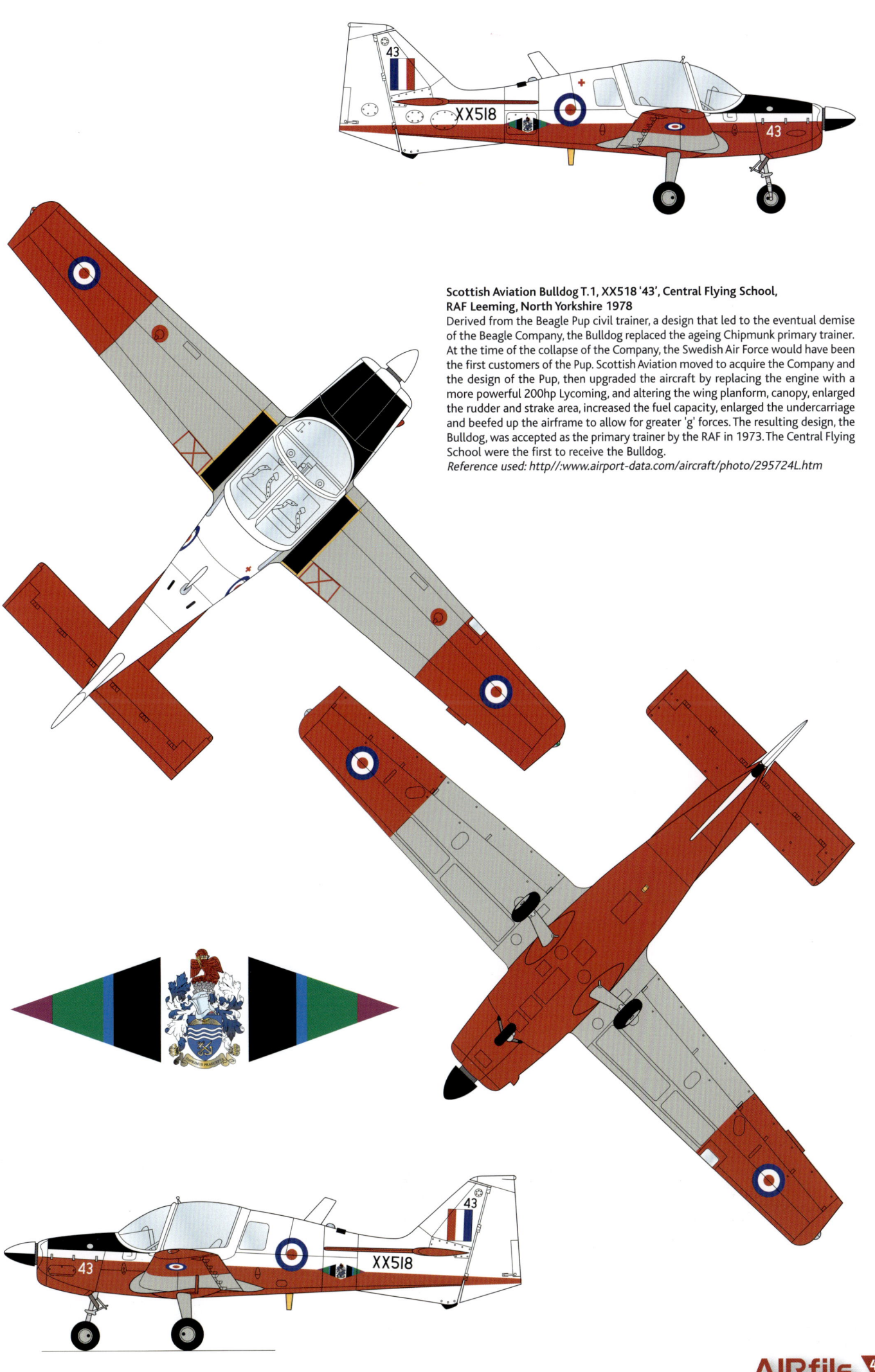

Scottish Aviation Bulldog T.1, XX518 '43', Central Flying School, RAF Leeming, North Yorkshire 1978

Derived from the Beagle Pup civil trainer, a design that led to the eventual demise of the Beagle Company, the Bulldog replaced the ageing Chipmunk primary trainer. At the time of the collapse of the Company, the Swedish Air Force would have been the first customers of the Pup. Scottish Aviation moved to acquire the Company and the design of the Pup, then upgraded the aircraft by replacing the engine with a more powerful 200hp Lycoming, and altering the wing planform, canopy, enlarged the rudder and strake area, increased the fuel capacity, enlarged the undercarriage and beefed up the airframe to allow for greater 'g' forces. The resulting design, the Bulldog, was accepted as the primary trainer by the RAF in 1973. The Central Flying School were the first to receive the Bulldog.

Reference used: http://:www.airport-data.com/aircraft/photo/295724L.htm

Royal Aircraft Establishment

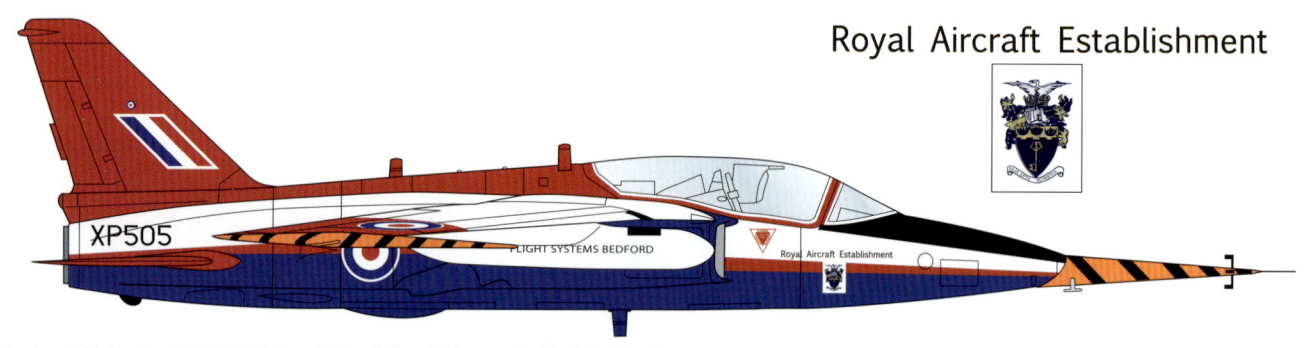

Hawker Siddeley Gnat T.1, XP505, Royal Aircraft Establishment, Bedford, Bedfordshire 1982
As a trainer, the Gnat was more than adequate, a long service life and reliability far outweighing the limited number built. As an aircraft with a potential to be used in other roles, it was severely limited. One Gnat that did find an alternative role was XP505, which came from the initial production batch of thirty aircraft. It was used by the Defence Research Agency at Bedford to record low level turbulence and wind gusting by means of the three prominent probes attached to the nose and wingtips. The recording equipment was installed in the only possible available space, namely the rear cockpit area. This one-off Gnat flew with the Flight Systems Squadron at the RAE from 1969 until it was sold to the London Science Museum in 1984, and was the last Gnat to fly in military service.
Reference used: p113 'Testing Colours' by Adrian M Balch, Air Life Publishing Ltd, 1993

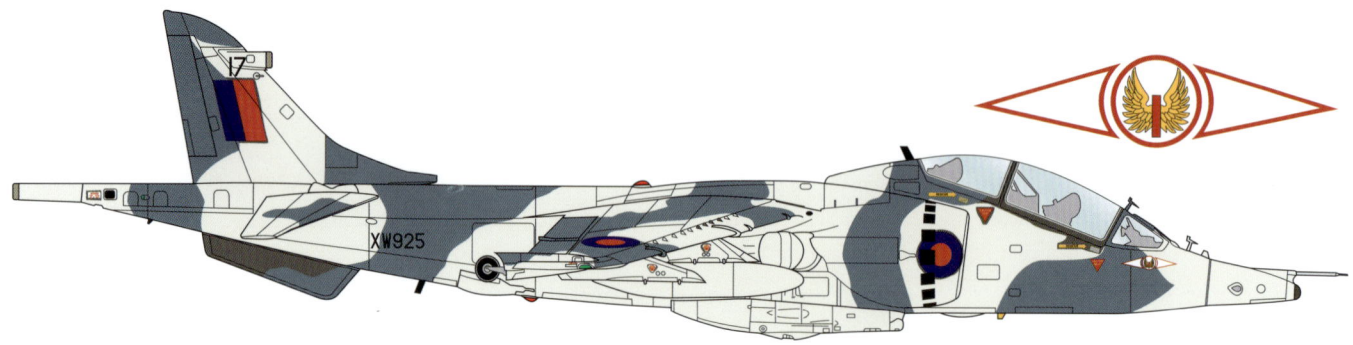

BAE Harrier T.4, XW925 '17', No 1 Squadron, Tromso, Norway, for Exercise 'Anorak Express', March 1982
Originally built as a T.2 and flying for the first time in 1971, XW925, like all early T.2s, was converted first to T.2A standard, and then to T.4. These upgrades included fitting the more powerful Pegasus 103 engine, laser ranging and marked target seeker nose and passive radar warning receiver to the leading edge of the tail fin. 'Anorak Express' was a regular NATO exercise held in Norway during the 1980s. Unfortunately XW925 ended its service career in a fatal accident at RAF Gutersloh in June 1989.
Reference used: p35 'Harrier' by Denis J Calvert, Aircraft Illustrated Special, Ian Allen Ltd

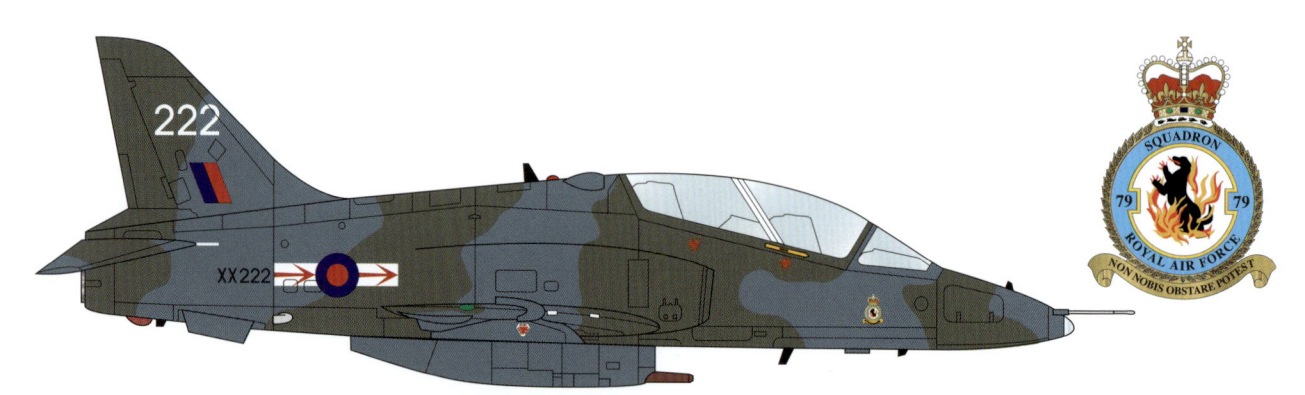

BAe Hawk T.1, XX222 '222', No 1 Tactical Weapons Unit, (No 79 (R) Squadron), RAF Brawdy, Wales 1984
In the past, an RAF trainer was one of two things: either it started as a trainer and finished as a trainer, or it had been a front line aircraft and had been altered or converted into a trainer. The Hawk has broken this tradition. The reliability of the Adour engine and the future potential of the design began to be recognised when Hawks were assigned to the Tactical Weapons Unit. It was seen that this highly manoeuvrable aircraft could be used as a point defence fighter, much like the Hunters that the Hawk replaced, carrying two Sidewinder missiles. Eighty-eight T.1 Hawks were so converted and it was the first step towards a trainer being turned into a fighter. XX222 has the tactical wrap around camouflage used by the TWUs at this time. A year later it would become one of the aircraft to be converted to carry missiles.
Reference used: p119 'Hawk Comes of Age' by Peter R March, The RAF Benevolent Fund Enterprises 1995

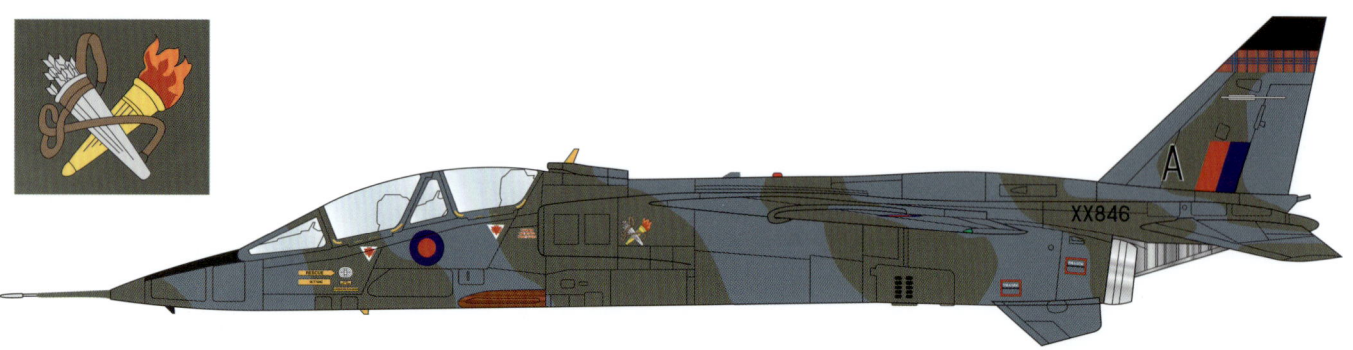

SEPECAT Jaguar T.2A, XX846 'A', No 226 Operational Conversion Unit, Jaguar Operational Conversion Unit, RAF Lossiemouth, Moray, Scotland, August 1984
The Jaguar, like the Gazelle, was a French design that was adapted to fulfill the needs of both the RAF and the *Armee de l'Air*. The original Breguet Br.121 was developed during the mid 1960s, the five variants being reduced to two basic types, a single seat attack version and a two seat trainer version. Thirty-five (or 3thirty-eight, depending on the reference) Jaguar T.2 aircraft were built for the RAF, and the first one to enter service went straight to the Jaguar Conversion Team, established in July 1973 specifically for the re-training of FGA pilots. Almost a year later, it was re-named the Jaguar Operational Conversion Unit, and by October 1974 was once again renamed, now known as 226 OCU. At the time XX846 was flying, tactical wrap-around camouflage was de riguer. Note the tartan tail band and the badge on the intake.
Reference used: www.abpic.co.uk/photo/1297234/

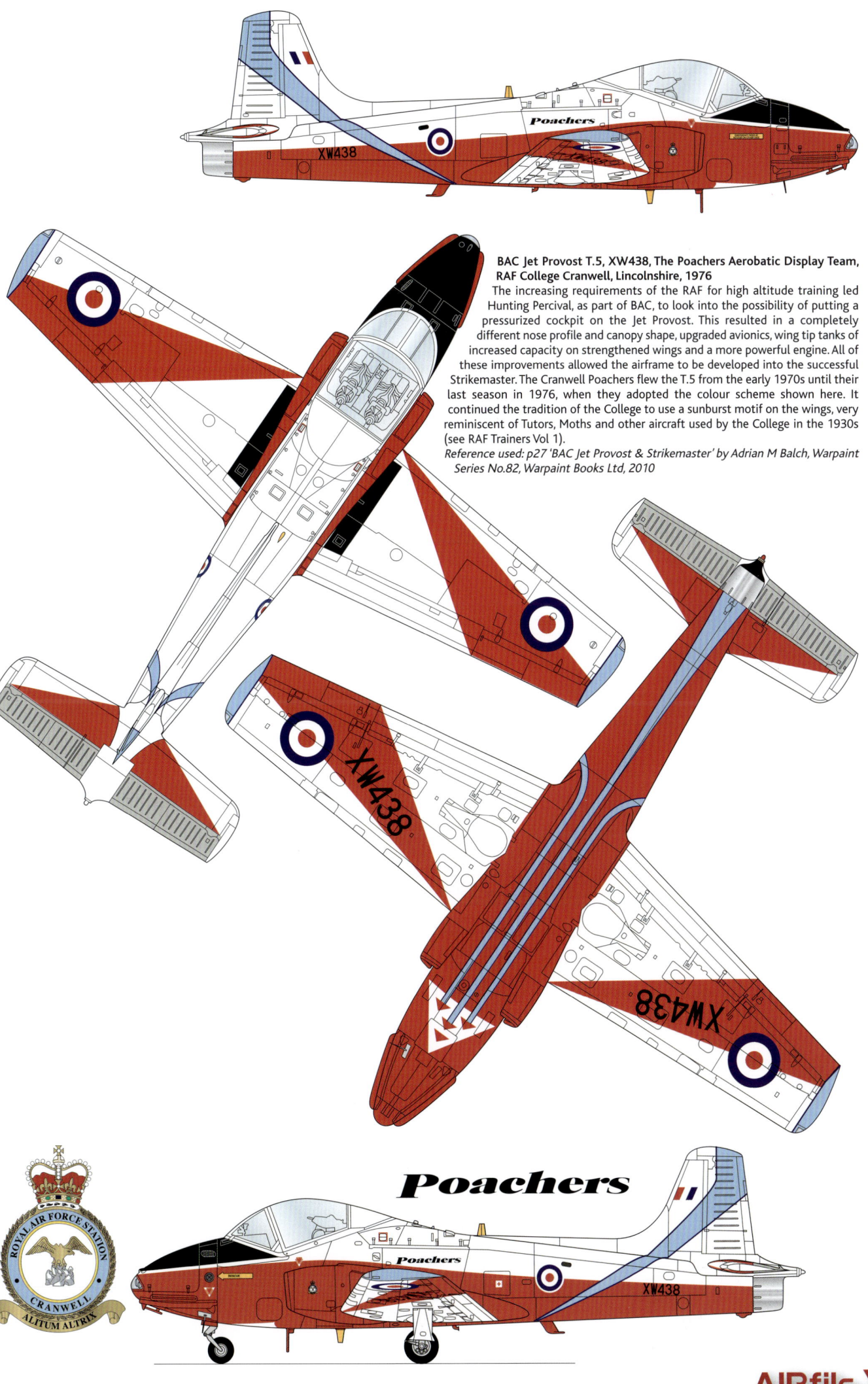

BAC Jet Provost T.5, XW438, The Poachers Aerobatic Display Team, RAF College Cranwell, Lincolnshire, 1976

The increasing requirements of the RAF for high altitude training led Hunting Percival, as part of BAC, to look into the possibility of putting a pressurized cockpit on the Jet Provost. This resulted in a completely different nose profile and canopy shape, upgraded avionics, wing tip tanks of increased capacity on strengthened wings and a more powerful engine. All of these improvements allowed the airframe to be developed into the successful Strikemaster. The Cranwell Poachers flew the T.5 from the early 1970s until their last season in 1976, when they adopted the colour scheme shown here. It continued the tradition of the College to use a sunburst motif on the wings, very reminiscent of Tutors, Moths and other aircraft used by the College in the 1930s (see RAF Trainers Vol 1).

Reference used: p27 'BAC Jet Provost & Strikemaster' by Adrian M Balch, Warpaint Series No.82, Warpaint Books Ltd, 2010

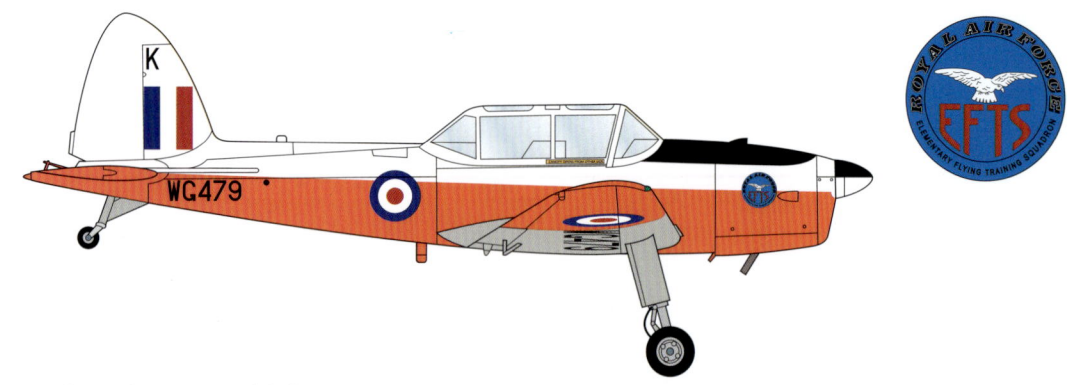

De Havilland DHC-1 Chipmunk T.10, WG479 'K', Elementary Flying Training School, Swinderby, Lincolnshire 1989
The Elementary Flying Training Squadron was established on 1 June 1987. Prior to this date it had been known as the Flying Selection Squadron, a separate adjunct of the Flying Training School at Cranwell, and had started flying from Swinderby in June 1979. After completion of this course on the venerable Chipmunk, the trainee pilot would move on to the Tucano. For more than sixty years the Chipmunk has served the RAF, and this simple, robust and reliable trainer continues to serve to this day, examples flying with the Battle of Britain Memorial Flight, to give jet pilots experience of 'tail dragger' aircraft, before they lay hands on the precious Spitfires and Hurricanes.
Reference used: p49 'Air Experience', Airforces Monthly, Key Publishing June 1989

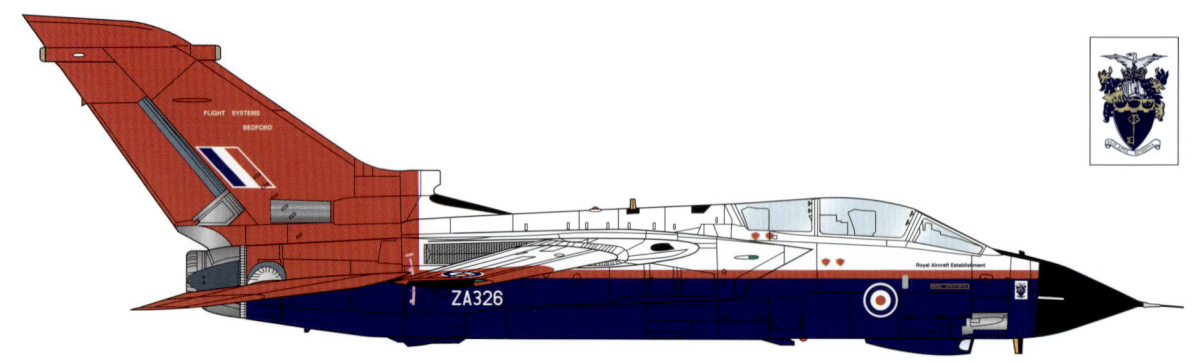

Panavia Tornado GR.1T, ZA326, Flight Systems Division, RAE Bedford, Bedfordshire, July 1989
Unfortunately, ZA326 suffered from a production line fire at the Warton factory where its rear end was badly damaged. This delayed its entry into squadron service and after a rebuild, the aircraft was assigned to the Royal Aircraft Establishment in 1983. Its work with the Flight Systems Division included laser terrain following trials. Subsequently, ZA326 joined the Defence Research Agency fleet at Boscombe Down, when its Bedford base closed in 1989. It is the sole 'Rasberry Ripple' Tornado flying and currently flies on various trials as part of the civilian operated QinetiQ fleet from Boscombe Down, Wiltshire.
Reference used: 'Testing Colours' by Adrian M Balch, Airlife Publishing Ltd., 1993

Panavia Tornado F.3T, ZE786 'DT', No 11 Squadron, RAF Leeming, North Yorkshire, 1990
The Panavia Tornado Air Defence Variant (ADV) was developed with the requirement for a long-range interceptor to replace the Lightning F.6 and Phantom FGR.2. The RAF specification for the ADV variant was the F.2 and this first flew in March 1984. After serious problems with the aircraft's radar, the F.2 aircraft were redesignated for training purposes with No 229 OCU and the updated variant, the F.3, became the prime operational interceptor with the front line squadrons. As with the GR.1s and GR.4s, a small number of F.3 aircraft were converted to dual-control and released to units as in-squadron trainers. Again as with the GR.1Ts and GR.4Ts, very little external differences identify these aircraft in their training role.
Reference used: 'Tornado' by Ian Black, Airlife Publishing Ltd., 1990

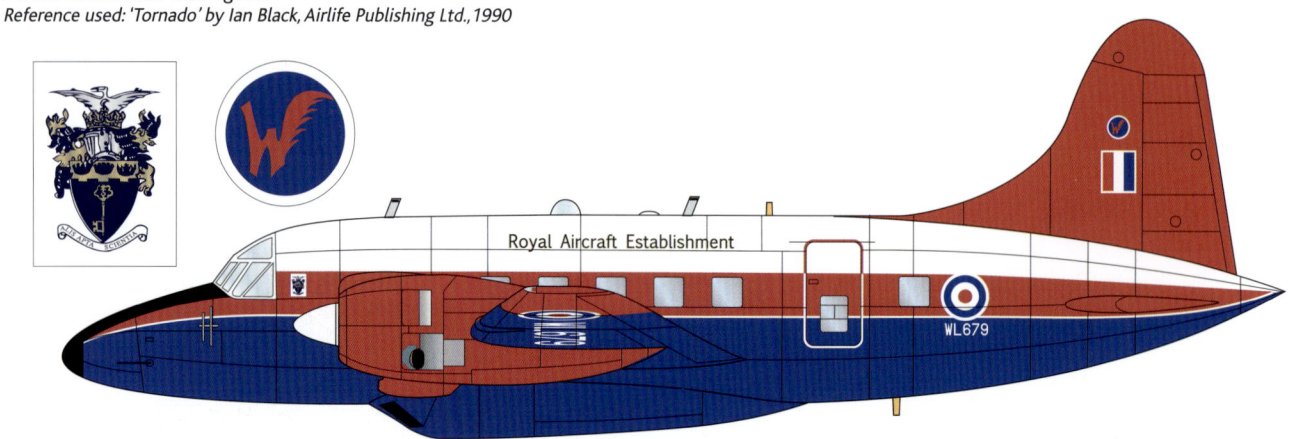

Vickers Varsity T.1, WL679, Royal Aircraft Establishment, Farnborough 1991
This Varsity, WL679, has the honour of being the very last of the type in service. Built in 1953, the aircraft never went to any of the Schools, being used by test units for the entire period that it flew, which was a grand total of 37 years. The Radio Flight at Farnborough made use of it from 1954 to 1968. It then spent some time at the Radar Research Establishment, before returning to the RAE at Farnborough in 1977. It stayed with the RAE until retirement in 1992, at which time it went to Cosford Aerospace Museum, acquiring the attractive raspberry ripple scheme during this latter period.
Reference used: 'Testing Colours' by Adrian M Balch, Airlife Publishing

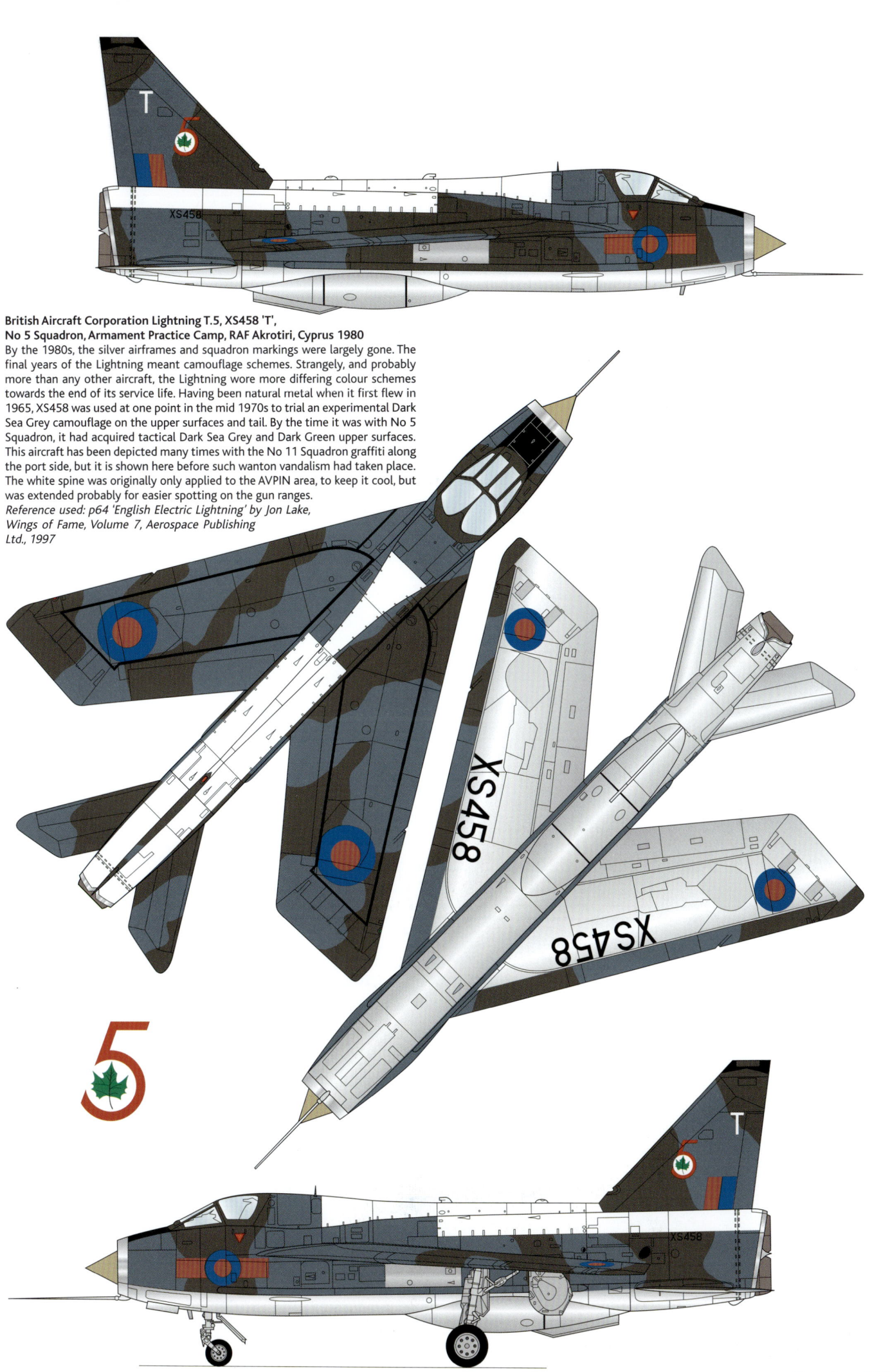

**British Aircraft Corporation Lightning T.5, XS458 'T',
No 5 Squadron, Armament Practice Camp, RAF Akrotiri, Cyprus 1980**

By the 1980s, the silver airframes and squadron markings were largely gone. The final years of the Lightning meant camouflage schemes. Strangely, and probably more than any other aircraft, the Lightning wore more differing colour schemes towards the end of its service life. Having been natural metal when it first flew in 1965, XS458 was used at one point in the mid 1970s to trial an experimental Dark Sea Grey camouflage on the upper surfaces and tail. By the time it was with No 5 Squadron, it had acquired tactical Dark Sea Grey and Dark Green upper surfaces. This aircraft has been depicted many times with the No 11 Squadron graffiti along the port side, but it is shown here before such wanton vandalism had taken place. The white spine was originally only applied to the AVPIN area, to keep it cool, but was extended probably for easier spotting on the gun ranges.
*Reference used: p64 'English Electric Lightning' by Jon Lake,
Wings of Fame, Volume 7, Aerospace Publishing
Ltd., 1997*

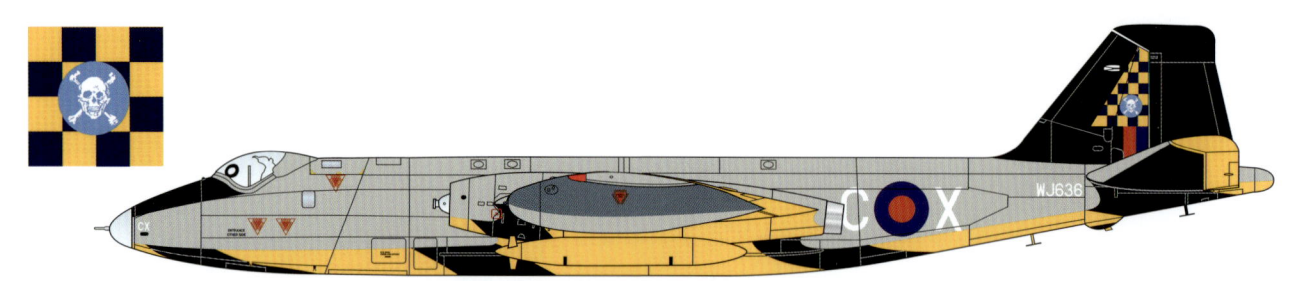

English Electric Canberra TT.18, WJ636 'C-X', No 100 Squadron, RAF Wyton, Cambridgeshire, August 1990
Once the Canberra had an efficient winch/towing system in the form of the Rushton equipment, it proved itself to be a highly effective target tower. Flying up to a height of 48,000 feet, and towing a target over 6 miles behind, allowed for realistic missions for fighters with both infra red and radar guided missiles. The targets could carry both radar reflective lenses that gave a radar return so it appeared many times larger than it actually was, and flares that gave a heat source for missiles such as Red Top. No 100 Squadron became the primary target towing squadron in 1972, and used Canberras into the 1990s until they were replaced by Hawks. The reference photo for WJ636 contrarily shows it to be carrying an RDF banner target container. Also of note are the camouflaged wing tip tanks.
Reference used: p204 'English Electric Canberra, by Ken Delve, Peter Green & John Clemons, Midland Counties Publications, 1992

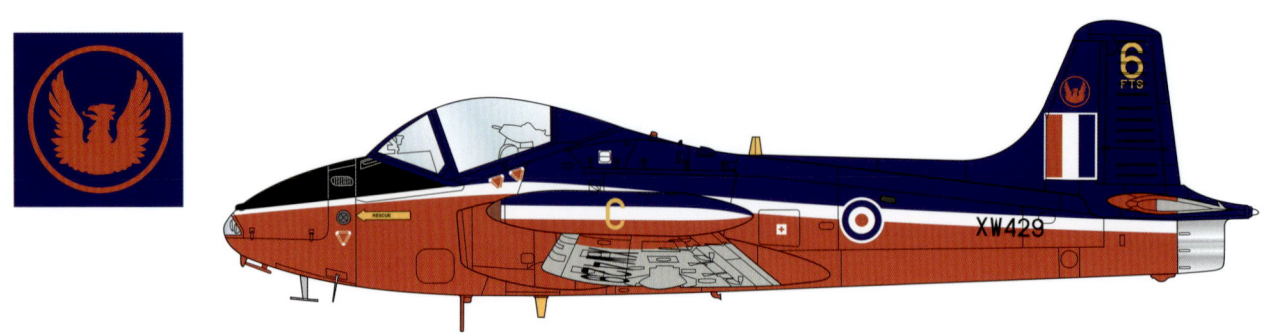

BAC Jet Provost T.5B, XW429 'C', No 6 Flying Training School, RAF Finningley, South Yorkshire, June 1990
As one of 110 T.5 Jet Provost aircraft built, XW429 was delivered to the RAF on 22 June 1972. No 6 FTS was responsible for the training of RAF navigators and used the Jet Provost during the low level flying phase. The designation T.5B is an unofficial one, as it is basically a T.5A converted for navigator training. No 6 FTS was one of the last two schools to use the Jet Provost, and the aircraft was retired from RAF use in 1993, after fifteen years of service.
Reference used: www.abpic.co.uk/photo/1283470/

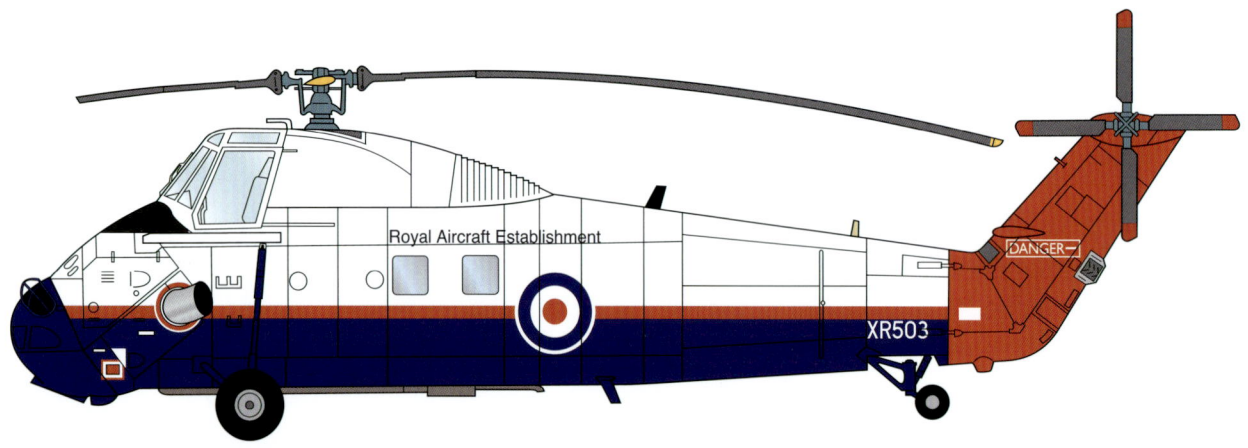

Westland Wessex HC.2, XR503. Defence Research Agency, Boscombe Down, 1992
XR503 still wears RAE titles despite the fact that the RAE had been merged into the Defence Research Agency on 1 April 1991. The research organisation of the Ministry of Defence later became known as the Defence Evaluation and Research Agency (DERA) and later still, was part-privatised, resulting in the curiously named QinetiQ. This helicopter was last known to be allocated to the Defence Fire Training and Development Centre at Manston in Kent as a ground instructional airframe.
Reference used: http://www.abpic.co.uk/photo/1154789/

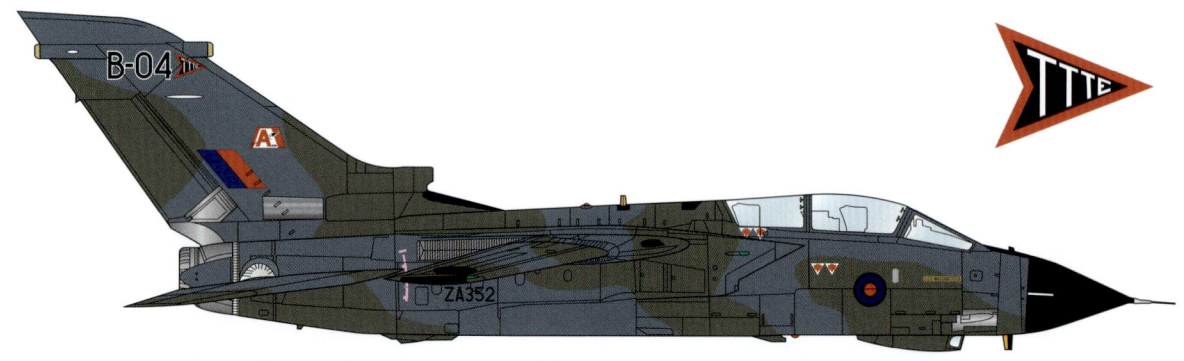

Panavia Tornado GR.1T, ZA352 'B-04', Tri-National Tornado Training Establishment, RAF Cottesmore, Rutland, August 1993
To reflect the joint international production of the Tornado between the UK, Germany and Italy, the Tri-National Tornado Training Establishment (TTTE) was formed in 1981 to train RAF, *Luftwaffe* and Italian Air Force pilots on the new aircraft. The unit was made up of three squadrons with all staff and students being tri-nationally mixed. A-Squadron was headed by a German, B-Squadron by a Brit and C-Squadron by an Italian squadron commander. There was also a Standardization Squadron (S-Squadron) which was responsible for follow-on training, training of instructor pilots and conducting check flights. Before its closure in 1999 the unit was training 300 crews a year when at its height.
Reference used: www.abpic.co.uk/photo/1043577/

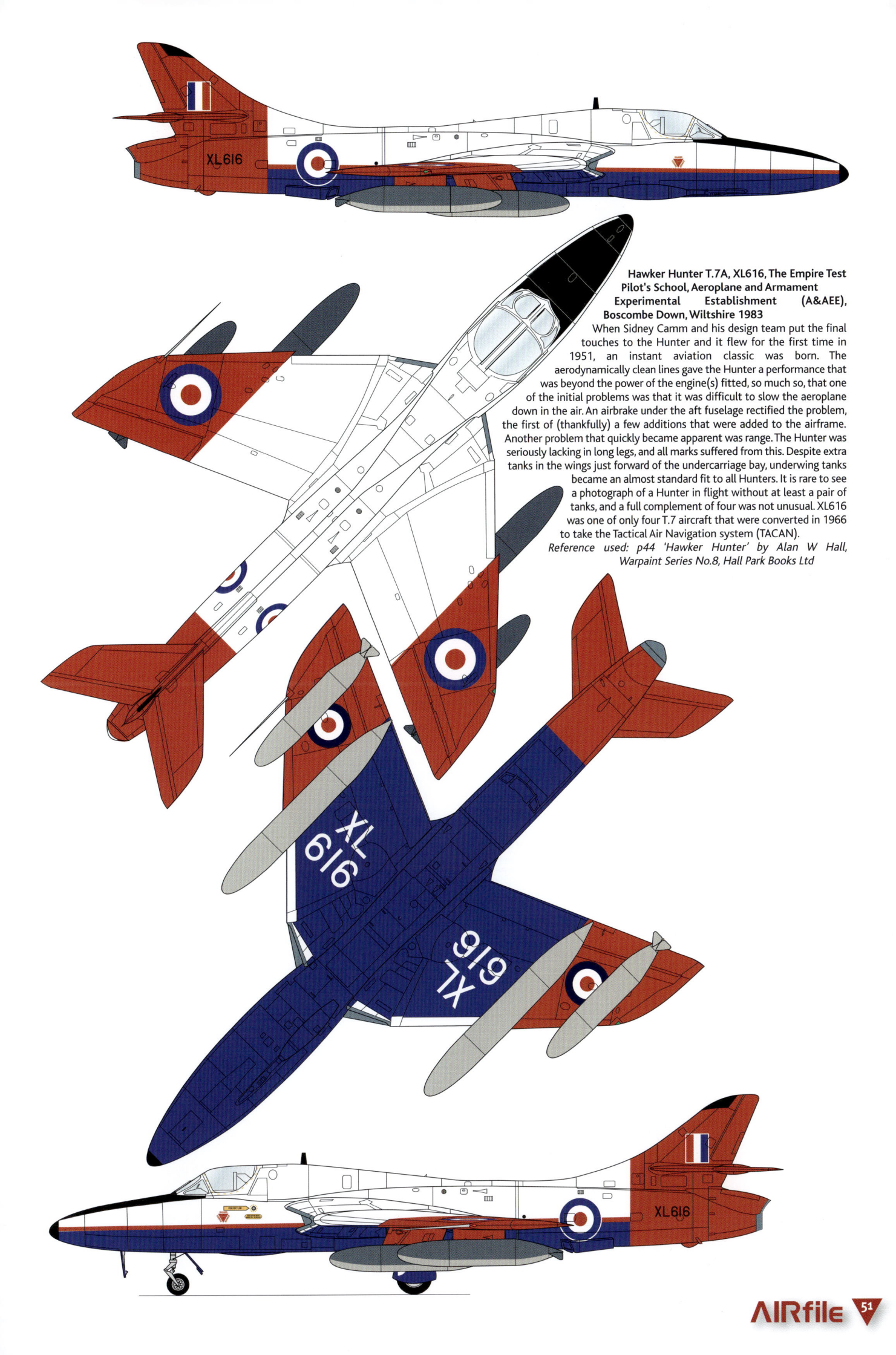

Hawker Hunter T.7A, XL616, The Empire Test Pilot's School, Aeroplane and Armament Experimental Establishment (A&AEE), Boscombe Down, Wiltshire 1983

When Sidney Camm and his design team put the final touches to the Hunter and it flew for the first time in 1951, an instant aviation classic was born. The aerodynamically clean lines gave the Hunter a performance that was beyond the power of the engine(s) fitted, so much so, that one of the initial problems was that it was difficult to slow the aeroplane down in the air. An airbrake under the aft fuselage rectified the problem, the first of (thankfully) a few additions that were added to the airframe. Another problem that quickly became apparent was range. The Hunter was seriously lacking in long legs, and all marks suffered from this. Despite extra tanks in the wings just forward of the undercarriage bay, underwing tanks became an almost standard fit to all Hunters. It is rare to see a photograph of a Hunter in flight without at least a pair of tanks, and a full complement of four was not unusual. XL616 was one of only four T.7 aircraft that were converted in 1966 to take the Tactical Air Navigation system (TACAN).

Reference used: p44 'Hawker Hunter' by Alan W Hall, Warpaint Series No.8, Hall Park Books Ltd

Scottish Aviation Bulldog T.1, XX619 'B', Yorkshire Universities Air Squadron, RAF Church Fenton, North Yorkshire 1993
The majority of the 130 Bulldog T.1 trainer aircraft that were built for the RAF went to the University Air Squadrons. These establishments offer their students the opportunity to gain flying experience, with a possibility of joining the RAF at a future date. The Bulldog was ideal for initial training, with side-by-side seating and a large canopy that gave unparalleled views, a characteristic that comes in useful for trainee navigators. The Yorkshire Universities Air Squadron was formed in March 1969 by combining Leeds and Hull UASs. The Tutor T.1 trainer was also used alongside the Bulldogs.
Reference used: http://abpic.co.uk/photo/1159117/

Westland Wessex HC.2, XR519 'WC', No 2 Flying Training School, RAF Shawbury, Shropshire 1993
Westland continued their successful run of adapting Sikorsky designs with the S-58, by replacing the original radial engines with turboshaft engines. In the case of the HC.2 for the RAF, two of these engines were fitted, and the mark entered service with the RAF in 1964 with No 18 Squadron at Odiham. Seventy four were built and the last was delivered in July 1965. XR519 was from the initial batch of thirty aircraft, and was used by No. 2 FTS to give trainee pilots advanced flying training after the preceding basic training on Gazelles. After graduating on the Wessex, the trainee pilots would move to an OCU where combat flying would be taught.
Reference used: 'On Eagles Wings - 75th. Anniversary of the Royal Air Force' by Tom Wakeford & Ian Rentoul, Concord Publications Co. 1993

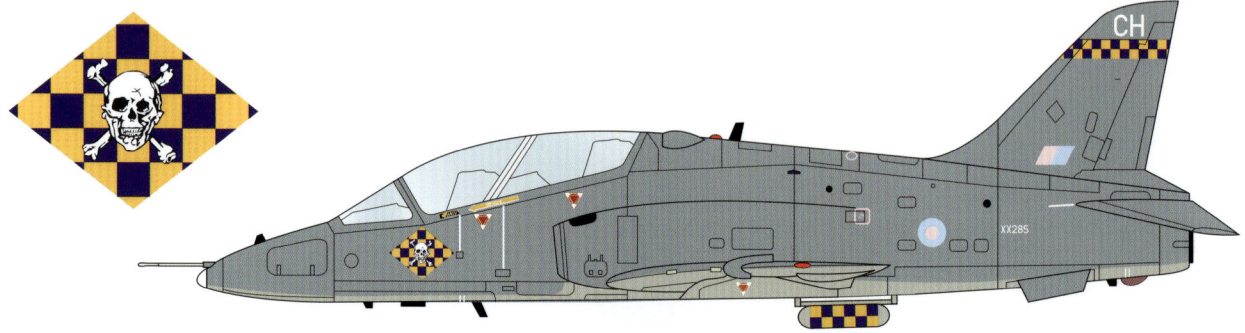

BAe Hawk T.1a, XX285 'CH', No 100 Squadron, RAF Finningley, South Yorkshire, June 1994
By the early 1990s, it was becoming obvious that the venerable Canberra, for so long the premiere target towing and electronic target aircraft, would have to be replaced. It was no longer representative of the current fast jets, and also the cost was becoming prohibitive. At the same time a surplus amount of Hawk aircraft became available, also as a result of the same cost cutting measures, and meant that the trainer could fulfill the 'tugging and spoofing' duties formerly carried out by the Canberra. XX285 carries a Luneberg lens under the fuselage, giving the aircraft a larger than normal radar return. This allows the trainee ground radar operators to quickly identify the aircraft as a 'hostile' and react accordingly for lifelike missions.
Reference used: http://www.abpic.co.uk/photo/1290578/

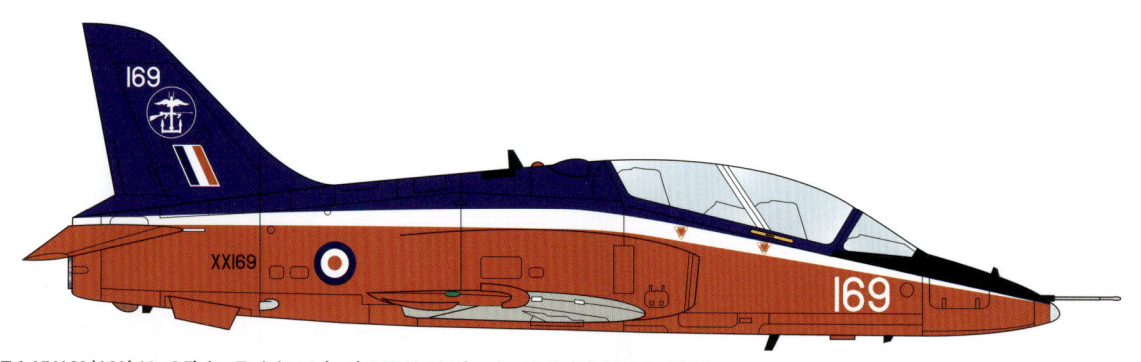

BAE Hawk T.1, XX169 '169', No 6 Flying Training School, RAF Finningley, South Yorkshire, July 1994
By the mid 1990s, RAF trainers were beginning to be re-painted in the new overall gloss black scheme. This was the result of a series of trials known as 'Longview 2' to establish a colour that could be easily seen in the air and against the ground. XX169 still retains the attractive blue/white/grey/red scheme, and is one of two (the other being XX168) to carry the badge of the Joint Forward Air Controller Training and Standards Unit, with all three services represented by the wings, rifle and anchor. Within two years Finningley had closed, another victim of the money saving measures being pursued by the Government.
Reference used: http://www.abpic.co.uk/photo/1078872/

Hawker Hunter T.7A, XL568 'ZF', No 12 Squadron, RAF Honington, Suffolk 1984

The success of the single seat versions of the Hunter led the Hawker Company to believe that if a two seat trainer version were to be built, it also would sell well. In the event, the RAF order was disappointing, a mere sixty-five ordered initially. Cutbacks meant that this was reduced to fifty-five, and of these, ten would go to the Royal Navy as T.8s, leaving a grand total of just forty-five aircraft which the RAF made use of. Paradoxically, although few in number, these T.7s had a long service life. XL568 was upgraded in 1966 with the TACAN system, probably also having Buccaneer instrumentation installed and at some point was fitted with a Royal Navy T.8 aft fuselage that incorporated the tail arrestor hook. This particular piece of equipment was never intended to be used ship-board (specifically as regards the RN T.8s), but could be used on airfields that had an arrestor wire facility. As No 12 Squadron was at this time flying Buccaneers, training with an arrester hook on a Hunter was logical. The wrap around tactical camouflage is unusual and rare for a two seat Hunter, and is rather compromised by the under wing fuel tanks. Note also the over painting of the fin cap and nose cone.

Reference used: p46 'Hunter Squadrons of the Royal Air Force and Fleet Air Arm' by Richard L Ward, Linewrights Ltd, 1985

Short Tucano T.1, ZF406., Central Flying School, RAF Cranwell, Lincolnshire, 1994
Before being accepted by the RAF, there were changes to the airframe that had been requested. Replacing the original Pratt and Whitney engine with a more powerful Garrett unit had been an initial selling point to bring the RAF around, but this increase in power required a four bladed propeller to make best use of the 1100shp from the engine. Bird strike resistant canopy and wing leading edges were fitted, a ventral air brake and a cockpit that would mirror that fitted to the Hawk; all of these changes meant that the RAF Tucano had very little commonality to the original EMB 312. ZF406 was painted overall blue for the CFS Tucano Display Team for the 1994-95 season. (Note: the blue scheme looks to be slightly lighter than Roundel Blue).
Reference used: http://www.abpic.co.uk/photo/1045663/

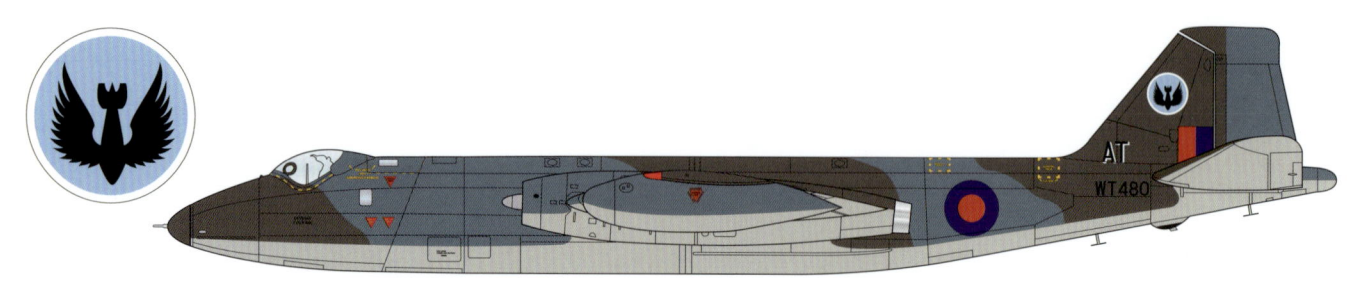

English Electric Canberra T.4, WT480 'AT', No 39 (1 PRU) Squadron, RAF Wyton, Cambridgeshire, May 1995
WT480 looks very different to when it flew with the Central Flying School some 35 years earlier. In the intervening years, the aircraft flew with almost a dozen units and squadrons in the RAF, and along the way acquired camouflage colours. No 39 Squadron became associated with the Canberra in 1958, and continued to fly them until their retirement, using the photo reconnaissance variants. WT480 would have been on strength with the squadron in the primary role for which it was designed, as a check and refresher aircraft for pilots and crew. The Canberra gave the RAF good value for money, with some of the airframes flying for three and four decades, and many of them were re-sold overseas once their time serving their country was over.
Reference used:http://www.planepictures.net/netshow.php?id=784920

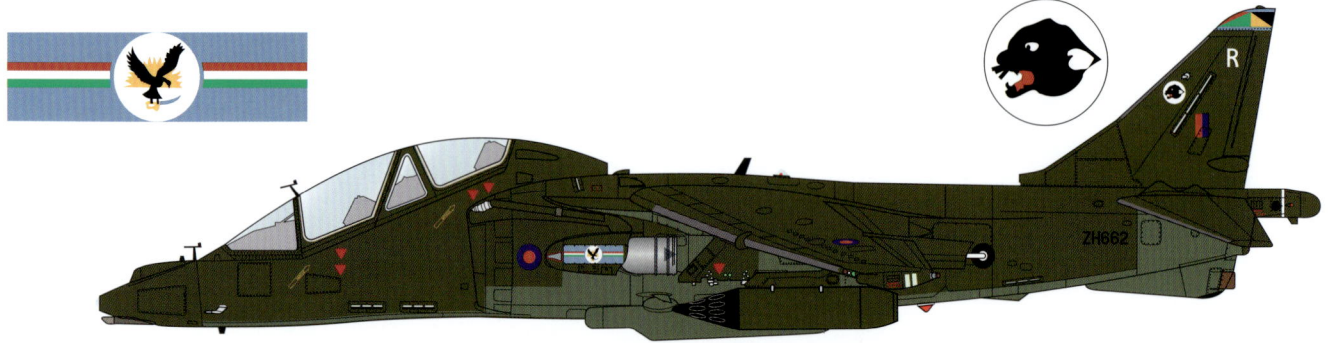

BAE Harrier T.10, ZH662 'R', No 20 (Reserve) Squadron, Harrier Operational Conversion Unit, RAF Wittering, Lincolnshire, July 1996
With the formation of Joint Force Harrier and the decision to withdraw the FAA's Sea Harriers, the personnel of the RAF's Nos 1 and 4 Squadrons and the Royal Navy's 800 and 801 Naval Air Squadrons, later known as the Naval Strike Wing, were absorbed within No 20(R) Squadron into a joint RAF/RN unit, manned 50/50 by each service. ZH662 was painted in the attractive two tone green that was carried by the GR.5 and GR.7 aircraft as they were introduced into service.
Reference used: http://www.abpic.co.uk/photo/1261889/

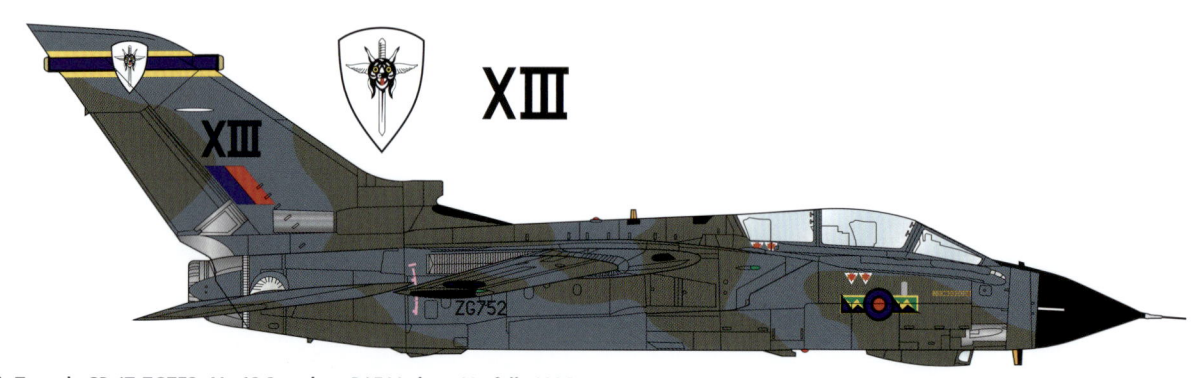

Panavia Tornado GR.4T, ZG752, No 13 Squadron, RAF Marham, Norfolk, 1996
A total of 142 aircraft were upgraded from GR.1 spec to GR.4 standard from 1997 to 2003. Amongst these were a number of twin-stick aircraft, distributed around the Tornado units to continue the in-squadron training and update role started by the GR.1Ts. The 'T' suffix was entirely unofficial, used mainly by air force personnel to identify the aircraft providing the training role. The external differences, to the layman, were slight. The GR.4 had two chin pods, the port side cheek cannon was removed and a different head box configuration was used on the ejection seats.
Reference used: www.abpic.co.uk/photo/1037422/

English Electric Canberra TT.18. WH734. Flight Refuelling Ltd, Royal Aircraft Establishment, Llanbedr, Wales, 1988

Like many aircraft used by the RAF, the Canberra was used as a Target Tug as it was gradually retired from front line duties. Initially, the Canberra was not ideally suited for use as a Target Tug, for despite the size of the bomb bay, there was no way to carry and deploy the targets. In fact, the only way the Canberra could tow a target was to use what was known as the 'snatch' method. This involved having the target laying on some sort of carrier or launch pad in the pick up area. The tow cable was laid out on the ground behind the target, to a distance of about 4,000 feet. At the end of the cable there would be a loop, and this was suspended between two 12ft poles. The Canberra had a pick up hook attached just aft of the bomb bay, and a small wing and fin arrangement half way down the hook ensured that it was angled away from the fuselage. The aircraft would come barreling across the pick up area at not much more than 12 feet above the ground, hook the loop from between the poles and perform an immediate climb. The cable and target would then be lifted almost vertically into the air behind the aircraft. The Canberra only became an effecient tow aircraft when the Rushton winch system was used, and WH734 can be seen here carrying one under each wing. This aircraft was built in 1953 as a B.2, and was converted to TT.18 standard in 1976.

Reference used: *'Testing Colours'* by Adrian M Balch, Airlife Publishing Ltd, 1993

Short Tucano T.1, ZF145 '145', No 7 Flying Training School, RAF Church Fenton, North Yorkshire 1990

After three decades in service, the venerable Jet Provost was in dire need of being replaced. Also, the JP was proving to be expensive, and a cheaper alternative was deemed necessary. Official thoughts turned to the possibility of utilising a turbo prop trainer, resulting in a tender known as Air Staff Target 412. The majority of the designs proffered were quickly eliminated, leaving just two main contenders, the Pilatus PC-9 and the Embraer 312 Tucano. Political factors meant that the winning design had to be built locally, so Pilatus joined forces with BAe and Embraer teamed up with Shorts of Belfast. A final call for a 'best price' offer saw the Tucano as the winner, and the opportunity to have the aircraft built in Northern Ireland, which would help some way to lowering unemployment there, helped to swing the deal. The contract for 130 Tucano aircraft with a new Garrett engine was signed in March 1983, and the RAF began to take delivery of the Tucano from 1987. ZF145 was the eleventh aircraft to be delivered and is shown as it was used by 7 FTS as their display aircraft for the 1990 season, with the then standard red/white/grey colour scheme, embellished with blue trim and a stylised Toucan on the fin.
Reference used: http://www.abpic.co.uk/photo/1270295/

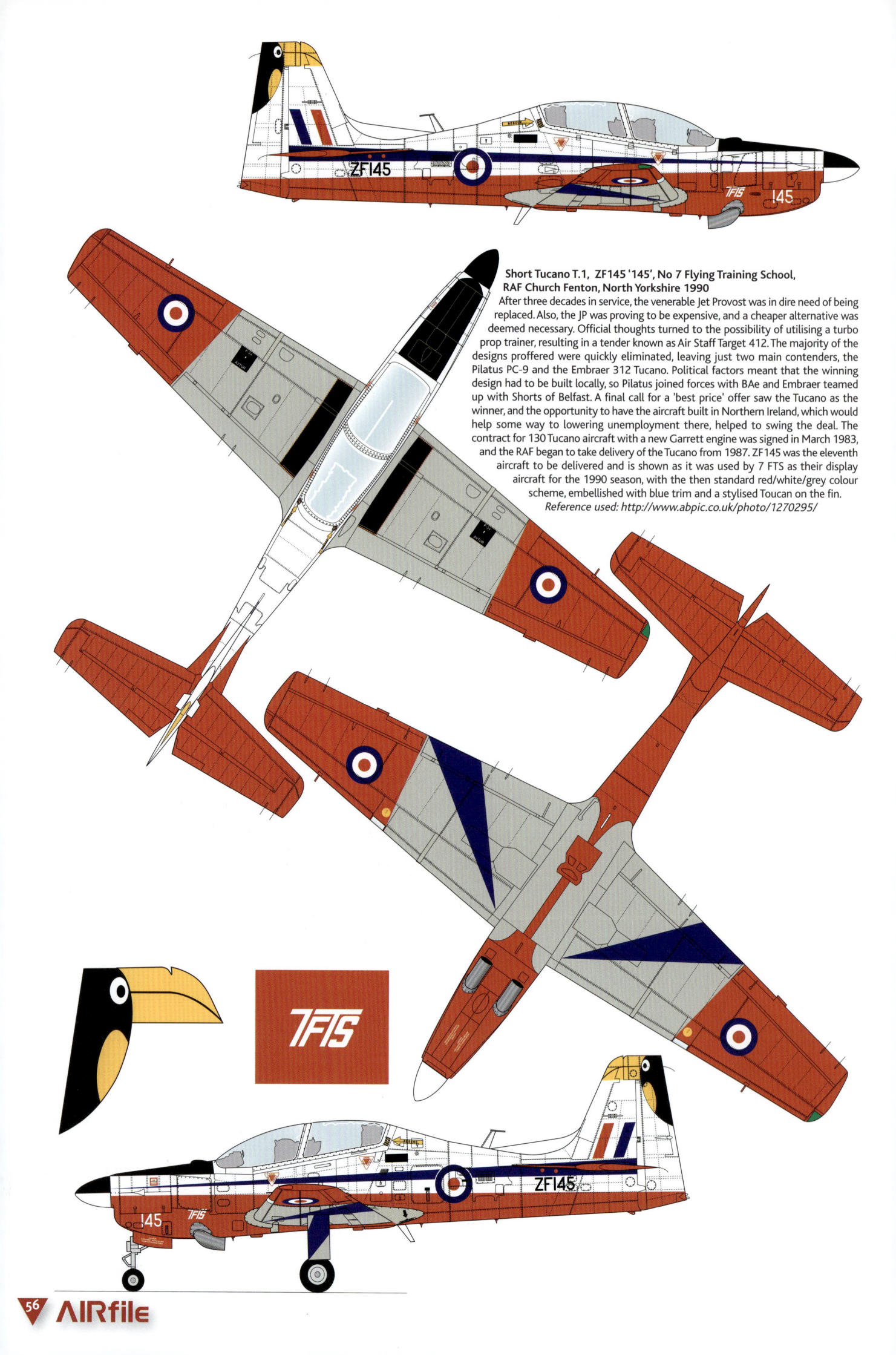

Panavia Tornado GR.1T, ZD742 'CZ', No 17 Squadron, RAF Bruggen, Germany 1990

ZD742 was given special markings in 1990 to commemorate the 75th. anniversary of No 17 Squadron. The black and white zig-zag markings on the wings are a tribute to the upper wing markings used by the squadron on their 1930s period biplanes. The squadron played a major part in the RAF forces in Germany between 1976 to 1999 operating Canberras, Phantoms, Jaguars and finally the Tornado at RAF Bruggen. The squadron was reformed in April 2005 at RAF Coningsby in Lincolnshire to operate the Typhoon T.1 and F.2.

Reference used: 'Tornado' by Ian Black, Airlife Publishing Ltd., 1990

BAE Systems Jetstream T.1, XX482 'J', No 45 (R) Squadron, RAF Finningley, South Yorkshire, 1992

The Jetstream was the swansong of the Handley Page company. Originally seen as the saviour of Handley Page Ltd, this potentially world class aircraft resulted in the demise of the company due to spiralling costs. This, and the fact that Sir Frederick Handley Page refused to become part of the conglomerates of BAC or Hawker Siddeley, meant that Handley Page went into liquidation in 1969, one of the last independent aircraft manufacturers. In 1971, a company was formed to continue production of the Jetstream, appropriately called Jetstream Aircraft Ltd, but this lasted for only a short time. The design and production rights were then acquired by Scottish Aviation Ltd, who produced twenty-six airframes for the RAF. XX482 was the first aircraft to be built at Prestwick (although the fuselage had already been constructed by Handley Page), and went straight to No 5 Flying Training School at RAF Oakington. The aircraft served with 5 FTS until they disbanded at the end of 1974, when all Jetstreams were put in to storage. XX482 was subsequently refurbished and is shown here in the markings of No 45(R) Squadron.

Reference used: www.abpic.co.uk/photo/1044839/htp

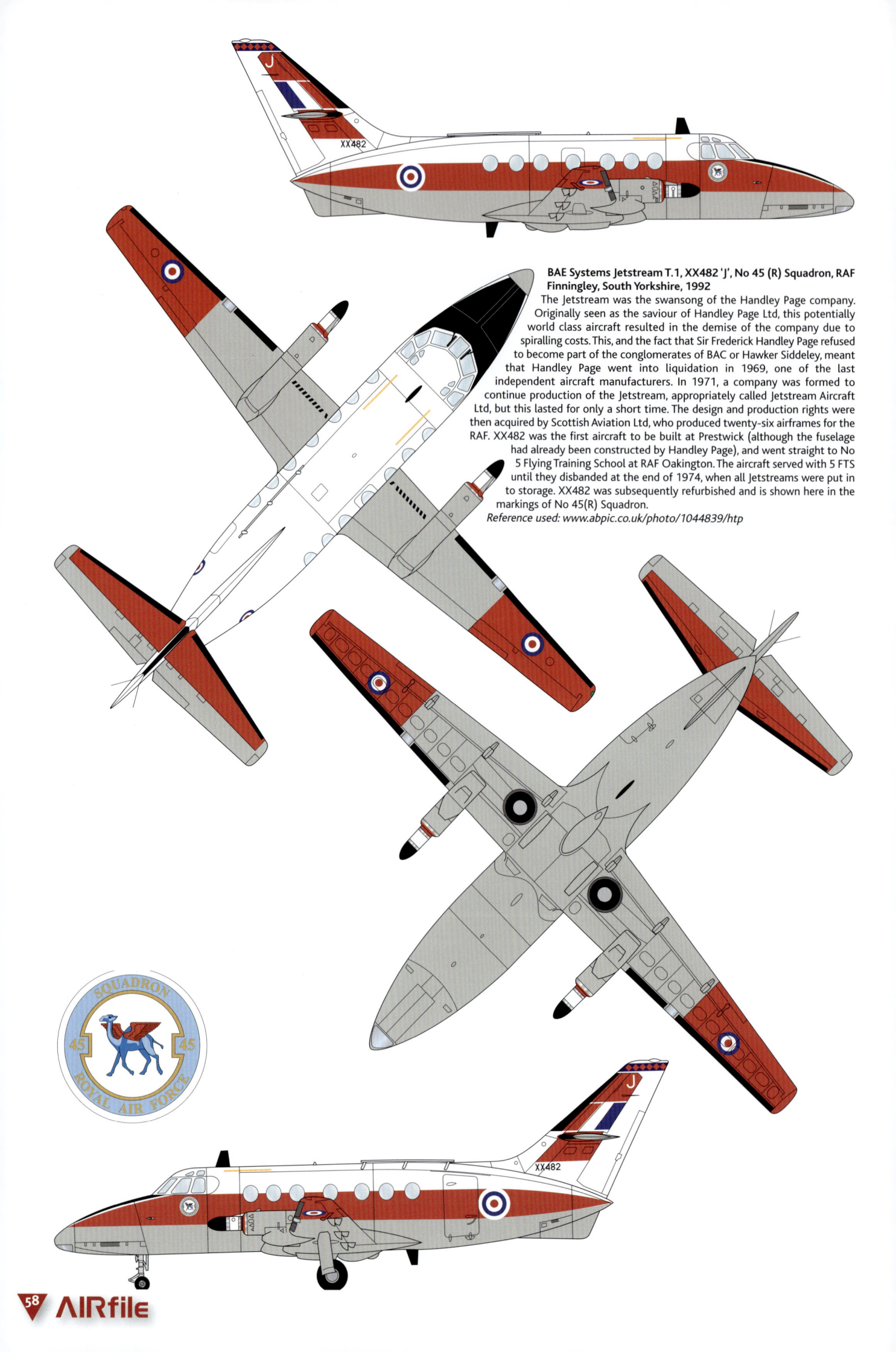

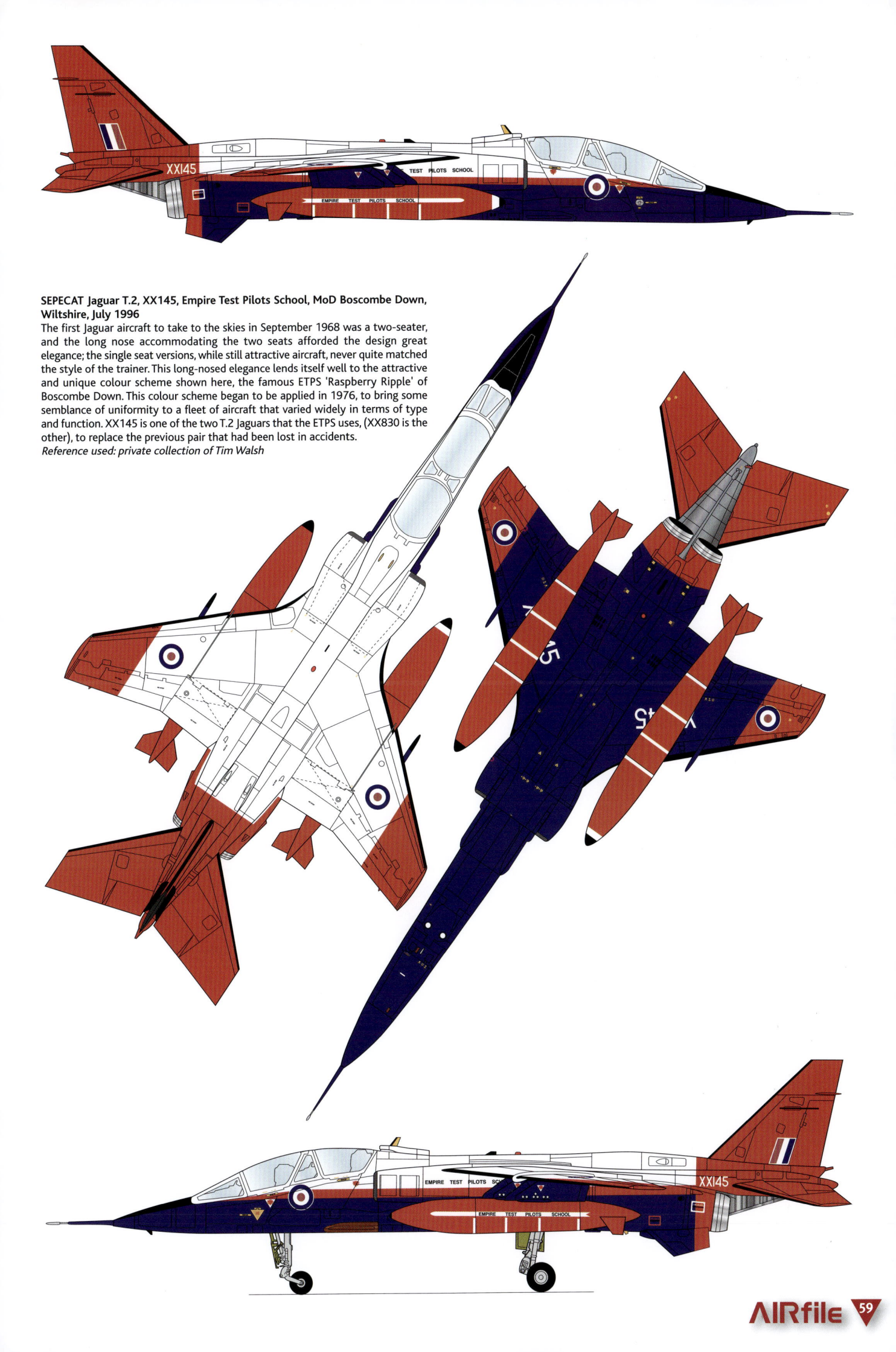

SEPECAT Jaguar T.2, XX145, Empire Test Pilots School, MoD Boscombe Down, Wiltshire, July 1996

The first Jaguar aircraft to take to the skies in September 1968 was a two-seater, and the long nose accommodating the two seats afforded the design great elegance; the single seat versions, while still attractive aircraft, never quite matched the style of the trainer. This long-nosed elegance lends itself well to the attractive and unique colour scheme shown here, the famous ETPS 'Raspberry Ripple' of Boscombe Down. This colour scheme began to be applied in 1976, to bring some semblance of uniformity to a fleet of aircraft that varied widely in terms of type and function. XX145 is one of the two T.2 Jaguars that the ETPS uses, (XX830 is the other), to replace the previous pair that had been lost in accidents.

Reference used: private collection of Tim Walsh

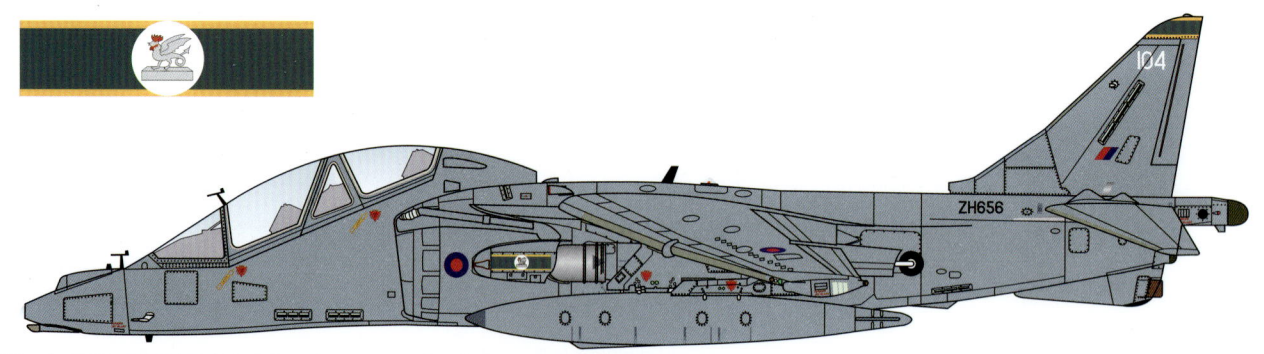

BAE Harrier T.10, ZH656 '104', No 3 Squadron, RAF Laarbruch, Germany, July 1998
A dedicated two-seat trainer was quickly found to be necessary to match the capabilities of the new GR.5/7 Harriers. Upgrading (again) the now well worn and obsolescent T.4 aircraft was never really an option, so from the beginning of January 1995, the RAF began to take delivery of thirteen T.10 aircraft. This was basically a TAV-8B, but fitted with full GR.7 cockpits and weapons capabilities. No 3 Squadron would soon give up their Harriers for the first single seat fighter to serve with the RAF since the Lightning, being the first Squadron to operationally fly the Eurofighter Typhoon.
Reference used: http://www.abpic.co.uk/photo/1240353/

BAE Systems Jetstream T.2, XX475, DERA West Freugh, Wigtownshire, Scotland. 2000
RAF West Freugh is one of a series of bases in the UK used by the Defence Evaluation Research Agency (DERA). Its earlier role was as an armaments training school in the handling and deployment of bombs and missiles. This now runs alongside its modern role as a Satellite Communications Ground Station. In July 2001 DERA officially became known as QuinetiQ (pronounced kinetic), a privately run organisation working for the MOD. Jetstream T.2 XX475 was used in a monitoring, testing and communications role during its service at RAF West Freugh.
Reference used: private collection of Tim Walsh

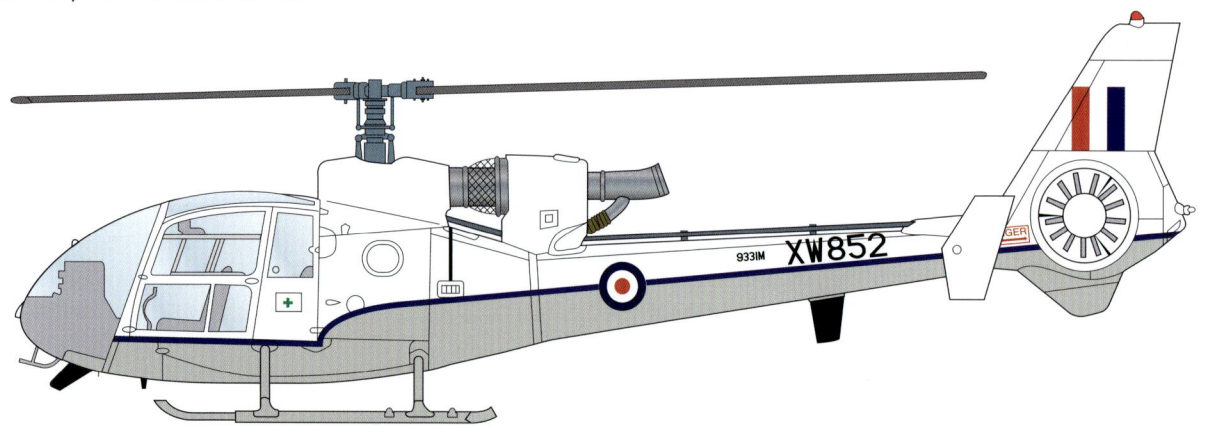

Aerospatiale SA.341 Gazelle HCC.4, XW852/(9331M), No 1 School of Technical Training, RAF Cosford, Shropshire, September 2004
The majority of the Gazelle aircraft flying with the RAF were the HT.3 variant, but a few were configured for communication work. The service life of XW852 was with No (TR) Squadron, based at RAF Northolt, with the express use of carrying VIP passengers on short flights. During this period, No 32 Squadron were known as 'The Royal' Squadron, and still is, but ceased any Royal transport role in 1999. After retirement, XW852 was given a maintenance serial and was used as a training airframe.
Reference used: http://www.abpic.co.uk/photo/1258776/

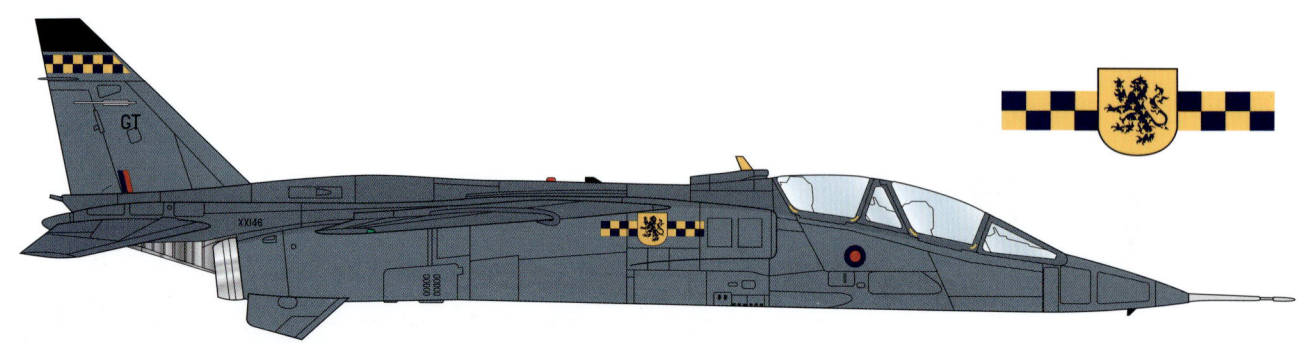

SEPECAT Jaguar T.2A, XX146 'GT', No 54 Squadron, RAF Coltishall, Norfolk 2004
While the majority of Jaguar training was undertaken by 226 OCU, frontline Jaguar Squadrons had at least one T.2 on the books for in squadron refresher and conversion training. No 54 Squadron began flying Jaguars in 1974, and continued to fly them right up to 2005, when the squadron was re-assigned to a new role, but without any aircraft, namely to train aircrew for the ISTAR and Rivet Joint reconnaissance platforms. It also trains 'crews' for the MQ-9 Predator drones flying from Waddington. A sad conclusion for a squadron that cut its teeth in combat in 1916 over the countryside of France and Belgium, an association that is apparent in the Squadron badge, with the lion of Belgium covered with French Fleur de Lys
Reference used: www.abpic.co.uk/photo/1139717/

BAe Hawk T.1, XX226, No 74 (Reserve) Squadron, No 4 Flying Training School, RAF Valley, Wales, September 1997

No 74 Squadron was the last RAF Squadron to fly the Phantom in 1992. The unit then became a Reserve Squadron flying with No 4 FTS, thereby allowing No 74 Squadron to continue to exist. Two other Reserve Squadrons also flew as part of No 4 FTS, namely Nos 208 and 234, and they too began to apply relevant squadron markings, and as a result the badge of 4 FTS, the pyramid and the palm tree, disappeared. By 1997, the majority of the Hawks, although not all, had adopted the overall gloss black trainer scheme.
Reference used: http://www.abpic.co.uk/photo/1235886/

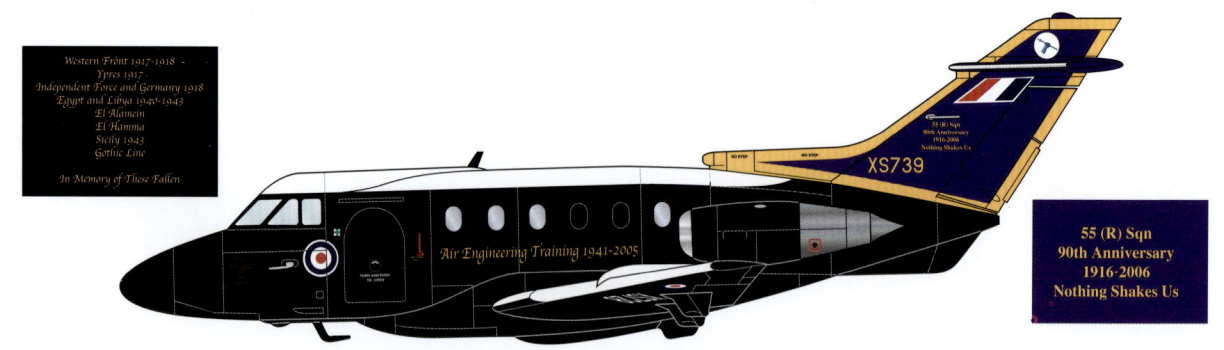

Hawker Siddeley Dominie T.1, XS739, No 55 (Reserve) Squadron, RAF College, Cranwell, Lincolnshire, July 2006
The primary role of the Dominie was to train navigators, air electronics operators and flight engineers, a role it filled admirably for over 45 years. In 1995, the Dominies of 6 FTS moved to 3 FTS, and in 1996, 6 FTS was disbanded. It was at Cranwell that all the aircraft of this type became known as the 'Dominie Squadron', and in November of 1996 it was re-named as No 55 Squadron. As can be seen, No 55 Squadron celebrated their 90th Anniversary with a brightly coloured tail fin and their roll of battle honours on the nose. The nickname of the squadron is 'The Spearpoints', from when they were the lead for 'Q' Force. No 55 Squadron reinforced the Army of the Black Sea and helped in the defence of the Dardanelles and Constantinople against the Turkish Nationals in 1920.
Reference used: www.abpic.co.uk/photo/1010327/

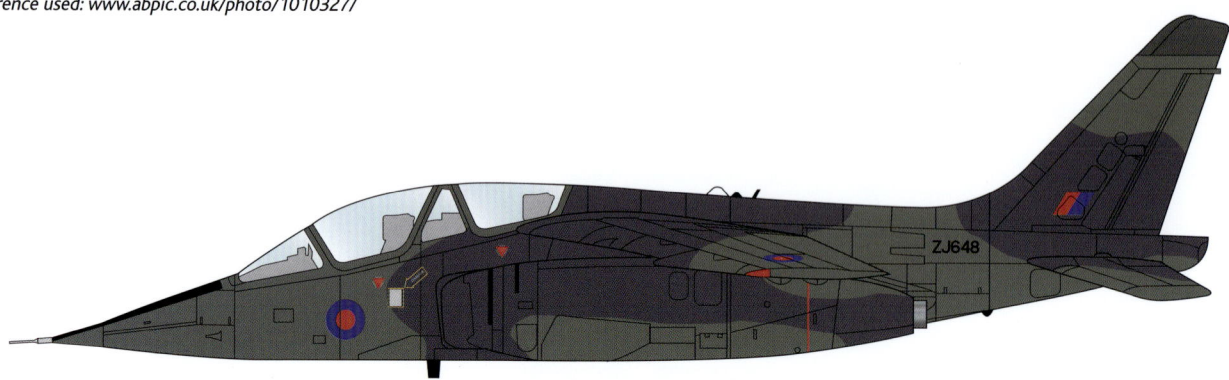

Dassault-Dornier Alpha Jet A, ZJ648, Empire Test Pilots School, QinetiQ, MoD Boscombe Down, Wiltshire, July 2006
At the end of the 1960s, both the German and French Air Forces were looking for a replacement for the Lockheed T-33 jet trainer. In 1969, an informal agreement was reached between the two countries to jointly design a new trainer. This agreement was officially approved in 1972, and in rapid time Dassault were able to deliver the first prototype in 1973, and the second prototype was delivered to the Germans by Dornier in January 1974. Over a quarter of a century later, Alpha Jets began flying with the RAF, (although under the auspices of the civilian company QinetiQ), and ZJ648 is one of a dozen used at Boscombe Down, still retaining the original German camouflage.
Reference used: http://www.abpic.co.uk/photo/1061064/ & p107 'Air Power Analysis', International Air Power Review, Volume 25, AIRtime Publishing 2008

Pilatus PC-9, ZG969 'Percy', BAE Systems, Warton, Lancashire 2007
The Pilatus PC-9 was one of four designs that had been considered by the RAF to replace the Jet Provost. Unfortunately for Pilatus, the Tucano was chosen in 1985 to become the new trainer for the RAF, even though British Aerospace were in partnership with the Swiss company. Despite failing to secure an indigenous order, this association paid off when Saudi Arabia signed a contract that included thirty PC-9 aircraft that came through Warton for modifications. ZG969 was the first of two PC-9s that the company used as a chase plane. Originally in the Royal Saudi Air Force colour scheme, 'Percy' was later painted in the smart red/blue scheme illustrated here.
Reference used: http://www.abpic.co.uk/photo/1040587/ & 'Pilatus-7/9/21: The Pilatus turbo trainers', International Air Power Review, Volume 21, AIRtime Publishing 2007

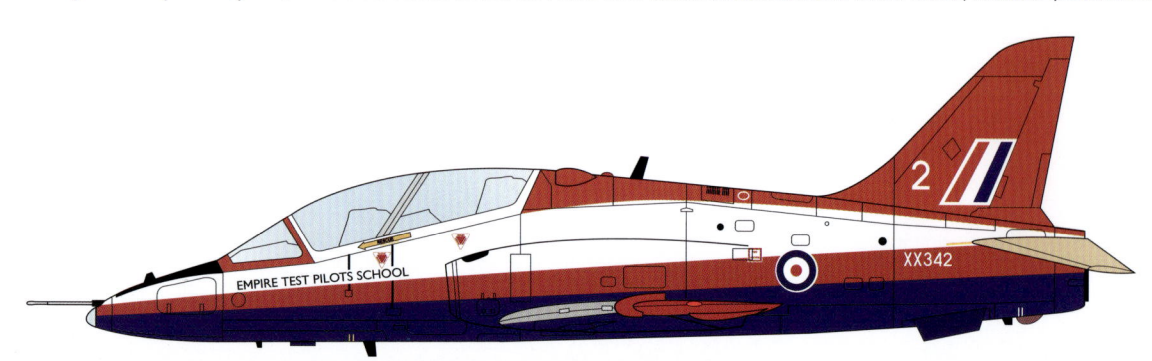

BAe Hawk T.1, XX342 '2', Empire Test Pilots School, QinetiQ, MoD Boscombe Down, Wiltshire, April 2009
During 1981, three Hawk T.1s were delivered new from the manufacturer to the Empire Test Pilots School. The first, XX341, became the ASTRA aircraft. The acronym stands for Advanced Systems TRaining Aircraft, with the front cockpit fitted out with computer software that allows the aircraft to take on various characteristics of different aircraft. The rear cockpit retains a standard Hawk configuration. The other two Hawks, XX342 and XX343, also received special instrumentation for recording flight performances, and also took over inverted spinning training from the retired Hunters, as well as handling and assessment missions. The reference photo for XX342 shows it to have a replacement white framed canopy and a yellow primer tailplane.
Reference used: http://www.abpic.co.uk/photo/1170765/

British Aerospace Harrier T.4, XW175, 'VAAC', Vector-thrust Aircraft Advanced Control (VAAC), QinetiQ, MoD Boscombe Down, Wiltshire, July 2008

Harrier T.4 XW175 took to the skies for the first time in July 1969, making it the oldest flying Harrier. One of two development two-seat aircraft (the other, XW174, had crashed just the month previously), it was used extensively for test purposes. Altering the basic Harrier design to accommodate a second seat caused directional problems, and XW175 was used to test the subsequent larger tail fin and larger strake under the tail. As of 2008/9, XW175 was being used as a test bed to investigate the shipborne rolling vertical landing concept that will be used by the new F-35 Lightning II aircraft that is planned for future service.
Reference used: http://www.abpic.co.uk/photo/1119503/

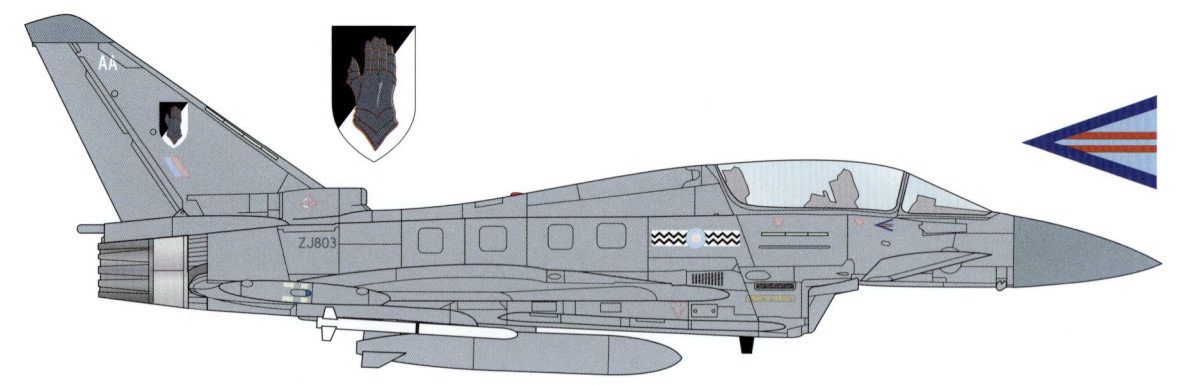

Eurofighter Typhoon T.1, ZJ803 'AA', No 17(R) Squadron, RAF Coningsby, Lincolnshire, 2005
On 30 June 2003, the RAF took delivery of the first Typhoon aircraft, ZJ803, and it eventually went to No 17 (R) Squadron. This historic squadron was re-formed on 1 September 2002 to be the Operational Evaluation Unit for the new fighter, and although for the first year of their existence they were without aircraft, they worked closely with the BAE systems engineers so that when the squadron began to take deliveries of aircraft in December 2003, there were no major setbacks to the introduction of the Typhoon. The squadron is tasked with the eventual service use of various weapon payloads and establishing the tactics for their use.
Reference used: http://www.abpic.co.uk/photo/1177370/

Short Tucano T.1, ZF448 'BASUTO', No 72(R) Squadron, No 1 Flying Training School, RAF Linton-on-Ouse, North Yorkshire, August 2008
As the RAF moved into the new millennium, resources and Squadrons were gradually whittled down, and many units realised that there was every possibilty that they would not reach their centenary year. As a result, many squadrons with a claim to the beginning of British military aviation, chose to celebrate early. The colours worn by No 72 Squadron were blue bars edged in red, seen on the Gladiators flown just before World War Two, and post-war on their Meteors and Javelins. On ZF448 the usual bars either side of the fuselage roundel have given way to a blue and red chevron along the entire length of the fuselage, reminiscent of the arrow head marking carried by the Javelins.
Reference used: the private collection of Paul Lister

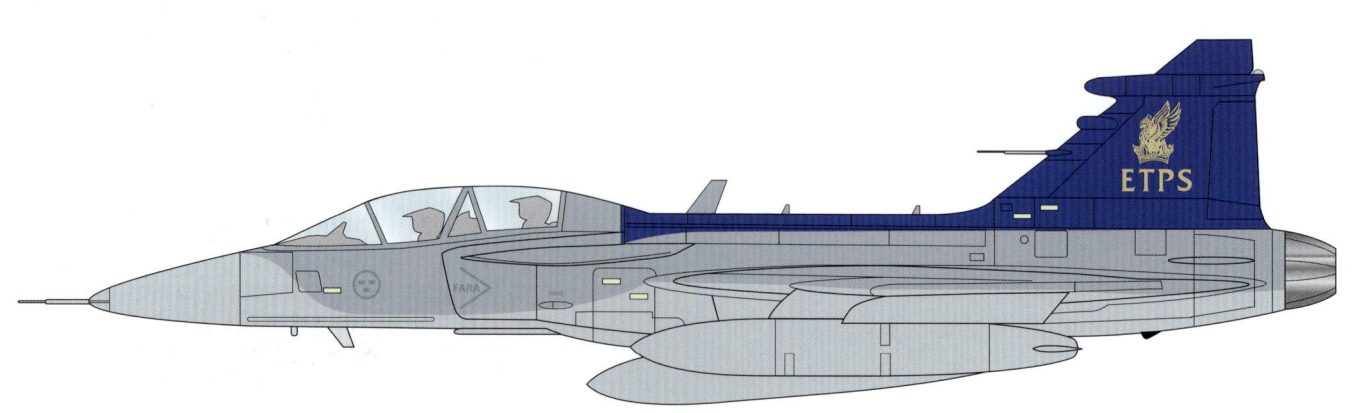

Saab JAS 39B Gripen 39802, on loan to the Empire Test Pilots School, QinetiQ, MoD Boscombe Down, Wiltshire, 2008
The two-seat version of the Gripen first flew in April 1996. Unlike many modern two-seat trainers, the Gripen has a fully combat capable rear cockpit, allowing either pilot to fly combat missions. The only piece of equipment lacking in the rear is the Head Up Display, but information transmitted from the HUD is shown on the other displays. In 1999, the ETPS began using the Gripen for fast jet experience training, as this dual seat capability gave pilots a training regime unavailable on other aircraft. The ETPS became a formal user of the Gripen in 2005, when a contract was signed to lease out a set number of hours on the aircraft, allowing students to gain flying time on a fourth generation jet.
Reference used: http://www.abpic.co.uk/photo/1118585/

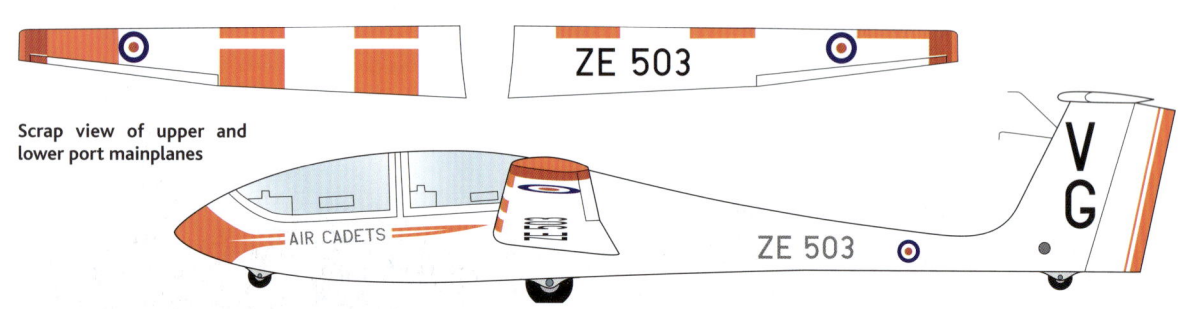

Scrap view of upper and lower port mainplanes

Grob G-103 Viking T.1, ZE503 'VG', No 625 Volunteer Gliding Squadron, Hullavington Airfield, Wiltshire, April 2009
The Grob Viking T.1 is the RAF version of the G103A Twin II Acro built by the German company, Grob Aircraft. The T.1 is the RAF's current sailplane trainer for the Air Cadet Corps. It has tandem seating for a crew of two and is constructed using the latest techniques in industrial glass-reinforced plastic for light weight and strength. It is used for basic training, high-performance flying and simple aerobatic flying by eleven of the Volunteer Gliding Squadrons within the UK. No 625 Volunteer Gliding Squadron was founded at RAF South Cerney in August 1958 operating five winch launched gliders - two Slingsby Sedberghs and three Kirby Cadet 3s. The current fleet at 625 VGS is seven Grob Viking T.1s
Reference used: http://www.abpic.co.uk/photo/1296801/

Eurocopter AS.350BB Squirrel HT.1 ZJ265 '65', Defence Helicopter Flying School, RAF Shawbury, Shropshire, February 2009

The Ecureuil (Squirrel), was chosen in the mid 1970s to be the replacement for the Alouette series of helicopters and was one of the first designs to make extensive use of plastics as part of the airframe. In 1997, the DHFS began flying the Squirrel from Shawbury. This School is run by FB Heliservices Ltd under a fifteen year contract, and replaced all the helicopter training units then in existence within the RAF, Army Air Corps and the Royal Navy. A lesser known duty of the Squirrel helicopters is the ferrying of Red Arrow pilots to and from the various venues at which they are displaying.
Reference used: www.abpic/photo/1160119/

10th ANNIVERSARY
1997 - 2007

Beechcraft B200 Super King Air, G-RAFP, (ZK456) Serco Limited (No 45(R) Squadron, No 3 Flying Training School), RAF Cranwell, Lincolnshire, June 2009
In 2003, Serco Limited were awarded a large contract to provide a range of flight training and support services to RAF Cranwell. It was, in effect, an innovative aircraft leasing solution whereby Serco introduced the Beech King Air B200 to RAF service. Initially, all King Airs run by Serco Ltd were civil registered with G-RAF plus a single letter identifier. From 2005 onwards, they have gradually been given RAF serial numbers. G-RAFP had its civil registration cancelled in November 2010 and transferred to the RAF as ZK456.
Reference used: http://www.abpic.co.uk/photo/1177800/

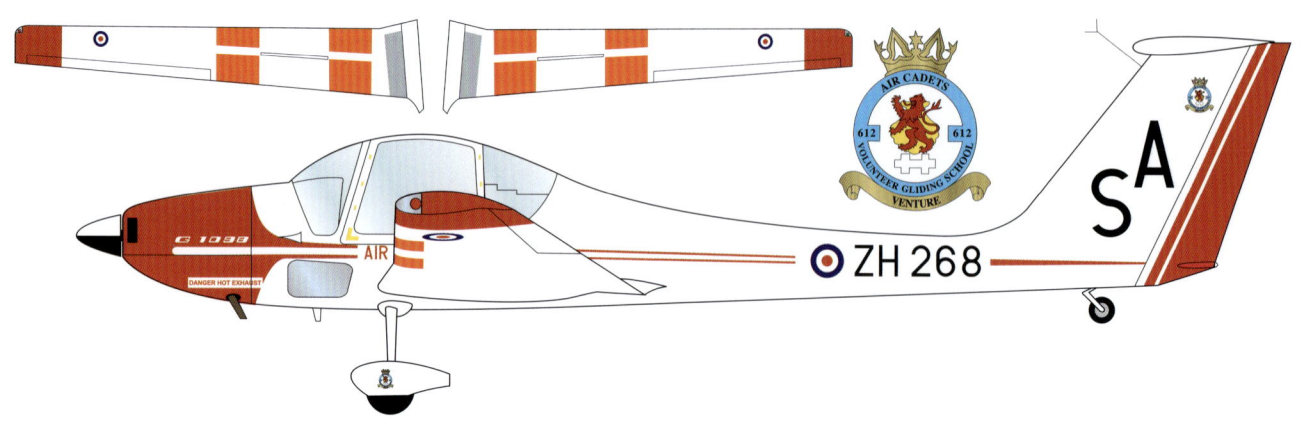

Grob Vigilant T.1, ZH268 'SA', No 612 Volunteer Gliding Squadron, Abingdon, Oxfordshire 2010
The Grob 109B motor glider, known by the RAF as the Vigilant T.1, is used by the Air Cadet Organisation to give basic flying and gliding training to air cadets. The aircraft is built in Germany, but it has been modified to meet the RAF's training requirements by the inclusion of an additional throttle in the cockpit and an increase in the maximum take-off weight. The Vigilant is currently used by sixteen Volunteer Gliding Squadrons (VGSs), located at various sites around the UK. Their role is to train air cadets in basic flying techniques and to enable them to reach a standard where they are able to fly solo.
Reference used: http://www.107aircadets.org/news_archiveY.php

SEPECAT Jaguar T.2A, XX141 'T', No 284 Squadron, Aircraft Maintenance Instruction Flight, RAF College, Cranwell, Lincolnshire, May 2010
At least six retired Jaguars, both twin stick and single, are used by the Aircraft Maintenance Instruction Flight at Cranwell for the training of ground personnel in the movement, handling and marshalling of aircraft. They are maintained in a taxiable condition and kept in a pristine gloss black training livery. These aircraft have been given the nickname of 'Lincolnshire Land Shark' as they prowl around the taxiways and perimeter tracks. The ejection seats have been disabled, and the armament stores and flares that they carry are inert, but to all intents and purposes, they are 'hot' aircraft.
Reference used: www.airliners.net/photo/UK---Air/Sepecat-Jaguar-T2A/1424979/L/

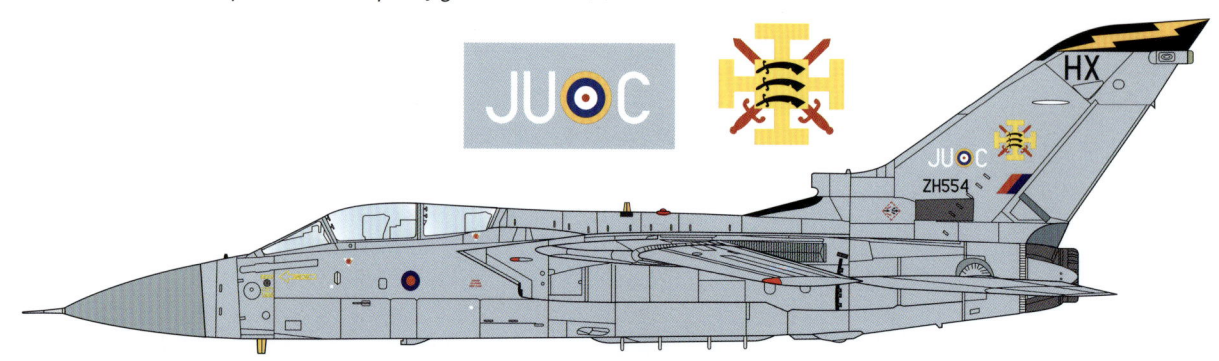

Panavia Tornado F.3T, ZH554 'HX' 'JU•C', No 111 Squadron, RAF Leuchars, Scotland, 2011
Tornado ZH554 carried additional commemorative codes 'JU•C', celebrating the 70th Anniversary of the Battle of Britain in 2011. No 111 Squadron was the last Tornado F.3 unit to stand down in March 2011, with the type having completed a service life spanning 25 years. No 111 Squadron had been based at RAF Leuchars since 1990 and had been the sole UK unit flying F.3s since July 2009. Their role at Leuchars has been taken over by No 6 Squadron flying Eurofighter Typhoons. In all, the RAF took delivery of 152 air defence variant Tornados, which at the height of their use equipped seven frontline squadrons, plus operational conversion and evaluation units. Notably, however, the F.3 was never used to fire a shot in anger.
Reference used: www.jetphotos.net/viewphoto.php?id=6914037&nseq=2

Panavia Tornado F.3T ZE735 'TG', 'The Firebirds', No 56(R) Squadron, RAF Leuchars, Fife, Scotland, April 2008

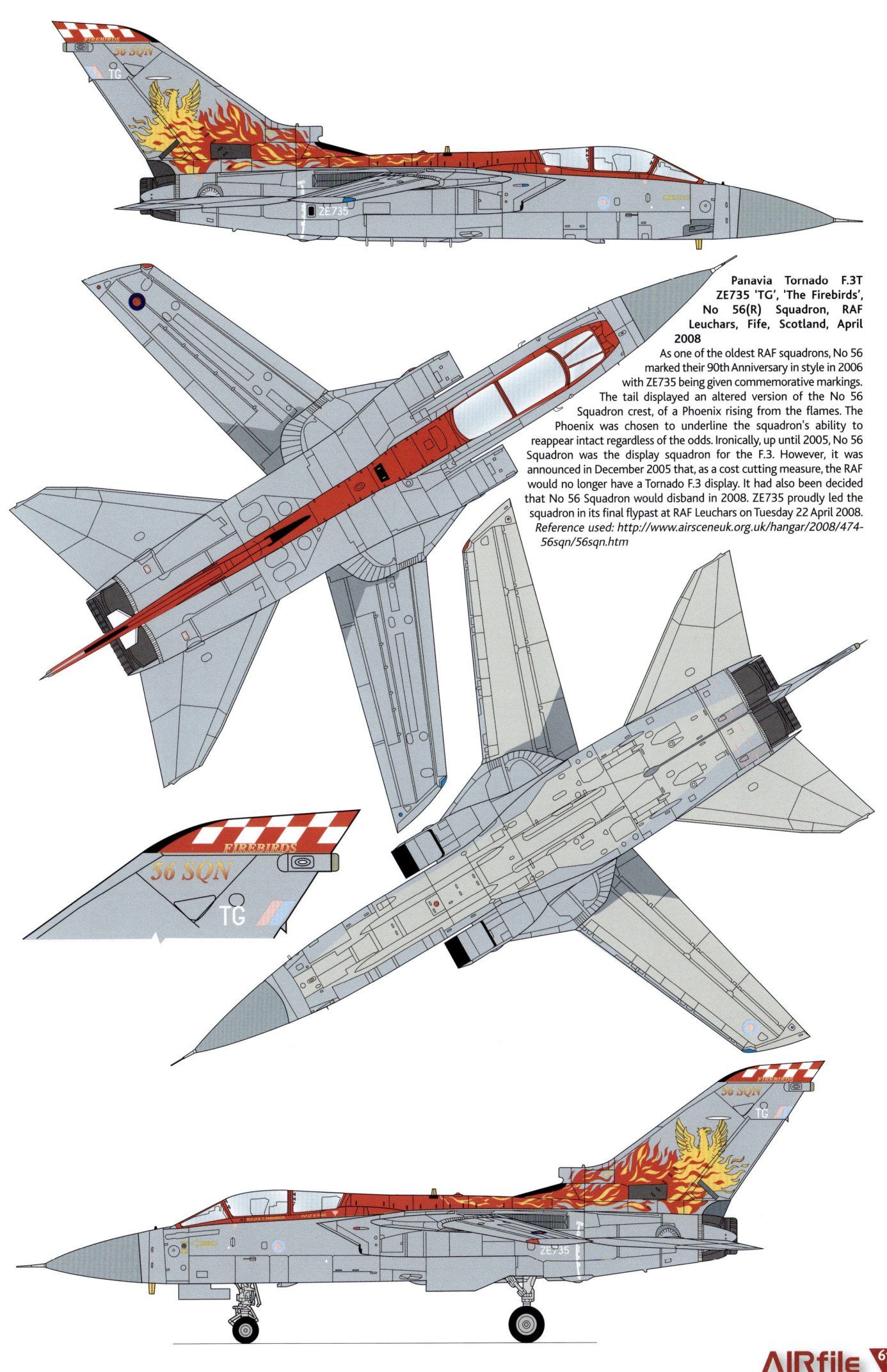

As one of the oldest RAF squadrons, No 56 marked their 90th Anniversary in style in 2006 with ZE735 being given commemorative markings. The tail displayed an altered version of the No 56 Squadron crest, of a Phoenix rising from the flames. The Phoenix was chosen to underline the squadron's ability to reappear intact regardless of the odds. Ironically, up until 2005, No 56 Squadron was the display squadron for the F.3. However, it was announced in December 2005 that, as a cost cutting measure, the RAF would no longer have a Tornado F.3 display. It had also been decided that No 56 Squadron would disband in 2008. ZE735 proudly led the squadron in its final flypast at RAF Leuchars on Tuesday 22 April 2008.
Reference used: http://www.airsceneuk.org.uk/hangar/2008/474-56sqn/56sqn.htm

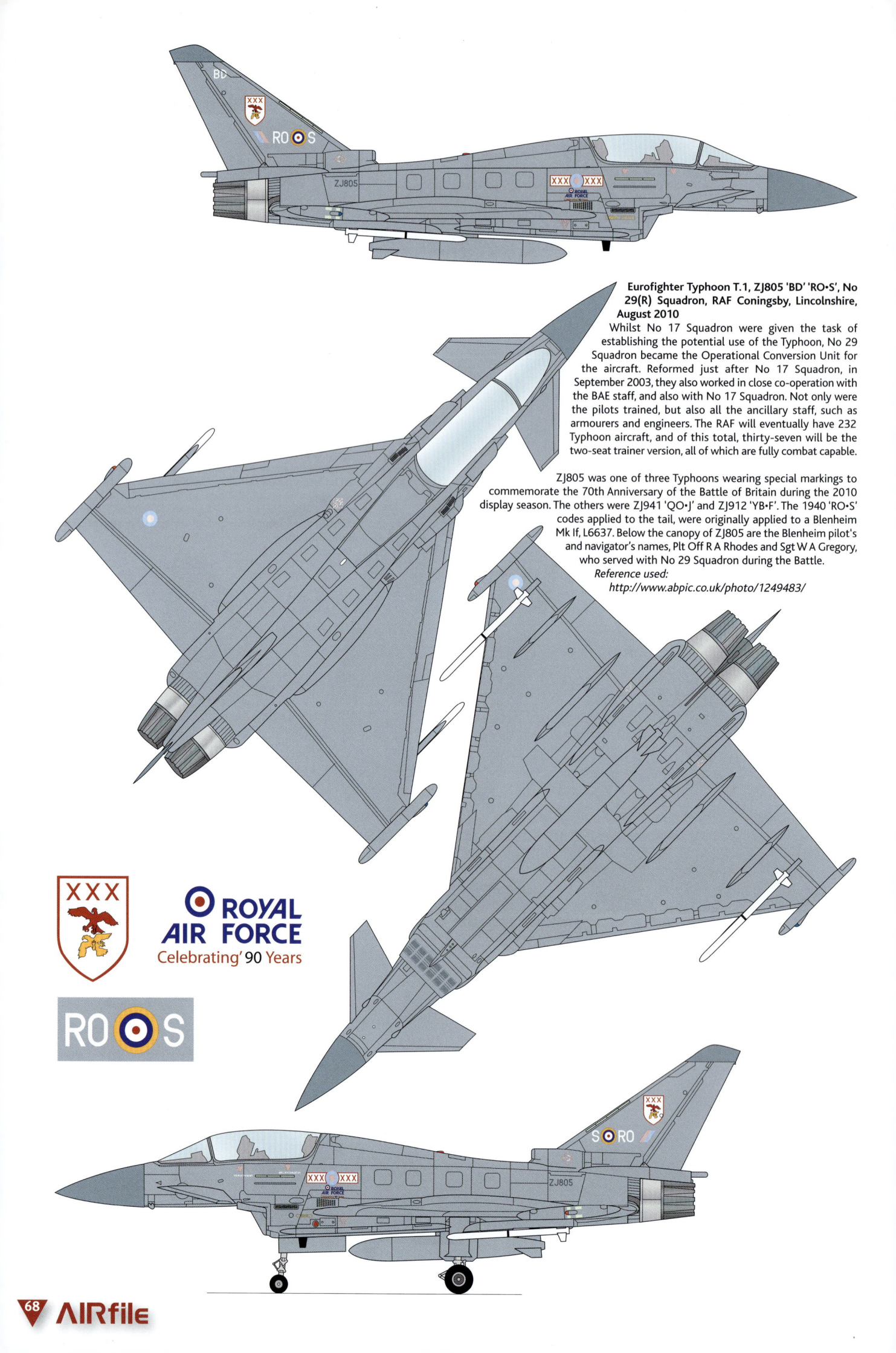

Eurofighter Typhoon T.1, ZJ805 'BD' 'RO•S', No 29(R) Squadron, RAF Coningsby, Lincolnshire, August 2010

Whilst No 17 Squadron were given the task of establishing the potential use of the Typhoon, No 29 Squadron became the Operational Conversion Unit for the aircraft. Reformed just after No 17 Squadron, in September 2003, they also worked in close co-operation with the BAE staff, and also with No 17 Squadron. Not only were the pilots trained, but also all the ancillary staff, such as armourers and engineers. The RAF will eventually have 232 Typhoon aircraft, and of this total, thirty-seven will be the two-seat trainer version, all of which are fully combat capable.

ZJ805 was one of three Typhoons wearing special markings to commemorate the 70th Anniversary of the Battle of Britain during the 2010 display season. The others were ZJ941 'QO•J' and ZJ912 'YB•F'. The 1940 'RO•S' codes applied to the tail, were originally applied to a Blenheim Mk If, L6637. Below the canopy of ZJ805 are the Blenheim pilot's and navigator's names, Plt Off R A Rhodes and Sgt W A Gregory, who served with No 29 Squadron during the Battle.
Reference used:
http://www.abpic.co.uk/photo/1249483/

Royal Air Force Celebrating 90 Years

BAE Systems Harrier T.12A, ZH665 '113', No. 4 (AC) Squadron, Joint Force Harrier, RAF Cottesmore, Rutland, December 2010

The continued whittling away of the Royal Air Force and the Royal Navy and many of the aircraft they used, led to the creation of the Joint Force Harrier. This allowed the RAF and the Royal Navy to pool their resources and saved the Government money (by retiring the entire fleet of Sea Harrier FA.2 aircraft). Half of the JFH were the RAF Squadrons of No 1(F) and No IV(AC), whilst the Royal Navy complement comprised No 800 NAS and No 801 NAS. These two Navy units later became known as the Naval Strike Wing. Also part of the JFH was No 233 OCU (No 20 (R) 'shadow' Squadron). The up-grading of the Harrier T.10 to T.12 standard that began in January 2008 was futile, as all Harriers were retired at the end of 2010 in another cost cutting exercise, a full eight years before they were due to leave service. ZH665 is shown as she participated in the British Harrier retirement flypast at RAF Cottesmore flown by Sqn Ldr Andy Chisholm and Flt Lt Darren Kups.
Reference used: http://www.airforcesreview.com/reports/The-Final-Day-of-the-Harrier/

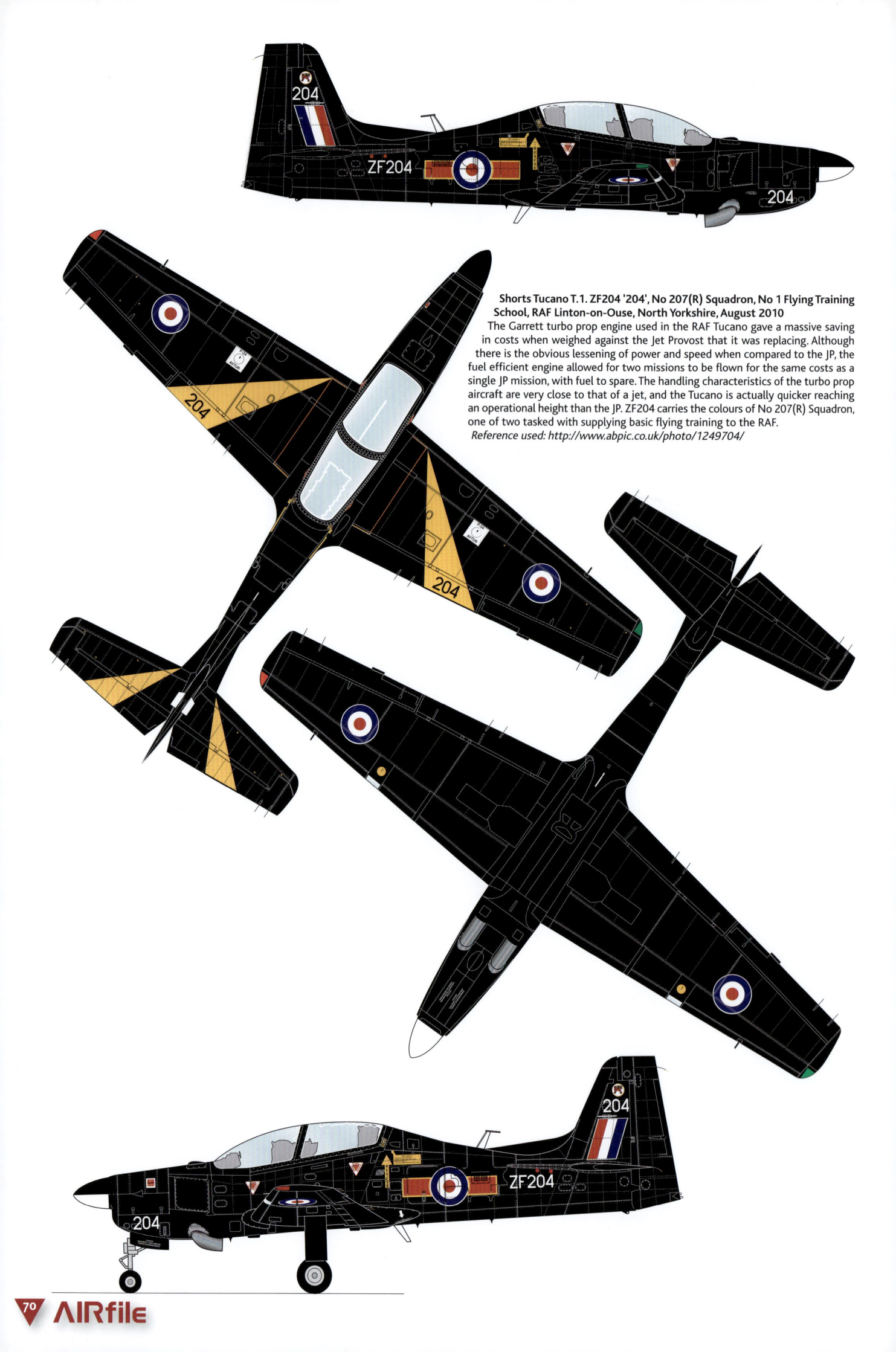

Shorts Tucano T.1. ZF204 '204', No 207(R) Squadron, No 1 Flying Training School, RAF Linton-on-Ouse, North Yorkshire, August 2010

The Garrett turbo prop engine used in the RAF Tucano gave a massive saving in costs when weighed against the Jet Provost that it was replacing. Although there is the obvious lessening of power and speed when compared to the JP, the fuel efficient engine allowed for two missions to be flown for the same costs as a single JP mission, with fuel to spare. The handling characteristics of the turbo prop aircraft are very close to that of a jet, and the Tucano is actually quicker reaching an operational height than the JP. ZF204 carries the colours of No 207(R) Squadron, one of two tasked with supplying basic flying training to the RAF.
Reference used: http://www.abpic.co.uk/photo/1249704/

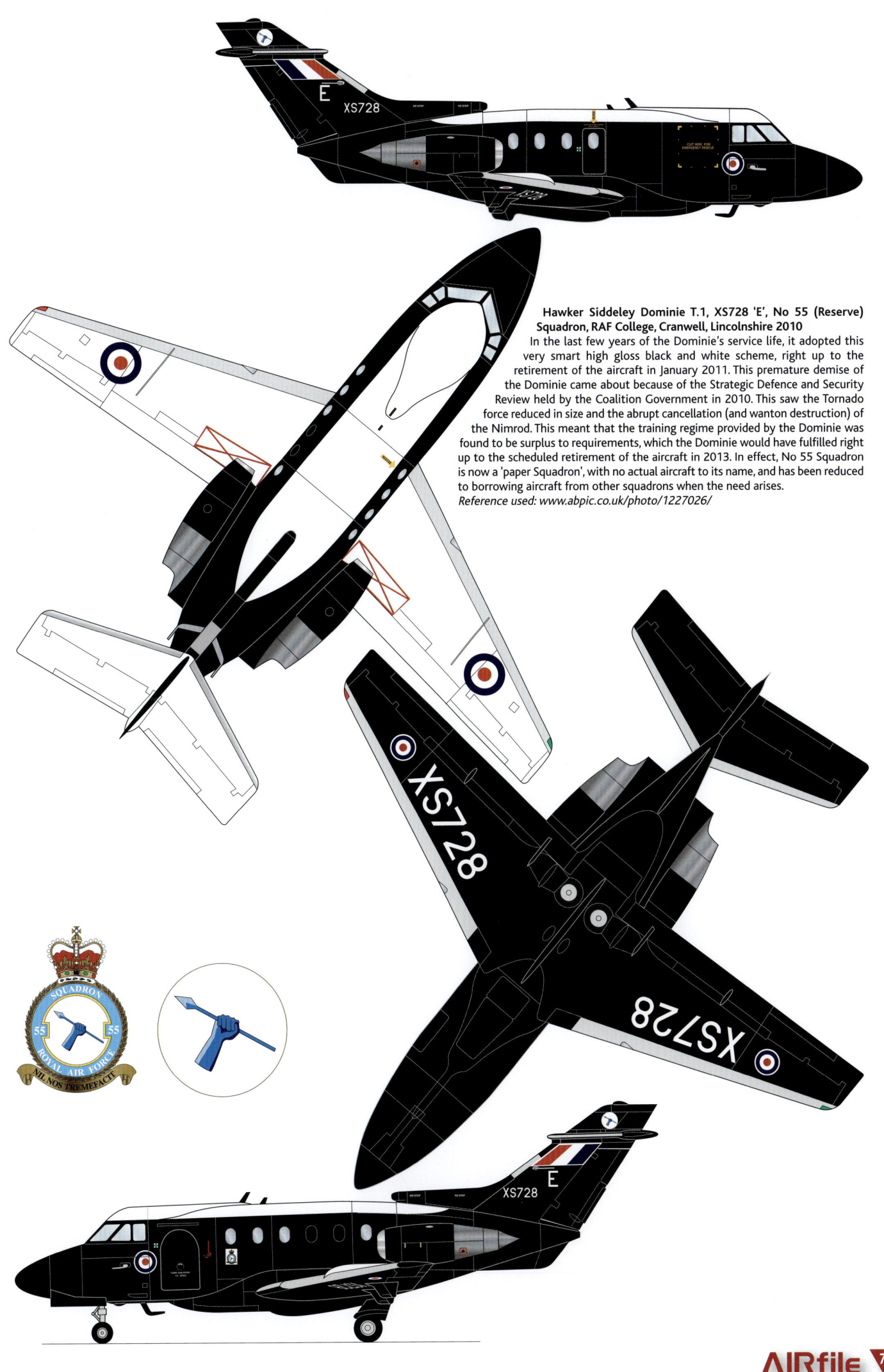

Hawker Siddeley Dominie T.1, XS728 'E', No 55 (Reserve) Squadron, RAF College, Cranwell, Lincolnshire 2010

In the last few years of the Dominie's service life, it adopted this very smart high gloss black and white scheme, right up to the retirement of the aircraft in January 2011. This premature demise of the Dominie came about because of the Strategic Defence and Security Review held by the Coalition Government in 2010. This saw the Tornado force reduced in size and the abrupt cancellation (and wanton destruction) of the Nimrod. This meant that the training regime provided by the Dominie was found to be surplus to requirements, which the Dominie would have fulfilled right up to the scheduled retirement of the aircraft in 2013. In effect, No 55 Squadron is now a 'paper Squadron', with no actual aircraft to its name, and has been reduced to borrowing aircraft from other squadrons when the need arises.
Reference used: www.abpic.co.uk/photo/1227026/

Bell Griffin HT.1, ZJ240 'U', No 60 (Reserve) Squadron, Defence Helicopter Flying School, RAF Shawbury, Shropshire 2011
After almost fifty years since the model was first introduced, the iconic lines of the Huey can still be seen in the latest incarnation, the Griffin HT.1. These are used by the DHFS for multi-engined helicopter training after initial training on the Squirrel. The Griffin is a development of the Bell 212, which was the first twin engined helicopter to be designed by Bell. It was a way of prolonging the service life of the design, giving it more power and greater safety margins. In 1978 the design was upgraded again by fitting a four blade rotor, and was designated Model 412. The RAF began using the equivalent, the HT.1, in 1997 under the auspices of FBHeliservices.
Reference used: http://www.abpic.co.uk/photo/1307792/

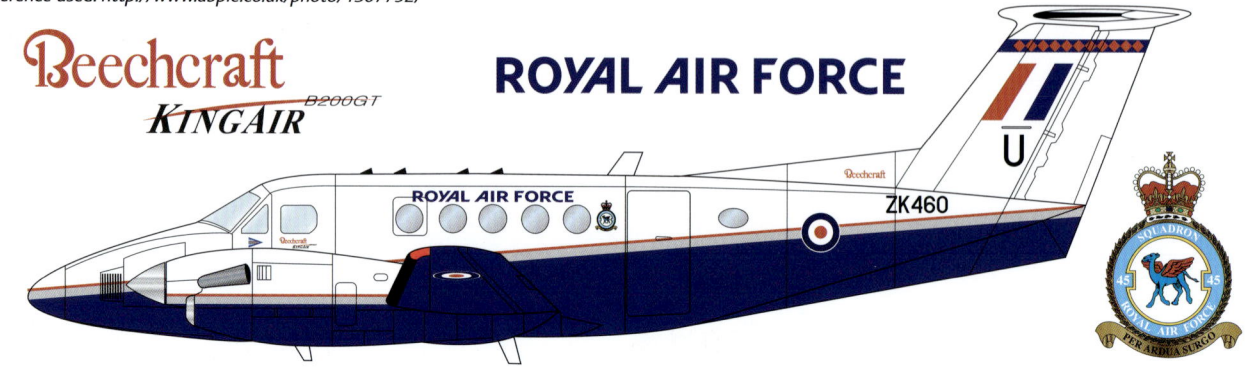

Beechcraft B200GT Super King Air, ZK460 'U', No 45(R) Squadron, No 3 Flying Training School, RAF Cranwell, Lincolnshire, 2012
Entering RAF service in 2004, the King Air fleet currently comprises seven King Air B200s and three B200GTs. The B200GT features a fully electronic 'glass cockpit' which makes it more applicable to modern RAF aircraft or those about to enter service such as the KC-30A Voyager and A400M Atlas. The B200GT is fitted with a new version of the Pratt & Whitney PT6A-52 which provides improved performance for the same power output as the B200 series. ZK460 is part of the RAF King Air Display team for 2012, proudly wearing the recently introduced red cheat line, squadron badge and Royal Air Force logo.
Reference used: http://www.abpic.co.uk/photo/1300785/

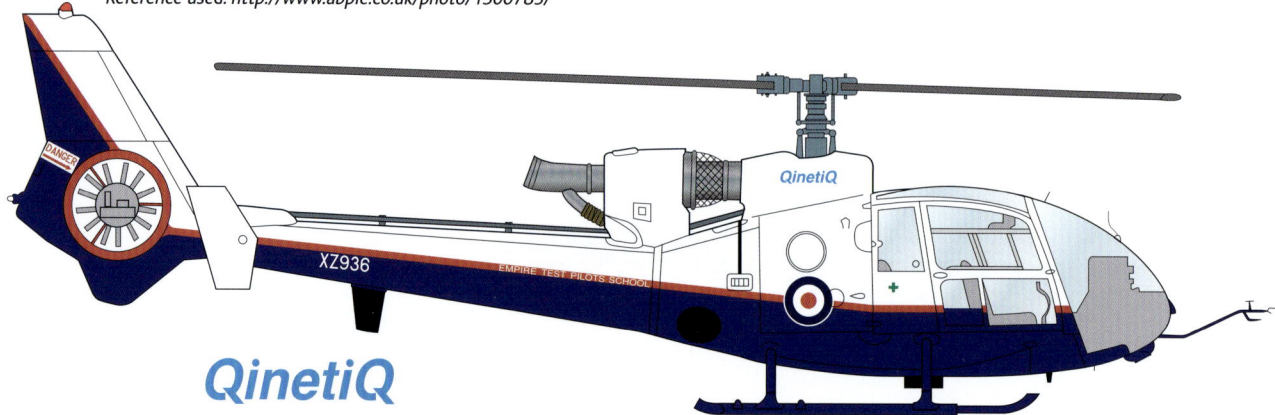

Aerospatiale SA.341D Gazelle HT.3, XZ936, Empire Test Pilots School, QinetiQ, MoD Boscombe Down, Wiltshire, February 2012
The Gazelle was liked by both pilots and engine fitters. The former had an aircraft that was simple to fly (ideal for trainee helicopter pilots), yet fairly powerful for its size with the Astazou engine. The latter were able to perform engine maintenance at a comfortable height without any major bending or squatting. The Gazelle was known as a reliable aircraft as regards both engine and airframe. XZ936 sports the latest variation of the famous 'Raspberry Ripple' colour scheme, and as it is the only one of the type to fly with the ETPS, it is the only Gazelle in these colours, although not as attractive as the scheme it initially wore when it joined over two decades previously.
Reference used: http://www.abpic.co.uk/photo/1335399/

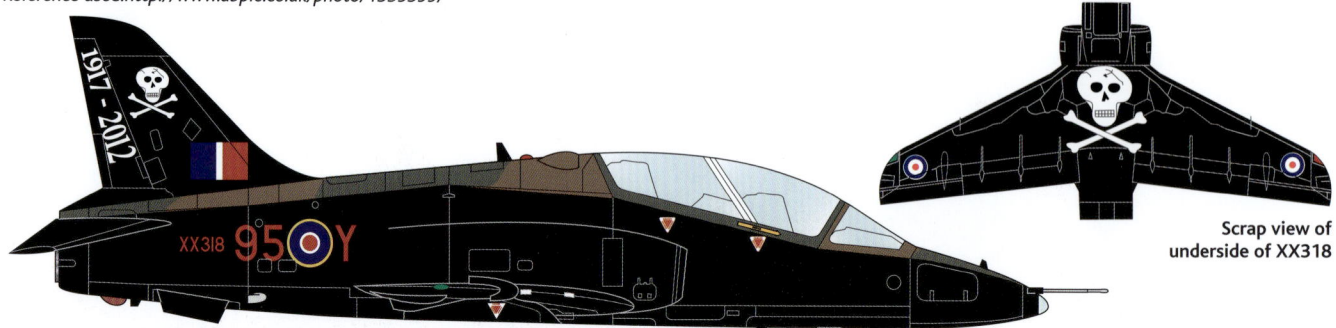

Scrap view of underside of XX318

BAe Hawk T.1A, XX318 '95•Y', No 100 Squadron, RAF Leeming, North Yorkshire, July 2012
No 100 Squadron can lay claim to be the first squadron to be specifically created in 1917 as a night bomber unit. Initially using FE.2bs, they also had several BE.2s, and the original 'skull and crossbones' was first seen on these aircraft. XX318 was painted up to celebrate 95 years of the squadron, with the date on the rudder, wartime Dark Earth and Dark Green camouflage on the spine, with the relevant style of roundel and fin flash. The '95•Y' in red on the fuselage side has the appearance of a wartime code, but actually just points out the 95 years. The white 'skull and crossbones' on the fin was also to be found on the underside of the aircraft.
Reference used: http://www.abpic.co.uk/photo/1358555/

BAe Hawk T.1A, XX263, No 208 (Reserve) Squadron, No 4 Flying Training School, RAF Valley, Wales, 2010

2010 was the anniversary year for No 4 FTS, having served continuously since being re-formed in 1960. The palm tree and the pyramid badge made a return on this specially decorated display Hawk, having had to make way for the individual Reserve Squadron markings that had taken precedence. No 4 FTS was initally formed back in 1921, flying DH.9s, Avro 504s and others (see 'RAF Trainers' Volume 1), and was disbanded and reformed several times in the intervening years.

Reference used: http://www.abpic.co.uk/photo/1283255/

De Havilland Chipmunk T.10, WK518 'K', Battle of Britain Memorial Flight,
RAF Coningsby, Lincolnshire 2011

The BBMF have two de Havilland Chipmunks on charge, and these are the last in RAF service. They are used primarily for the conversion and continuation training of BBMF pilots on tailwheel aircraft. As single engined, 'tail-dragger' aircraft are now obsolete to the RAF, pilots new to the Flight commonly arrive with no previous tailwheel aircraft experience. The aircraft are also used for the delivery of small spare parts, delivery or collection of pilots and also the reconnaissance of new venues. Of the two aircraft, WK518 has been with the BBMF the longest, and is 59 years old. WK518 was first delivered to the RAF in January 1952 going to the RAF College at Cranwell. Other units who have operated WK518 include the University Air Squadrons of Liverpool, Manchester, Cambridge, Hull, Leeds and London Universities, the Cottesmore Station Flight and No 1 Air Experience Flight, from which it was delivered to the BBMF in April 1983.

Reference used: http://www.raf.mod.uk/bbmf/theaircraft/

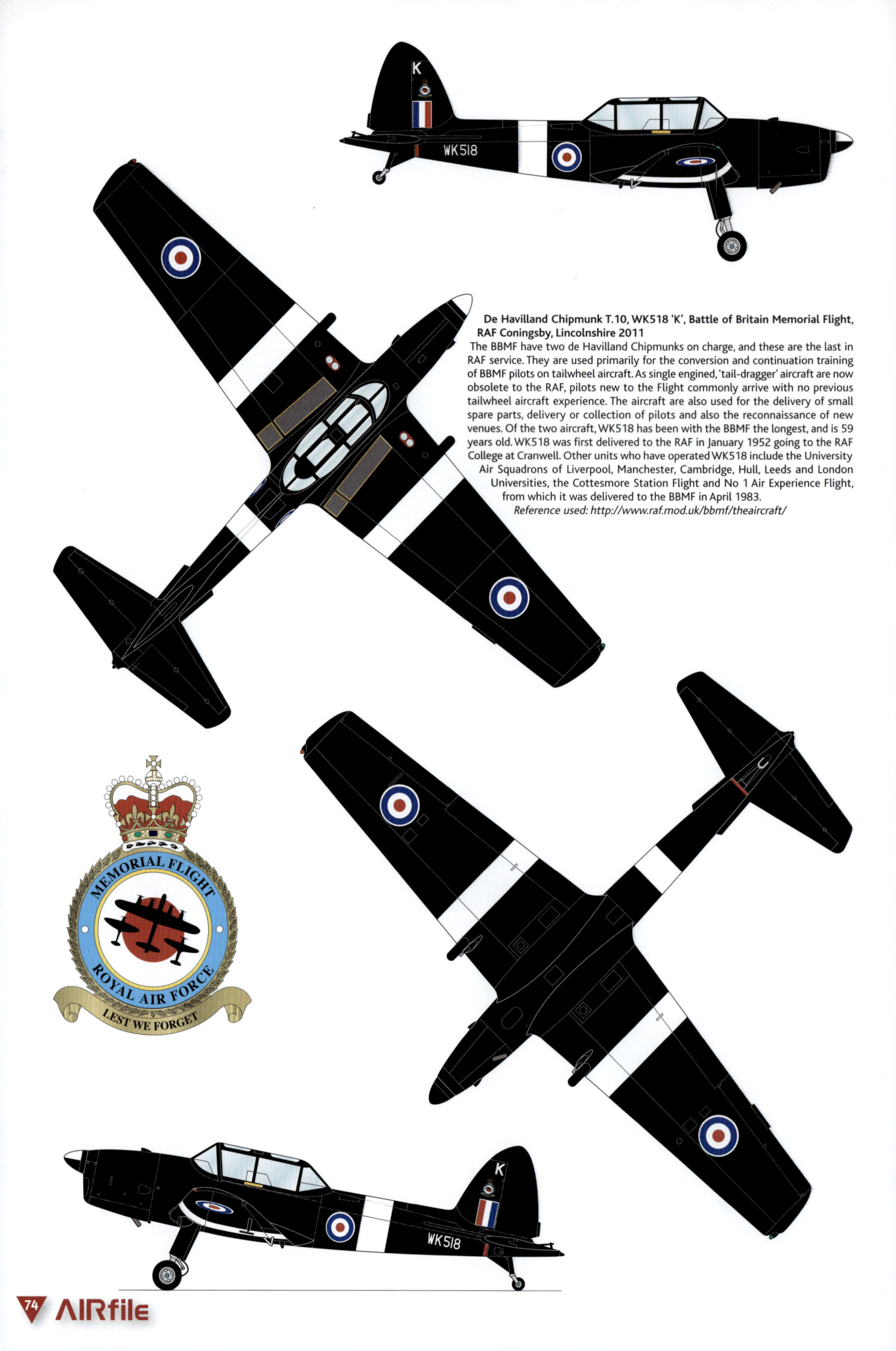

Grob G-115E Tutor T.1, G-BYXN, RAF Tutor Display, No 1 Elementary Flying Training School, RAF Cranwell, Lincolnshire 2011, flown by Flt Lt Shaun Kimberley during the 2011 display season

When the Scottish Aviation Bulldog T.1 was retired from RAF University Air Squadrons and Air Experience Flights in 2001, a new system was put in place for the provision of the UAS and AEF training. The aircraft were to be owned and operated by private industry, but contracted to the Ministry of Defence. The aircraft chosen was the Grob 115E, designated Tutor T.1 by the MoD. The Tutor fleet is owned and maintained by Babcock International, a large engineering and services corporation. Confirming this, the aircraft carry British civilian registrations but also display RAF roundels. Some 117 Tutors are currently providing flying experience to fourteen University Air Squadrons, twelve Air Experience Flights, four RAF Reserve Squadrons, the Defence Elementary Flying Training School and also 727 Naval Air Squadron.

No 1 EFTS is based at the RAF College Cranwell. The School is responsible for fixed wing elementary flying training for pilots of all three UK armed forces and for pilots from some overseas countries too. With G-BYWL, G-BYXN is one of two Grob Tutor aircraft that are used for the RAF Tutor Solo Display. Each year a new pilot is selected from the CFS instructors to perform the aerobatic displays seen by thousands at the various air displays the solo team attend.
Reference used: www.abpic.co.uk/photo/1245337/ and private collection of Tim Walsh

AIRfile 75

Dassault-Dornier Alpha Jet A, ZJ647 '47', Empire Test Pilots School, QinetiQ, MoD Boscombe Down, Wiltshire, July 2011
The Alpha Jet was a collaboration between Dornier and Dassault to create an interim trainer for pilots moving on to the Jaguar, in the French Air Force, and the Tornado in the German Air Force. ZJ647 is one of twelve that were bought by the civilian company QinetiQ from the German *Luftwaffe*. Of these, five are held in storage, whilst the other seven are flown from Boscombe Down as part of the Aircraft Test and Evaluation Centre, of which QinetiQ is a partner. QinetiQ was formed on 2 July 2001 out of what used to be the Defence Evaluation and Research Agency. ZJ647 has the standard gloss black trainer scheme, although with white wing tips, the company name along the nose as well as carrying RAF roundels, and an oddly rendered serial number under the port wing only, where it should read from the leading edge, and not from the trailing edge.
Reference used: http://www.abpic.co.uk/photo/1302196/

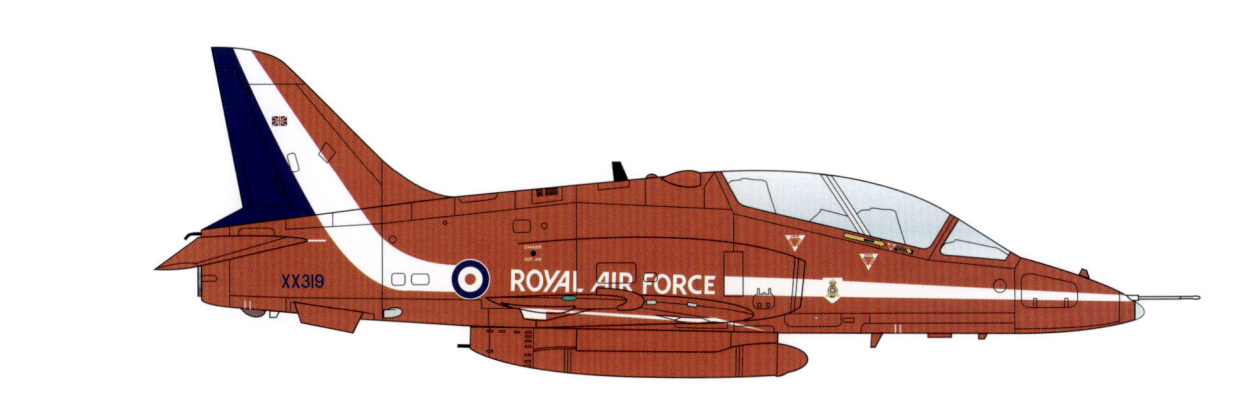

BAe Hawk T.1A, XX319. Red Arrows, RAF Display Team, RAF Scampton, Lincolnshire, July 2012

The British Aerospace Hawk has become one of the best selling trainer aircraft around the world, with seventeen countries having bought the design up to now, either in the original two-seat configuration, the up-graded T.2, or the single seat fighter version. The US has taken the design and altered it to their own needs for the US Navy. One of the main reasons for this global success is the (not unintentional) flying of the flag by the world famous Red Arrows, spending many months displaying the virtues of their aircraft around the world. The Red Arrows have used the Hawk as their mount since 1979, with their first full display taking place in 1980.
Reference used: http://www.abpic.co.uk/photo/1361304/

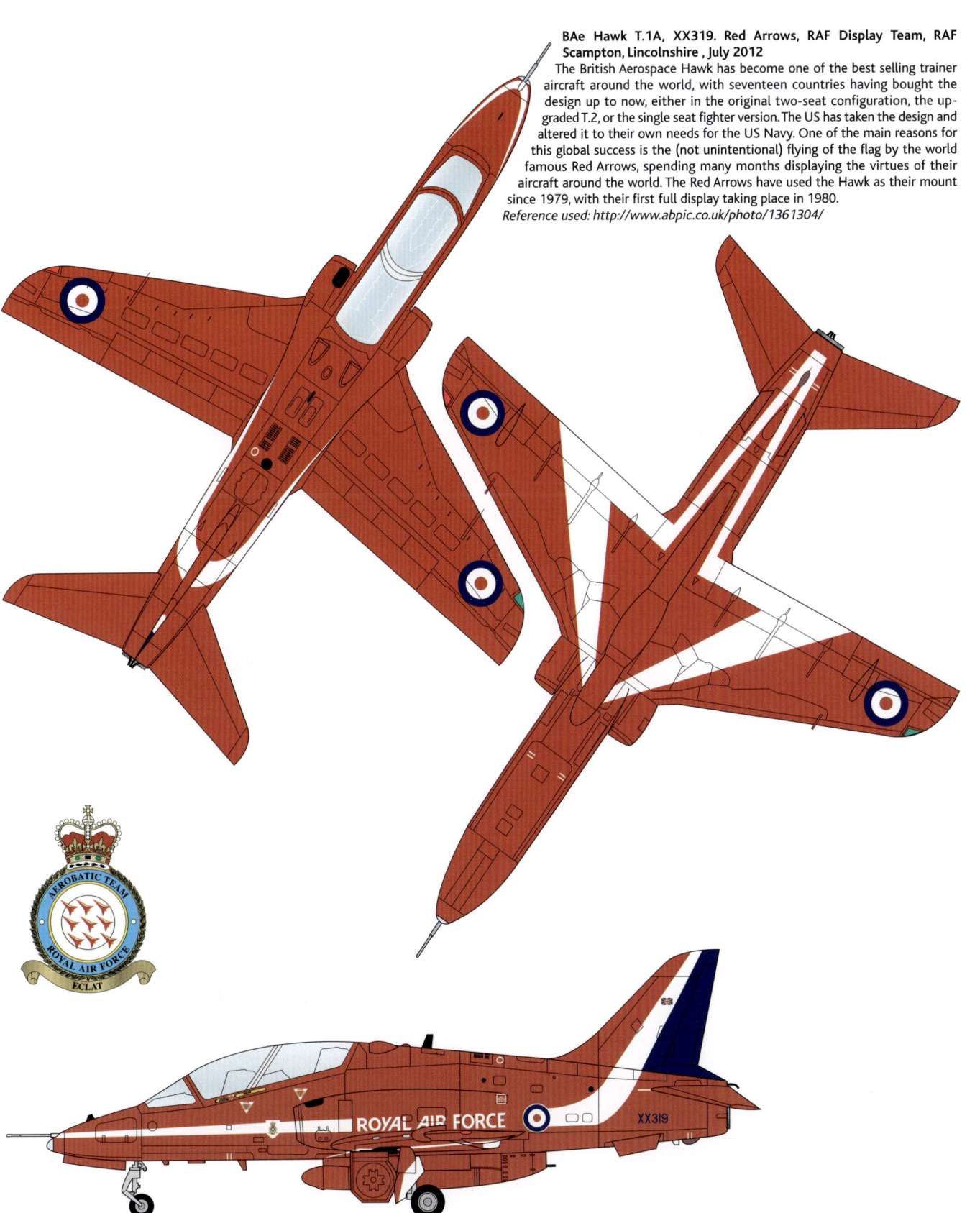

BAe Hawk T.2, ZK020 'K', No IV (R) Squadron, RAF Valley, Wales, August 2012
As previously noted, the potential of the Hawk design and the Adour engine, meant that it was logical for the aircraft to be developed into a fully combat capable aircraft. The wing was redesigned with more hard points and a greater camber on the leading edge, to become known as the combat wing. Laser ranging and forward looking infra red systems were added to a lengthened nose, and these systems were linked to an all new glass cockpit. A taller tail fin helped to compensate for the longer nose, and 'smurfs' (side mounted unit root fins) were added just in front of and below the tail planes to alleviate the tail plane from stalling. This original problem had been solved by removing an inboard portion of the double slotted flaps.

Known in the RAF as the Hawk T.2, the mere twenty-eight that have been purchased will be expected to take over all the training requirements previously fulfilled by the original 176 Hawk T.1s, for the foreseeable future. ZK020 carries the centenary year markings of No IV Squadron, one of the very few units that will reach their one hundredth year.
Reference used: http://www.abpic.co.uk/photo/1360239/

Short Tucano T.1, ZF269 '269', Silver Jubilee Display Scheme. No 1 Flying Training School, RAF Linton-on-Ouse, June 2012

This colour scheme used on ZF269 needs no explanation, other than to say it is quite stunning, and is indicative of the commemorative and anniversary schemes that the Tucano and the BAe Hawk have carried in these last few years. Incredible as it seems, the next Strategic Defence and Security Review due in 2015 may see the demise of the Tucano. The numbers in use have been drastically curtailed, and 2015 might see the few that are left being replaced entirely, or having to soldier on in the face of more possible cost cutting measures.
Reference used: http://www.abpic.co.uk/photo/1354655/

General Atomics MQ-9 Reaper, ZZ203/UK08-133, No 39 Squadron, Creech Air Force Base, Nevada, USA 2012

No 39 Squadron was reformed on 1 January 2007 as the RAF's first Unmanned Aerial Vehicle (UAV) squadron. The Reaper has a 'crew' of three – a pilot, sensor operator, and mission co-ordinator/image analyst, who remotely control each mission, by satellite link, from Creech AFB. In support, there are 'in-theatre' ground crew, who carry out maintenance, ordnance and launch and recovery activities. There are currently thirty-one RAF personnel qualified to pilot the Reaper. The MoD state that a further sixteen will be trained for the task between October 2012 and September 2013. Also, as of October 2012, No XIII Squadron has been reformed at RAF Waddington as the second RAF UAV Squadron. It will operate its five Reapers from a new control facility at Waddington, with the plan to eventually base all UAV operations out of this UK air base. All the pilots, at the moment, are experienced combat pilots, but the UAV concept of remote control from a hi-tech ground station, starts to question the need for existing skill levels (and expense) of flying training. In 2011 the RAF conducted an experimental training programme in the United States, 'Project Daedalus', which included a group of four non-aircrew, these being two air traffic controllers, a fighter controller and a policeman, to fly the MQ-1 Predator. These four were amongst the top-rated in their class beating pilots with fast jet experience. There is now some consideration in training the four up to fly the MQ-9...

Reference used:
http://globalmilitaryreview.blogspot.co.uk/2011/10/rafs-mq-9-reaper-unmanned-aerial.html

ROYAL AIR FORCE